Mr. Jefferson's Women

JON KUKLA

ALFRED A. KNOPF · NEW YORK

2007

THIS IS A BORZOI BOOK
PUBLISHED BY ALFRED A. KNOPF

Copyright © 2007 by Jon Kukla
All rights reserved. Published in the United States by Alfred A. Knopf,
a division of Random House, Inc., New York, and in Canada
by Random House of Canada Limited, Toronto.
www.aaknopf.com

Library of Congress Cataloging-in-Publication Data
Kukla, Jon, [date]
Mr. Jefferson's women / by Jon Kukla. — 1st ed.
p. cm.
Includes bibliographical references and index.
ISBN 978-1-4000-4324-8
1. Jefferson, Thomas, 1743–1826—Relations with women.
2. Jefferson, Thomas, 1743–1826—Political and social views.
3. Women—United States—Social conditions—18th century.
4. Sex role—United States—History—18th century.
5. Women's rights—United States—History—18th century.
6. Presidents—United States—Biography.
I. Title. II. Title: Mister Jefferson's women.
E332.2.K85 2007
973.4'60922—dc22   2007006348
Manufactured in the United States of America
First Edition

For Marion, Edna, and Marie,
Connie, Mimi, Margreda, Cindy, and Ruth,
Amy, Jennifer, Elizabeth, and Kaia

Let us view the disadvantages of sending a youth to Europe. . . .
He is led by the strongest of all the human passions into a spirit for
female intrigue destructive of his own and others happiness, or a
passion for whores destructive of his health, and in both cases learns
to consider fidelity to the marriage bed as an ungentlemanly prac-
tice and inconsistent with happiness.

—Thomas Jefferson to John Banister, Jr., 1785

The appointment of a woman to office is an innovation for which
the public is not prepared, nor am I.

—Thomas Jefferson to Albert Gallatin, 1807

Were our State a pure democracy, in which all its inhabitants
should meet together to transact all their business, there would yet
be excluded from their deliberations: 1. Infants, until arrived at
age of discretion. 2. Women, who, to prevent depravation of morals
and ambiguity of issue, could not mix promiscuously in the public
meetings of men. 3. Slaves, from whom the unfortunate state of
things with us takes away the rights of will and of property.

—Thomas Jefferson to Samuel Kercheval, 1816

CONTENTS

APPENDIXES

ILLUSTRATIONS

A NOTE ON TEXTS

This book relies heavily on documentary sources, both from manuscripts and from a variety of published editions with differing editorial policies. For the text, so-called accidentals are consistently presented in accord with accepted canons of modern documentary scholarship: sentences begin with capital letters; terminal periods in abbreviations are omitted unless retained in modern usage; superior letters are brought to the line of the text; ampersands and *&c* are generally spelled out; and Jefferson's persistent use of *it's* for *its* is silently corrected. When quoting from modern documentary editions, I generally suppress apparatus used to identify interlineations, encoded words, and readings supplied by a reliable editor. When it is important for the reader to be aware of the original orthography, I comment upon it in the text or notes. Underscored words from manuscript sources are set in italics, and italics are retained from printed sources when originally used for emphasis rather than typographic decoration. The notes identify those instances in which I employ italics to convey my own emphasis within a quotation. All my interpolations in quoted passages are presented within brackets, including the occasional substitution of a noun for a pronoun (e.g., *Jefferson's* for *his*) or a third-person for a first-person pronoun (e.g., *her* for *my*). Signatures are presented in SMALL CAPS.

For appendixes A and C, which present significant sources about which controversy sometimes arises, the editorial policy is more literal: ampersands are retained; interlineations are reported in notes; deleted words are shown as ~~struck through;~~ and all the vagaries of punctuation and capitalization are retained. As in my text, all editorial interpolations within quoted texts are presented within square brackets. Explanatory comments in the appendixes are presented in italic type within decorative brackets *{thus}*.

Mr. Jefferson's Women

THOMAS JEFFERSON BY MATHER BROWN, 1786

The earliest known portrait of Thomas Jefferson, this likeness derived from sittings with the artist Mather Brown in 1786 during Jefferson's tenure as American minister to France. Jefferson wears the fashionable attire and powdered hair expected of a diplomat to the court of Louis XVI. In the background, the female allegorical figure of Liberty holds a Phrygian cap on a liberty pole—popular symbols of freedom during the American Revolution and the French Revolution. John and Abigail Adams displayed this portrait in their London home when Adams served as the American minister to Great Britain. She told Jefferson that it "dignifies a part of our room, tho it is but a poor substitute for those pleasures which we enjoy'd some months past," when Jefferson and the Adamses were often together in Paris.

Courtesy of the National Portrait Gallery, Smithsonian Institution
(NPG.92.110), bequest of Charles Francis Adams.

CHAPTER ONE

Mr. Peterman's Shirt

Jefferson disliked stuffy people, stuffy houses, stuffy societies. So he changed a few things. Law. Gardening. Government. Architecture.

Of the thousand castles, mansions, chateaux you can walk through today, only Monticello, only Jefferson's own mansion, makes you feel so comfortable you want to live in it.

—J. Peterman Company

THOMAS JEFFERSON did wear simple and comfortable shirts like the one that inspired a clever advertising copywriter for the J. Peterman Company's retail catalogue. The claim that the style is "99% Thos. Jefferson. 1% Peterman"[1] may stretch the truth. Simple muslin work shirts were as common among Jefferson's Virginia contemporaries as they were inside the great house at Monticello. Still, the rest of the copywriter's pitch rings true.

Jefferson was an inventor.

He liked comfort.

And he did change a few things.

In 1776 Jefferson's words declared American independence and encouraged a candid world to hope that all men were created equal. Ten years later his Statute for Religious Freedom summoned Virginians to insist that "Almighty God hath created the mind free." Jefferson calculated the most efficient shape for the blade, or moldboard, of a plow. He modeled a new capitol for the commonwealth of Virginia, based on an ancient Roman temple, that established the classical revival as the standard for American public architecture. At Monticello he devised a mechanism, hidden beneath the floor between the entrance hall and parlor, to open both French doors simultaneously when either door was pushed. In the valley below Monticello he established Virginia's first secular university. Farther to the west, Jefferson's acquisition of the vast territory of Louisiana secured the navigation of the Mississippi River and changed the political geography of the nation and the world.

Jefferson did change a few things, but there were others that he left alone. He lived comfortably on a southern plantation as the master of about one hundred slaves, yet he contended that slavery was both a moral wrong and a political liability. He was content to hope that future generations might set things right for people of color. Comfort—whether in his mansion or in the muslin shirts that inspired J. Peterman—mattered to Thomas Jefferson. In his personal life, Jefferson was never entirely comfortable with strong and independent women. In politics, except for a brief moment in dialogue with Abigail Adams, his attitude toward women was immovable. Jefferson did nothing whatsoever to improve the legal or social condition of women in American society, and he was always wary of female influence in government.

ALMOST A decade ago I heard a distinguished panel of scholars discuss "Thomas Jefferson, Sally Hemings, and the DNA Evidence" at a historical conference in Fort Worth, Texas. The program committee had wisely placed the session in the large ballroom of the headquarters hotel. The place was full. DNA tests had recently confirmed a genetic relationship between Thomas Jefferson's family and one of Sally Hemings's children. That scientific evidence persuaded many previously skeptical historians (myself included) that the liaison between Thomas Jefferson and Sally Hemings—a connection first alleged by James Callender in 1802, reasserted by Fawn Brodie in 1974, and finally rehabilitated by Annette Gordon-Reed's persuasive book in 1997—was almost certainly true.[2]

The panel discussion in Fort Worth was informative, but I found the comments from historians in the audience more interesting. Someone in a tweed jacket was confident that "surely it was a loving relationship." Two or three questions later someone else prefaced her question with the rejoinder that "surely it was rape." In a conference at Charlottesville that same year, the late Winthrop Jordan witnessed a similar and, as he described it, "occasionally heated discussion, which centered on such terms as *rape, concubinage,* and *marriage*." Professor Jordan doubted "that anyone today will ever know enough about the emotional contents of the Hemings-Jefferson relationship to understand it thoroughly," and he suggested that "such labels do little to help our understanding."[3] Nevertheless, people do ask the question.

As I listened to those earnest scholars venturing their opinions about the nature of Jefferson's relationship with Hemings, my reaction was somewhat different from Professor Jordan's. With the evidence so meager, it was obvious that despite our training, many of us in the audience were unthinkingly projecting contemporary values back into an earlier and perhaps different age. It also struck me that we historians would never get a handle on what Jordan called the "emotional contents of the Hemings-Jefferson relationship" without knowing more about how Jefferson interacted with other women. At the time I was busy writing about the Louisiana Purchase, but I made a mental note to consult Frank Shuffelton's comprehensive bibliography of nearly everything written about Jefferson since 1826, where I expected to find a reliable book about Jefferson and women to assuage my curiosity. Many months later, however, when at last there was time to rummage through Shuffelton's bibliography, I discovered that the book on Jefferson and women I had hoped to find was not there. This book, *Mr. Jefferson's Women*, is basically one I wanted to read.

Many of my conclusions surprised me. To the fullest degree that the extant sources permit, I have sought to understand the significant women in Jefferson's life not only through his eyes but also from historical evidence that is completely independent of his perceptions. Relationships between people, then or now, never entirely match the perspective of only one participant. The result, I think, is not a book that could be written by a young scholar. It is certainly not one I could have researched and written thirty-odd years ago when I began my first explorations of Virginia's history. A few decades of work in the primary sources (and the accumulated joys and bruises of life) make a difference.

THOMAS JEFFERSON's personality was complex to the point of paradox. A sphinx according to one able biographer, he was a grieving optimist to another. For a man with so many talents and interests, the list of descriptive phrases could go on and on. In respect to his relationships with women, Jefferson was always self-absorbed and often a bit frightened. Both in private life and in public policy, Jefferson was less uncomfortable with married women than with their undomesticated sisters. Winthrop Jordan got it right almost four decades ago when he observed that for Jefferson "intimate emotional engagement with women seemed to represent . . . a gateway into a dangerous, potentially explosive world" and "female passion must and could only be controlled by marriage."[4] After the wife of his neighbor and friend spurned his repeated advances, Jefferson married a widow. After her death, it was the talented and flirtatious wife of a fashionable artist who reawakened the widower's heart in Paris. Finally, the light-skinned half sister of his late wife proved the exception to Winthrop Jordan's formulation: marriage was not the only available means of control for the women in Jefferson's life or polity. Enslavement also sufficed.

In the age of the American Revolution, gentlemen like Jefferson were acutely conscious of their personal as well as their political independence. Personal independence began with self-control. The most sublime compliment that one gentleman could offer to another, Virginians believed, was "that he was a master of himself!" In his relationships with women, Jefferson struggled for self-control throughout his early adulthood and once again in Paris. In Virginia during the Revolution, he was largely indifferent to women's aspirations for educational opportunity, a voice in public life, or relief from the patriarchal strictures of English property law. During his years as minister to the court of Louis XVI, however, he became alarmed by the conduct of French women at court, in their salons, and eventually in the streets. When Jefferson returned from Europe, he was convinced that women posed a serious menace to republican government and American liberty.[5]

Jefferson may have been comfortable in simple cotton shirts, but his lifelong uneasiness around women is evident in his earliest surviving correspondence with friends from college. These letters, complained Jefferson's sympathetic biographer Dumas Malone, "disclose a great deal which the mature man would not have relished." "Worst of all," he added, "they are full of references to girls." Then or now, no sensible adult relishes all memories of adolescence. Comfortable or not, however, adolescence is where we must begin. There is scarcely any evidence from which to speculate about Jefferson's youthful relationships with his mother and sisters. Our inquiry about Thomas Jefferson and the women in his life must begin in the circle of his college friends and the young women they sought to impress, to woo, and to marry. It begins not with a philosophic statesman relaxing in Mr. Peterman's shirt but with an awkward youth imagining himself in "a suit of Mecklenburgh Silk" as he prepared for "the ball." With an introverted youth asking his fraternity brother about a party he had missed—and wondering, with a self-consciousness that he never outgrew, "how I should have behaved?"[6] Our inquiry about Thomas Jefferson and women in the age of the American Revolution begins with his friends and classmates in Williamsburg and with the young women they admired, dated, and wed.

WILLIAMSBURG IN 1760

WILLIAMSBURG, the home of the College of William and Mary since 1693 and capital of Virginia from 1699 to 1780, was the metropolis of Thomas Jefferson's youth. The town stands midway between the James and the York Rivers, some thirty miles inland from the Chesapeake Bay and six miles northeast of Jamestown, the colony's initial settlement and first capital. In 1698, after fire had consumed the statehouse in Jamestown for the third time, Virginians had given up on the swampy island and moved their capital to higher ground at Middle Plantation, where their college had recently been chartered. The new town was named for England's Protestant hero and king, William III, whose late queen, Mary Stuart, had shared with him the namesake honors of the college.

"By going to the College," sixteen-year-old Jefferson assured one of his guardians on New Year's Day in 1760, "I shall get a more universal Acquaintance which may hereafter be serviceable to me." He supposed that he could pursue "studies in Greek and Latin as well there as here." *Here* was Shadwell, his mother's plantation on the Rivanna River below the mountain on which he would one day build his architectural master-piece, Monticello. Jefferson's father had died three years earlier. A skilled surveyor and explorer, famous for the *Map of Virginia* published with his partner, Joshua Fry, Peter Jefferson may have passed along some of his

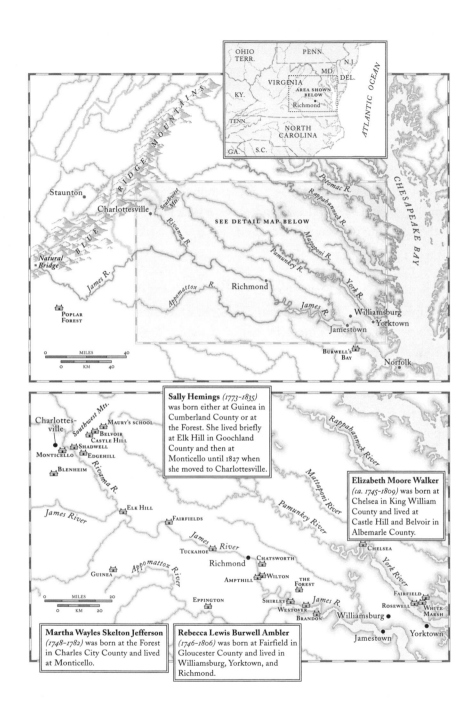

Sally Hemings *(1773–1835)* was born either at Guinea in Cumberland County or at the Forest. She lived briefly at Elk Hill in Goochland County and then at Monticello until 1827 when she moved to Charlottesville.

Elizabeth Moore Walker *(ca. 1745–1809)* was born at Chelsea in King William County and lived at Castle Hill and Belvoir in Albemarle County.

Martha Wayles Skelton Jefferson *(1748–1782)* was born at the Forest in Charles City County and lived at Monticello.

Rebecca Lewis Burwell Ambler *(1746–1806)* was born at Fairfield in Gloucester County and lived in Williamsburg, Yorktown, and Richmond.

technical skills to his eldest son. Nevertheless, that son now looked to the College of William and Mary as the place where he could "learn something of the Mathematics."[7]

Jefferson owed his presence in Williamsburg to the encouragement of his uncle and guardian, Peter Randolph of Chatsworth, a former clerk of the House of Burgesses and then a member of the prestigious Governor's Council. Jefferson had visited his uncle in eastern Henrico County during the New Year's holiday. Two weeks later, in the earliest of Jefferson's surviving letters, he advised John Harvie, another of his legal guardians, that his uncle "said he thought it would be to my Advantage to go to the College."[8] Later in life, as one of his own descendants prepared for college, Jefferson recalled that "at fourteen years of age the whole care and direction of myself was thrown on myself entirely, without a relative or a friend qualified to advise or guide me." Reflecting upon "the various sorts of bad company with which I associated from time to time," Jefferson expressed (with perhaps some grandfatherly exaggeration) astonishment "that I did not . . . become as worthless to society as they were."[9] Late in March 1760, Williamsburg supplanted Albemarle County as the geographic center of the adolescent Jefferson's circle of friends.

With perhaps two thousand permanent residents and another hundred at the college, Williamsburg in 1760 was a small provincial town. As the capital of Great Britain's oldest and largest American colony (with its population of about 340,000 souls), the village nevertheless had pretensions to greatness. Williamsburg was the seat of Virginia's royal governor and his council. It regularly played host to the colonial legislature and General Court. Its college was the third oldest in the colonies, younger only than Harvard and Yale. More significant, it was from Williamsburg that the imperial governors of the self-declared monarchs of four dominions—England, Scotland, Wales, and Ireland—claimed sway south to the Carolina line, west across the Allegheny Mountains to the Mississippi River, and north to the Great Lakes. For six years Virginia's western forests had been one of the front lines in a raging imperial war between Great Britain and France and their respective colonies and Native American allies. Quebec in 1759 had fallen to the heroic forces under General James Wolfe. The British were on their way to a victorious conclusion of the Great War for Empire. George II was nearing the end of his thirty-three-year reign. His heir would be crowned king in the autumn of 1760. All around town, Britain's oldest colony declared its pride with heraldic crests blazoned on the walls of its public buildings, wrought in iron and gilt over the gate of the Royal Governor's palace, painted on the doors of his carriage, published in the masthead of the weekly newspaper, and engraved on the bookplates of the council library. Beneath the quartered emblems of the Crown's other dominions, the motto read *En Dat Virginia Quintam*—Behold Virginia, the Fifth Dominion. Arriving in Williamsburg in the spring of 1760, the teenage Thomas Jefferson had reason to regard the small capital town as a metropolis peopled with universal and serviceable acquaintances—and a beckoning gateway to the wider world.

Thomas Jefferson was nearly seventeen on March 25, 1760, when he moved into his lodgings at the College of William and Mary. With reddish-blond hair and a fair complexion, Jefferson was a lanky student well on the way to his adult height of six feet two inches. The eldest son of Peter and Jane Randolph Jefferson, he had been born 120 miles to the west in 1743, a year before the colonial legislature had created the county of Albemarle for the benefit of frontier citizens who were settling the Piedmont, the rolling plateau between the falls of Virginia's great tidal rivers—the James, Rappahannock, and Potomac—and the Blue Ridge Mountains.[10] Jefferson grew up far from the Georgian brick mansions of Tidewater Virginia. His father's family had been middling planters in Virginia since the early days of the colony,[11] but Peter Jefferson had married well. Through his mother, the future president was kin to the powerful Randolph family, with its connections throughout the sprawling tobacco plantations and riverfront mansions. He had two elder sisters, four younger sisters, and a younger brother (two other boys having died in infancy), but several of Jefferson's boyhood schoolmates were virtually siblings to him.[12]

Jefferson's earliest formal education was at an "English school" on the grounds of Tuckahoe plantation, high above the James River fifteen miles west of Richmond, the seat of his father's intimate friend and his mother's cousin William Randolph of Tuckahoe. Jefferson was two when William Randolph died and his parents moved their family to Tuckahoe, where, as promised, they raised Randolph's children as their own. Cousin, classmate, and virtual older brother, Thomas Mann Randolph of Tuckahoe remained among Jefferson's circle of friends in Williamsburg.[13]

At age nine Jefferson returned with his parents to Albemarle County, where he and four other boys comprised the senior class boarding at the Reverend James Maury's log-cabin school across the Rivanna near the Southwest Mountains. As young teenagers, Jefferson and his classmates Dabney Carr and John Walker slept many weeknights at school and many weekends at Castle Hill, Dr. Thomas Walker's home midway between Shadwell and Maury's school. In any speculation about Jefferson's relationship with his mother and sisters, the scant information we have about them must be weighed against the fact that Jefferson spent much of his youth with his schoolmates in neighboring households.

There were moments in Williamsburg when Jefferson felt that he had been "thrown upon a wide world, among entire strangers," despite the prominence of his Randolph uncles. On Nicholson Street, about six blocks from Jefferson's new lodgings, stood the home of his uncle Peyton Randolph, king's attorney general and later the powerful Speaker of the House of Burgesses and first president of the Continental Congress. A few blocks to the south, near Francis Street, workmen engaged by Clerk of the House John Randolph, the Speaker's younger brother, were erecting the grand residence later named Tazewell Hall by the family that bought it during the Revolution, when John Randolph sided with the king and moved to England.[14] We have no evidence that Peyton and John Randolph took any notice of their young nephew, but from their exalted position perhaps they exerted as much influence upon Jefferson as his favorite teachers. "Under temptations and difficulties," Jefferson recalled, "I would ask myself what would Dr. Small, Mr. Wythe, [or] Peyton Randolph do in this situation?"[15]

Within a year Jefferson welcomed two boyhood friends from the Reverend Maury's school—Dabney Carr and John Walker—to the College of William and Mary. Born in October 1743, Carr had entered Maury's school from western Louisa County and become the dearest of Jefferson's friends there. Six months younger than Jefferson, Carr studied at the college in Williamsburg for two years, then joined Louisa County's frontier militia for a year or so. In time the faces of both tragedy and comedy attested to his close friendship with Jefferson, who esteemed his "spotless integrity, sound judgment, handsome imagination" as well as his "pleasantry of conversation and conduct."[16] In 1765, when Carr married Jefferson's younger sister Martha and settled at Spring Forest in Goochland County, he also passed the bar and began practicing law in the county courts. He served one term in the colonial legislature and had a promising career in law and politics when he suddenly died of a "bilious fever" in 1773, five months shy of thirty. When Jefferson learned of his friend's death, he rushed home to arrange Carr's burial beneath an oak tree under which, as boys, they had talked and read together on carefree afternoons. At that serene location, which they had chosen as their final resting place, the grave of Dabney Carr became the first interment in the cemetery at Monticello. A more happy testimony to Carr's special place in Jefferson's affection was the only boyhood prank that memory attributes to Jefferson. Years after both men had died, one of the Reverend James Maury's younger sons showed his sister "the place designated for a race between Tom Jefferson's slow pony and Dabney Carr's swift horse." The joke was that Jefferson had set the date of the great race for February 30, "and not until the last day of the month did the others discover that they had been taken in."[17]

The other Albemarle County classmate who followed Jefferson to William and Mary in 1761 was John Walker, eldest son of the famed physician and explorer Dr. Thomas Walker.[18] Born in 1744 a few miles east of Shadwell, Jack Walker was a year younger than Jefferson. Their families were neighbors. The boys virtually grew up together. Dr. Walker was one of Jefferson's guardians after his father died.

ALTHOUGH JEFFERSON remained close to Carr and Walker, Williamsburg enticed him into new circles of acquaintances among the children of Tidewater Virginia's great families. Talent aside, Jefferson was the son of a successful frontiersman who had married up into the Randolph family. The first of his father's family ever to attend college, he was making friends among the upper tier of the Tidewater gentry, especially among the grandchildren of Virginia's most wealthy planter, the fabled Robert "King" Carter. Preeminent among Jefferson's new friends at the college was John Page. Born on April 17, 1743, at Rosewell plantation in Gloucester County, Page was four days younger than his new friend from Albemarle. A three-year veteran of the college when Jefferson arrived, Page had come to William and Mary at fourteen. He attributed his love of learning to the tutelage of his grandmother Judith Carter Page, daughter of the late "King" Carter, one of the few Virginians who had more land and money than the Pages. To his able tutor William Price, "who possessed the happiest faculty of explaining what he taught and rendering it agreeable," Page attributed his Whig political principles and familiarity with classical republicanism.[19]

Rosewell was the largest and one of the grandest houses in the colony. Three stories high, it had twenty-three rooms and three wide halls in the main house and six rooms in each wing. Situated on the north bank of the broad York River, two miles wide as it approaches Chesapeake Bay, Rosewell was readily accessible by private boat or the public ferry at Yorktown. Jefferson was soon familiar with the carved mahogany wainscoting that graced the walls of the house, and with the grand staircase wide enough to accommodate Page, Jefferson, and six of their friends walking abreast. Although the construction of Rosewell may have eroded the family's enormous wealth, if Tidewater Virginia had aristocrats, Jefferson's new friend John Page strolled easily among them.[20]

Three blocks from the college, at the corner of Duke of Gloucester Street and the Palace Green, the tomb of Page's great-great-grandfather and namesake stood prominently next to the front door of Bruton Parish Church. He had come to Virginia about 1650 and was the first of the family named to the Governor's Council. Eighty-two years had passed, but in the Williamsburg of 1760, John Page's ancestor was still remembered as the man who gave the land and the first donation of twenty pounds to build the church. Page's great-grandfather Matthew, also a member of the council, had been a founding member of William and Mary's board of visitors in 1693. His grandfather Mann Page was a member of the council and a judge of the Court of Admiralty. He married well twice—first to a daughter of the secretary of the colony; then, after her death, to King Carter's daughter Judith—and began the construction of Rosewell directly across the York River from Williamsburg. Page's father, Mann Page II, completed the house and represented the College of William and Mary in the colonial legislature during Jefferson's first five years in Williamsburg. John Page himself inherited Rosewell in 1765, and on the eve of the Revolution he followed his

Rosewell, the Page family seat, as depicted on a porcelain punch bowl imported from China. Probably commissioned by Jefferson's friend John Page of Rosewell about 1800, this punch bowl bears two images of the family mansion in Gloucester County, just across the York River from Williamsburg. Begun by John Page's grandfather in 1725 and finished by his father in 1737, Rosewell was intended to surpass the Governor's Palace in size and splendor. Jefferson was a frequent guest at Rosewell during the 1760s. The house burned in 1916, but Rosewell's towering ruins have been preserved.

Courtesy of the Minnesota Historical Society.

ancestors to a seat on the council, where he promptly antagonized the last royal governor, John Murray, earl of Dunmore, by siding with Jefferson and the colony's other patriots.

Jefferson and Page comprised one third of the membership of America's first collegiate fraternity, founded at William and Mary in November 1750. "The F.H.C. society [was] confined to six students only, of which I was a member," Jefferson recalled half a century later, "but it had no useful object, nor do I know whether it now exists." Later revived as the Flat Hat Club, Jefferson's fraternity was named for its ideals: *fraternitas, hilaritas,* and *cognitioque.* Jefferson and his fraternity brothers—John Page, Lewis Burwell, Jr., Warner Lewis, James McClurg, and Jack Walker—honored their commitment to friendship, mirth, and science with a secret handshake, a silver badge inscribed with the motto *Stabili-*

tas et fides, and parties in an upper room of favorite taverns on Duke of Gloucester Street, first the Crown and later the Raleigh.[21]

The family connections among Jefferson's new circle of Tidewater friends were complicated, even for members of the group: Anne Randolph of Wilton's nickname, Nancy Wilton, may well have distinguished her from William Fitzhugh's girlfriend, Anne Randolph of Arlington. Family connections were serious matters in the colony, but their tangles and twists were still amusing. Prompted by a marriage between a Carter and a Willis that created new links among the in-laws, a poem in the *Virginia Gazette* poked fun at the social fabric of the Tidewater gentry:

> My husband's my uncle,
> My father's my brother,
> I also am sister unto my own mother
> I am sister and aunt to a brother called John
> To whom wit and good nature combined doth belong,
> This paradox, strange as it may be to you,
> Any day that you please, I can prove to be true.

Printed beneath this lighthearted verse was the editor's comment: "N.B. The marriage is lawful."[22]

Lawful marriages were frequent within the circle of Jefferson's friends during the six years after his arrival in Williamsburg. At parties in Williamsburg and at weddings and other gatherings at their Tidewater mansions, Jefferson and his college friends danced and flirted with Frances and Judith Burwell, Alice Corbin, Susannah Potter, Anne Randolph, and Jenny Taliaferro. Their names and gossip fill Jefferson's early letters. "You have heard I suppose that John Page is courting Fanny Burwell," he wrote to William Fleming—and that "Will Bland and Betsy Yates are to be married Thursday." Was Susannah Potter "offended with me about something"? Jefferson asked Page—and "how did Nancy look at you when you danced with her at Southal's?" Writing to Page about a party at Blenheim, where Jenny Taliaferro sang and played the spinet piano, Jefferson thought she bore "a great resemblance [to] Nancy Wilton, but prettier."

"Remember me affectionately to all the young ladies," Jefferson implored Page—but especially to Rebecca Lewis Burwell.[23]

CHAPTER TWO

Rebecca Burwell

The imagination of a boy is healthy, and the mature imagination of a man is healthy; but there is a space of life between, in which the soul is in a ferment, the character undecided, the way of life uncertain, the ambition thick-sighted.

—John Keats, *Endymion* (London, 1818)

Let th'aspiring youth beware of love
Of the smooth glance beware; for 'tis too late,
When on his heart the torrent softness pours.

—Thomas Jefferson, notebook entry, ca. 1764

WHEN THOMAS Jefferson entered the College of William and Mary in March 1760, Ned Carter from Albemarle and Bob Carter from Westmoreland, aged twenty-seven and thirty-two respectively, were the only married members of his circle of friends.[1] Within a few years, as the group expanded to about thirty acquaintances in their mid-twenties, only Jefferson and one or two others remained bachelors. James McClurg, who graduated in 1762, did not marry until 1779, after a decade of medical study in Edinburgh, London, and Paris and a few years as surgeon general with Virginia's troops during the Revolution. John Edmunds's marital status remains unknown.

During his two years of college, Jefferson attended many of his friends' weddings. His friends continued to pair off during the two years he read law under the supervision of Virginia jurist George Wythe. With every new betrothal or wedding, Jefferson increasingly became the odd man out. The pace of their weddings did not relent until 1767, when Jefferson transferred his law practice from the county courts to the

General Court in Williamsburg. "Why cannot you and I be married too," Jefferson asked his friend John Page, "and to whom we would chuse?"[2]

From Shadwell, where he retreated after college to master his law books and begin a practice in the county courts, Jefferson frequently set aside Edward Coke's ponderous volumes about land tenures to pester his friends for news of their romantic adventures. "I hear that Ben Harrison has been to Wilton," he wrote Page, referring to the home of Nancy Randolph. "Let me know his success."[3] He wanted to be kept abreast of "everything which happened" and of "any news stirring in town or country [about] . . . deaths, courtships and marriages in the circle of my acquaintances." He passed along gossip whenever he heard it first. "Miss Willis is to be married next week to Daingerfield," he reported. "When is Brown to be married?"[4]

When Jefferson left the college in 1762, his own dreams of marital bliss were focused on the fair Rebecca Lewis Burwell, the youngest sister of a college classmate and F.H.C. brother. She was sixteen when she caught his eye, but in many respects she was more mature than he. Jefferson at nineteen was far more the adolescent—indeed medical science suggests that eighteenth-century boys matured several years later than boys do today.[5] Jefferson's hopes (realistic or not) were dashed when Rebecca Burwell declined his offer of marriage in 1763 and married twenty-one-year-old Jaquelin (Jack) Ambler the following spring. Her betrothal to a rival triggered the onset of Jefferson's recurrent and debilitating headaches. It fueled the misogyny of Jefferson's twenties and aroused a more predatory attitude toward women that ended in a series of unwelcome advances toward a married neighbor.

REBECCA BURWELL's eldest brother, Lewis Burwell, was the first of Jefferson's classmates to marry. In 1760 he wed John Page's sister Judith. From then until 1765 Jefferson's friends married at the pace of one or two a year. His boyhood friend Tom Randolph of Tuckahoe was next, marrying Anne Cary of Ampthill in November 1761. Eight months later Tom Nelson married Lucy Grymes at a ceremony conducted by Betsy Yates's father, rector of Bruton Parish and president of the college. Will Fitzhugh of Chatham married Anne Randolph of Arlington in April

*Anne Randolph, known to Jefferson and his friends as Nancy Wilton,
by John Wollaston, ca. 1755.*

Courtesy of the Virginia Historical Society.

1763, and Will Daingerfield went to the altar with Mary Willis that
autumn.

The pace of weddings quickened in the spring of 1764. Will Bland
married Betsy Yates in March 1764. Later in the year Jefferson's boyhood
friend Jack Walker married Betsy Moore at Chelsea, and Jack Ambler
married Rebecca Burwell. Two more of Jefferson's close friends were
married in 1765: John Page to Fanny Burwell at Burwell's Bay plantation
in Isle of Wight, and Dabney Carr to Jefferson's sister Martha at Shadwell in July. Two more bachelors went to the altar in 1766: F.H.C.
brother Warner Lewis married Mary Chiswell in May, and Will Flem-

ing wed Bettie Champe in October. The dates of the remaining marriages among Jefferson's friends are unknown, but classmate Frank Willis married Elizabeth Perrin, Westwood Armistead married a girl named Jenkins, and Ben Harrison of Brandon eventually *did* capture the heart and dowry of Nancy Wilton.

OFTEN A groomsman but never a groom, Jefferson may have met young Rebecca Burwell as early as 1760, when he attended her eldest brother's wedding in Gloucester County. Orphaned at ten, she was living in Yorktown with her aunt and uncle, Elizabeth and William Nelson, a senior member of the Governor's Council. Beautiful, vivacious, and blessed with an agile mind, Rebecca enjoyed dances and parties and "all the innocent gaieties of life." Behind those girlish charms was a serious young woman who had quietly found comfort in a deep religious faith after the deaths of her parents.[6]

We can only guess at the exact moment when Rebecca Burwell first caught Jefferson's eye, but she was often in Williamsburg, where the Nelsons kept a town house near the capitol, and her brother was Jefferson's classmate and friend. Perhaps their paths crossed at a wedding, a ball at the Royal Governor's palace, a party at Wetherburn's Tavern, or a dance at the Raleigh. We do know that on one of these occasions in the summer or autumn of 1762, Rebecca Burwell gave Tom Jefferson a small piece of paper bearing her silhouette—a treasure that he placed inside the cover of his pocket watch as if the timepiece were a locket. One other thing is certain. When Rebecca Lewis Burwell made her romantic debut in Jefferson's extant correspondence on Christmas Day 1762, the tall and awkward young man was utterly smitten for the first time in his life. Disaster soon followed.

In December 1762, when Jefferson left Williamsburg and headed home to Shadwell for the holidays, he visited his elder sister Mary and her husband, John Bolling, at Fairfields in Goochland County, about halfway between Richmond and Charlottesville. Retiring to bed on Christmas Eve, Jefferson hung his jacket on a bedpost and laid his pocket watch "in the usual place." The next morning he awoke feeling "overwhelmed by more and greater misfortunes than have befallen a descendant of Adam for these thousand years past." Rats and rain had attacked his possessions while he slept. "I am sure if there is such a thing as a devil in this world," Jefferson complained, "he must have been here last night."[7]

For starters, as Jefferson described his tribulations to John Page, there were "the cursed rats." They carried away half a dozen pieces of sheet music, "new minuets I had just got." They chewed up his wallet, "which was in my pocket within a foot of my head." They also stole a pair of embroidered silk garters, a loss mitigated only by his good luck in having recently won a new pair from Alice Corbin at a holiday party.

The rain did far more serious damage than the rats. "When I went to bed I laid my watch in the usual place," Jefferson grumbled. When he arose on Christmas morning, his watch was "afloat in water let in at a leak in the roof of the house." The loss of his timepiece was bad enough, but its ruin was attended by "something worse." Because Jefferson had carefully placed Rebecca Burwell's keepsake silhouette inside the cover of his pocket watch, the image was ruined:

> The subtle particles of water . . . so overcame the cohesion of the particles of the paper of which my dear picture and watch paper were composed that in attempting to take them out and dry them Good God! . . . my cursed fingers gave them such a r[ip] as I fear I shall never get over.

Although rain and clumsy fingers were the instruments of destruction, Jefferson blamed the loss on more nefarious forces. "This was the last stroke Satan had in reserve for me," he wrote. "I cared not for any thing else." Jefferson's only solace was his awareness that "although the picture be defaced, there is so lively an image of her imprinted in my mind that I shall think of her too often I fear for my peace of mind."[8]

For two years, from 1762 through the spring of 1764, Jefferson sustained an adolescent obsession with Rebecca Burwell. When Page went to a Williamsburg wedding that Jefferson could not attend, he wanted to know, "Was SHE there?" He dreamt of building a sailboat and naming it the *Rebecca*. He mused about constructing "a small house" at Shadwell, but was eager to alter the design if Rebecca agreed "to favor us with her company, in which case I will enlarge the plan as much as she pleases."[9]

By October of 1763 Rebecca Burwell was at the center of a two-part scheme that Jefferson pitched to Will Fleming as "the cleverest plan of life that can be imagined." The first step was plausible enough. Fleming and Jefferson could easily have moved closer to each other. "You exchange your land for Edgehill," Jefferson suggested (referring to a Randolph family plantation a few miles from Shadwell), "or I mine for Fairfields" (the house with the leaky roof a few miles across the James River from Fleming's residence in Cumberland County). Once they were neighbors, the rest of Jefferson's plan was simple: "You marry S[uke]y P[otte]r, I marry R[ebecc]a B[urwel]l, and [we'll] get a pole chair and a pair of keen horses, practise law in the same courts, and drive about to all the dances in the country together. How do you like it?"[10]

Fleming's reply is lost to history, but that does not matter. Before he could have replied, Jefferson had mustered up his courage to speak with Rebecca Burwell about marriage. And her answer was no.

WILLIAMSBURG's Raleigh Tavern was noted less for its beauty than for its convenience—on Duke of Gloucester Street midway between the capitol, Bruton Parish Church, and the Governor's Palace. Aside from these public buildings, the tavern's Apollo Room was the town's largest available space for meetings or events. Since midcentury the Apollo Room had served as a favorite venue for concerts, parties, dances, and the occasional lecture. Later it was destined for fame as the meeting place of Virginia legislators quarreling with royal governors and deliberating about independence.[11]

In the Apollo Room on Thursday, October 6, 1763, Tom Jefferson spent the evening dancing with Rebecca Burwell. He was now six months past his twentieth birthday. She was four months past her seventeenth. Before the party ended, Jefferson ventured to ask Rebecca to marry him. And from that moment—as Jefferson lamented the next morning in a letter to John Page—the evening became a disaster. "I had dressed up in my own mind, as moving language as I knew how and expected to have performed in a tolerably creditable manner," Jefferson groaned to Page, "but good God!"

In the actual presence of the young woman of his dreams, Jefferson was overwhelmed with what he could only describe as a "strange confusion!" All the eloquent sentiments he had prepared for the occasion crumbled into "a few broken sentences, uttered in great disorder, and interrupted with pauses of uncommon length." Morning found Jefferson in a "most melancholy fit." Aside from his letter to Page, no other evidence sheds light on that fateful Thursday evening in the Apollo Room. All we know is that Rebecca Burwell gave Jefferson a second chance to outline his dreams for their future "on another occasion" that autumn. "I then opened my mind more freely and more fully," Jefferson told Page, but apparently the second conversation was as confusing to Miss Burwell as it was to Page.[12]

Jefferson opened their second conversation by expressing a desire to consult her guardians before asking *her* consent to marriage! In effect the young attorney served notice that he would *in time* ask her to marry him—"Such questions would one day be asked"—when a more resolute man would have known to plead his love directly. Not a promising start. Then Tom told Rebecca that marriage would have to wait until he returned from a trip to England that he portrayed as imminent and described as a "necessity"—though it proved neither. What could Rebecca have thought as she listened to Tom describe an intended journey and "the delays which would consequently be occasioned"?[13] "Please marry me, but not yet" was the gist of Jefferson's second conversation with Rebecca Burwell in the autumn of 1763.

JEFFERSON'S CONDUCT can only have been puzzling to the woman he thought he loved. His infatuation with Rebecca Burwell sent him running along an odd course, as is evident when we look closely at his youthful correspondence with Page and Fleming. Consider the simple matter of Rebecca's name. At first Jefferson wrote of the fair "Miss Becca Burwell." Then he disguised her name with initials and dashes. He asked Page about "R. B." in a letter from Shadwell early in 1763, and he commented about "R——a B——l" in a letter to Will Fleming. By summer he had fastened on the nickname "Belinda."[14] All of these disguises—initials, dashes, and nicknames—were common in newspapers and private correspondence in eighteenth-century British America, but Jefferson soon went further. Early in 1764 he began using Greek letters to disguise her nickname, first by transliterating *Belinda* into Greek and then for good measure by writing that coded in reverse as αδμιλεβ.

Finally, in January 1764 when Jefferson replaced this Greek anagram with a convoluted Latin phrase, *campana in die*, something was seriously amiss.[15] It was not just the fact that Jefferson's final code word for Rebecca's name was a cumbersome pun on *Belinda* ("bell" *in die*, since *campana* is Latin for "bell"). The significant truths, of which Jefferson may not have been aware, were two. First, he had replaced a real girl and her real name with nicknames on paper that ended in a sophomoric verbal trick. Second, all of this occurred not in conversation with her, or in love letters to her, but in notes written to his buddy John Page.

Did Jefferson somehow regard Rebecca Burwell's name as too sacred to be written plain? No. His motive for disguising her name is familiar to anyone who survived high school. Jefferson and his gossipy friends were passing notes to one another at a distance, with the ever-present risk that some adolescent courier might be tempted to peek and tattle. "If this letter was to fall into the hands of some of our gay acquaintance," Jefferson commented to Page in July 1763, "your correspondent and his solemn notions would probably be the subjects of a great deal of mirth and raillery."[16] Each new layer of verbal disguise marked Jefferson's escalating need for secrecy and control. And inevitably—three months after the disastrous evening in the Apollo Room—one of his acquaintances *did* succumb to the temptations of curiosity and gossip.

After spending the holidays in Albemarle, Jefferson was back in Williamsburg on a dreary winter evening. He took a blank piece of paper and scrawled an anguished dateline at the top: "Devilsburg Jan: 19. 1764." Then he poured his feelings about "what has formerly passed between αδμιλεβ and myself" into a fervent letter to his confidant John Page.[17] He signed it, sealed it, and the next day entrusted his letter to Sukey Potter, who was to give it to Page at Rosewell on her way home to Middlesex County. At Yorktown, however, perhaps as she waited for the ferry, Miss Potter apparently encountered their friend Tom Nelson and entrusted *him* to carry Jefferson's letter the rest of the way to Page.

At some point between Williamsburg and Rosewell, the letter was opened, and its secrets soon were being whispered among Jefferson's acquaintances. He got wind of this over the weekend and became suspicious. On Monday he wrote Page again from "Devilsburg"—outlining his fears that their friends had peeked at his earlier revelations. This time he referred to Rebecca as "my dear *campana in die*, instead of αδμιλεβ," expressing regret that he had not used Latin in Thursday's note (as though their friends would have been misled by that ruse).[18]

By the early weeks of 1764, the real flesh-and-blood young woman named Rebecca Burwell had faded into the clever abstractions of Jefferson's correspondence as he sought to cloak the aftermath of the Apollo Room fiasco from his peers. The details of Jefferson's second conversation with Rebecca Burwell must have struck John Page as oddly as they do a modern reader.

Why did he tell Page that his entire second conversation with her was "managed in such a manner that I was tolerably easy myself *without doing anything which could give* [*her*] *friends the least umbrage, were the whole that passed* [*between us*] *to be related to them*"? What about the sentence, a few lines later, that proclaimed his devotion to Rebecca with all the passion of a legal brief: "After all the proofs I have given of my sincerity," she "can be under no apprehension of a change in my sentiments: and *were I to do as my friends advise me, I could give* [*her*] *no better security than* [*s*]*he has at present*"? Finally, what of the posturing declaration that "my fate depends on [Rebecca's] present resolutions: by them I must stand or fall: if they are not favorable to me, it is out of my power to say anything . . . that I have not said already: *so that a visit could not possibly be of the least weight*"?[19]

Jefferson's second conversation with Rebecca Burwell, as he summarized it to Page, was less a discussion of marriage than an exercise in emotional damage control. Consider the three italicized phrases just presented. Jefferson consciously "managed" the conversation so that, when it was reported to their friends, none could find fault or take offense. Despite advice to the contrary from Page and his friends,[20] and without ever mentioning love, Jefferson contended that he had done everything possible to demonstrate his "sincerity"—contending, further, that "a visit could not possibly be of the least weight." Despite the fact that he was writing to Page from Williamsburg—where the object of his affection was at that very moment either down the street or only a few miles away in Yorktown—Jefferson insisted that there was no reason for him to visit her. And all the while he wrote only to Page—never to her. Peculiar behavior for a young man in love.

Rebecca Burwell had the maturity to recognize that Jefferson's sentiments comprised something other than true and everlasting love. He was not ready for marriage. Rebecca knew that, and apparently so did many of their friends. His idolizing dreams had blinded him to the physical existence of the real girl. Even in the aftermath of their two unsuccessful discussions of marriage, Jefferson continued to fill his letters with romantic hopes that were entirely contradicted by his actions. "Can you believe it?" he admitted to Will Fleming in March of 1764. "I have been so abominably indolent as not to have seen her since last October."[21]

Indolence was not the issue. Jefferson was avoiding Rebecca Burwell—indeed we do not know when he ever saw her again. Presumably their paths crossed in later life, but as late as April of 1764 he was still avoiding her. When he learned that she had made an unexpected visit to Burwell's Bay plantation in Isle of Wight while his friend John Page was visiting his fiancée, Frances Burwell, Jefferson felt that he had made "the narrowest escape in the world." What if he, too, had been present? "I wonder how I should have behaved?" he admitted to Page. "I am sure I should have been at a great loss."[22]

Jefferson's mood of detachment, exemplified by his unwillingness to approach Rebecca Burwell in person, suggests elements of both confusion and emotional self-defense. "What would you advise me to do?" he asked Page from Albemarle. "Had I better stay here and do nothing, or go down and do less? . . . Inclination tells me to go, receive my sentence, and be no longer in suspence: but, reason says if you go and your attempt proves unsuccessful you will be ten times more wretched than ever." Jefferson's sustained absence seems especially puzzling after Page had alerted him, in July 1763, to the existence of a "rival" for Miss Burwell's affection.[23]

On the other hand, after the Apollo Room fiasco and their follow-up conversation, perhaps Jefferson was avoiding a public confirmation of what he already knew—and a catastrophe that could only leave him "ten times more wretched." In his intimate letters to Page and Fleming, he offered his absence and his anticipated trip to England as pretexts for Rebecca's decision. Perhaps these excuses made the pain of rejection less hurtful—or less embarrassing in the eyes of all those acquaintances who were pairing off so readily.

Rebecca's responses to Jefferson's proposals seem to have been forthright. If she even regarded Jefferson as a serious alternative to Jaquelin

Ambler, Rebecca Burwell may have been inclined to leave her "two speculating geniuses to their own conjectures," as her eldest daughter did when she was courted by "two of the Very Smartest Beaux in this country." For Rebecca in 1764 (as for her eldest daughter in 1785), the successful suitor was the one who "lost no opportunity" to declare his love and who did "everything in his power to ingratiate himself with [her] family"—not the awkward boy writing angst-ridden letters to his buddies.[24]

IN THE SPRING of 1764, regardless of his self-deceptions in the interim, Jefferson was forced to confront the truth. Near midnight on a lonely Tuesday evening in March, he fought off "a violent headache, with which I have been afflicted these two days," as he scrawled a hasty reply to a note from Will Fleming. Forget about marriage, Jefferson grumbled. Forget about living as neighbors and practicing law together. Forget about pole chairs and country dances. "With regard to the scheme which I proposed to you," Jefferson wrote, "I am sorry to tell you it is totally frustrated by Miss R. B.'s marriage to Jaquelin Ambler which the people here tell me they daily expect."[25]

The news of their betrothal was accurate. Rebecca Burwell and Jaquelin Ambler were married in Yorktown on May 24, 1764. Jefferson's rival was a gentleman with a bright future and an "athletic form and remarkable florid complection."[26] A year older than Jefferson, Jack Ambler had attended the grammar school at William and Mary in the 1750s and then graduated from the College of Philadelphia in 1761. After returning to Virginia, he had begun working toward a partnership in his wealthy father's mercantile business in Yorktown, down the street from the Nelson home where Rebecca grew up. After their marriage, Ambler inherited the family business when his father and one brother died in 1766, followed by his other brother in 1768. Heir to an estate valued at £14,940, Jaquelin Ambler promptly succeeded his father as collector of customs, a member of the vestry, and a justice of the peace. After independence, he served on the Virginia Board of Trade and then on the Council of State when Jefferson was governor. Elected state treasurer in 1782, Ambler held that office as well as positions of leadership within the Episcopal Church.[27] On January 10, 1798, Jack Ambler died of consumption (tuberculosis or a similar respiratory ailment, which had also killed his father and elder brothers) in Richmond.[28]

The couple shared a strong traditional Anglican faith. "On every Sunday that his church was open," Jaquelin Ambler "was the first to enter it," their eldest daughter wrote, "and often would be the almost solitary male at the Table of his God."[29] Their faith "had great weight in the selection he made of our Mother," she concluded, for never "were minds more congenial, and for upwards of thirty years they lived in the constant reciprocation of connubial affection."[30] Rebecca survived him by eight years. After her death on August 5, 1806, she was buried next to her husband in St. John's churchyard.

WHO WAS the fair and devout young lady who so captivated the adolescent Jefferson? Born on Tuesday, May 20, 1746, Rebecca Lewis Burwell was the youngest child of Eton- and Cambridge-educated Lewis Burwell of Fairfield, in Gloucester County. Her father was a grandson of Robert "King" Carter—but the Burwells themselves were "a long-tailed family," as one royal official described them. Their place in the colony began with its founding by the Virginia Company of London. Many Tidewater Virginia families had vague traditions about distinguished English forebears, but when the Burwells emblazoned their tombs with a coat of arms, its legitimacy had been formally certified by the College of Heralds in London after genealogical research (at no small expense) that few other proud colonials chose to risk. Rebecca's grandfather was probably the Virginian who, in 1698, first unrolled a colorful parchment (still proudly preserved by his descendants) entitled "A Genealogical Arbor of the ancient Family of BURWELL of Sutton in the County of Suffolk." It was festooned with no less than three colorful versions of the family arms.

Rebecca's father had been appointed to the Governor's Council during the administration of Sir William Gooch, and Rebecca was probably named in honor of that governor's wife. Two of her uncles, Carter Burwell and Robert Burwell, also served on the council. Her aunt Elizabeth, their sister, was married to councilor William Nelson of Yorktown. Before Governor Gooch's successor arrived in 1751, Rebecca's father served as acting governor and "president" of the council. In that capacity, when British authorities requested a new map of the colony, her father had selected Joshua Fry and Peter Jefferson for the task. "Considering that we are yet a country of woods," Burwell told Fry when their work was complete, "it is surprising how [you] could draw so beautiful a map of it."[31] Both social and geographic distance separated the frontier Jeffersons from the Tidewater Burwells.

Rebecca's mother, Mary Willis Burwell, had grown up at White Marsh plantation in Gloucester County. She had died from the complications of Rebecca's birth, her eighth child in nine years. Her eldest was Jefferson's classmate and F.H.C. brother Lewis Jr. Between them were five sisters—Elizabeth, Lucy, Anne, Judith, and Mary—and a brother, Nathaniel.

Childbirth was a dangerous enterprise in the eighteenth century, and the Burwell children at Fairfield were like many young Virginians who experienced the loss of their mother. Unlike her siblings, however, Rebecca was the child whose birth had *occasioned* her mother's death. We have no evidence as to whether that tragic circumstance brought her father closer to his innocent young daughter, kept him more distant, or made any difference at all. We do know that Lewis Burwell never remarried, or at least that he had not found a second wife before illness struck him down, too.

Rebecca's infancy surely was comfortable at Fairfield. At midcentury her father owned 7,800 acres in Gloucester County, as well as 168 slaves, 16 horses, and 259 cattle. But wealth could not buy health. At about the time of Rebecca's fifth birthday, her father began to exhibit symptoms of "a distemper in the Mind." It may have been a tumor or cancer, or perhaps some ominous mental illness foreshadowing the "malady" that afflicted his daughters and granddaughters. Nothing his doctors could offer, not even the healing waters of Virginia's medicinal springs, proved effective against its relentless advance. Lewis Burwell lingered at Fairfield for several years and finally died at forty-six on May 6, 1756—two weeks short of Rebecca's tenth birthday.[32]

Sometime during the years of her father's long illness Rebecca probably had been sent to Yorktown and placed in the care of her aunt Elizabeth and uncle William Nelson. "Having no daughter of her own," Elizabeth Burwell Nelson "took great delight in having the charge of" Rebecca.[33] The Nelsons clearly loved their orphaned niece as their own,

and her childhood memories of Yorktown were happy. She proudly
recalled the Nelson house as "a seat of wealth and elegance" that was
"unrivaled in Virginia," with "its commanding view, its vast expanse of
water," and its "beautiful neighboring country." The house in which
Rebecca spent her early teens was "a delightful residence for persons of
all descriptions, resorted to by travillers from every part of the world,
remarkable for its hospitality, and its Society so far the most polished in
Virginia."[34]

These were family stories that Rebecca's daughters remembered, celebrated, and shared with her granddaughters. Women of the Burwell
family regarded their history as a source of wisdom and example "that
you may hand down to your daughters." Young girls, they knew, "will
attentively listen to hear what Grand pa, and Grand ma said, where they
lived, and from whence they came."[35] The illness and death of her father
certainly deepened Rebecca's religious faith. Both the death of her
mother and the nurture of her guardian aunt may also have inclined
young Rebecca Burwell toward a greater appreciation of another notable
female ancestor.

PROMINENT AMONG the family stories to which Rebecca Burwell
attentively listened was the saga of her great-aunt Lucy Burwell, whose
independent spirit had delighted Virginians of both sexes for six
decades.[36] Any of a number of her father's kin might have told Rebecca
Lewis Burwell the story of her celebrated great-aunt—whose defiance
and humiliation of an imperious royal governor was a proud moment for
Virginia women—but surely Rebecca heard the story in detail from her
aunt and guardian, Elizabeth Burwell Nelson, who was also Lucy's
niece.

Born at Fairfield in November 1683, some sixty years before Rebecca's
birth at the same plantation, Lucy Burwell was said to have been the
prize of her father's "houseful of blooming daughters"—nine girls by his
two wives. "Her eyes have enough fire to inflame the coldest saint,"
wrote William Byrd II, "and her virtue is pure enough to chill the
warmest sinner."[37] Lucy was barely sixteen in the spring of 1699 when
she innocently caught the eye of Virginia's forty-four-year-old governor,
Francis Nicholson. An able career soldier, Nicholson was also known for

his temper and violent language. After a visit or two, Lucy showed no interest in her middle-aged suitor. By then, however, her feminine charms had swept the governor off his feet.

Nicholson regaled Lucy Burwell with letters. He addressed poems to his "Vertuous pretty Charming Innocent Dove, the only Center of my Constant Love." But Lucy Burwell simply did not care for Francis Nicholson. As he persisted, she spurned his displays of passion with embarrassment, his displays of temper with alarm. When Lucy declined to see him, Nicholson offered "Sacred Pledges of true Love, Which Age nor time shall ever move." Even Nicholson's love poems seemed fraught with menace.[38]

Lucy's indifference drove Nicholson crazy. He offered her father a seat on the council. It was politely declined. Her father (Rebecca's great-grandfather) was already a prominent member of the House of Burgesses and kin to a majority of the Governor's Council. "I have often told you that I left my daughter to make her own choice as to a husband," Colonel Burwell reminded the governor. Even "to gain a kingdom," Burwell said he could never "be guilty of such a horrible piece of Cruelty . . . as to force my daughter to marry against her will to the best man alive."[39]

For more than two years Nicholson reacted with temper tantrums and threats at reports that Lucy Burwell was being courted by younger rivals. His obsessive behavior—"passion etc. beyond the power of words to express"—inevitably had political implications. When he learned that Lucy loved someone else enough to marry him, Nicholson threatened to slit the throat of "the bridegroom, the minister, and the justice who issued the license." A friend in London warned Nicholson that his atrocious conduct was playing into the hands of his enemies: unlike in "some barbarous countries where the tender Lady is often dragged into the Sultan's arms, just reaking in the blood of her nearest relations," his friend asserted, "English women . . . are the freest in the world and will not be won by constraint."[40]

Nicholson ignored the advice. News of Lucy Burwell's engagement in 1703 to a promising young planter provoked the governor to violent threats against the extended Burwell family. Unfortunately for Nicholson, the family's bonds of kinship reached into virtually every great mansion in Tidewater Virginia—and some prominent places in England as well. Sir Robert Walpole, the preeminent leader of the House of Commons, regarded himself as kin to the Burwells of Virginia. That spring, six members of the Royal Council, four of them closely related to Lucy Burwell, petitioned Queen Anne for Nicholson's recall. They cited his "unusuall, insolent, and arbitrary methods of Government" as well as the "wicked and scandalous examples of [his] life."[41] Enhanced by reports of Nicholson's unruly courtship, the petition soon hit its mark.[42] The governor departed Virginia early in 1705. He would die in 1728, far away and unmarried. Nicholson was history.

Lucy Burwell was legend. She and her twenty nine year-old husband, Edmund Berkeley of Barn Elms, in Middlesex County, were married at Fairfield in December 1703. It was a happy marriage, blessed with six children, and they cherished each other until she died in 1716, victim of a local epidemic of measles that "spar[e]d few or none in the country and sent many to their long home."[43]

Although some had reservations about "obedient," the gentry women of eighteenth-century Virginia generally accepted the traditional marital roles—wife, "kind mistress and indulgent mother and obedient"—that were inscribed on Lucy Burwell Berkeley's tombstone.[44] As family history, however, Lucy's story also demonstrated that the choice of a husband, arguably the most public and independent act of her life, was the single decision within a woman's control that might determine her future happiness or misery.[45]

Women of the Ambler family into which Rebecca Burwell married after she declined Jefferson's proposal were also acutely conscious of their history. In the mid-eighteenth century the Amblers of Virginia revered a "dear Aunt Jaquelin" who lived at Jamestown and never married. "On account of her many great virtues," as Rebecca's daughter explained, their great-aunt Jaquelin's name "was given to my father, myself, and indeed to one in each of our families." Women in the Ambler family were expected to "understand that the name of a woman may be transmitted to posterity—and even to boys—tho' she never change her State of Celibacy."[46] Rebecca's husband's first name testified to that fact.

Rebecca Burwell also commemorated significant women in her family in the naming of her own daughters. Her eldest daughter, born in 1765, was Elizabeth Jaquelin Ambler—named to honor both Rebecca's guardian aunt and her eldest sister as well as her husband and his name-sake aunt. Her second daughter, Mary Willis, born in 1766, bore the maiden name of Rebecca's mother and the given name of her sister. Rebecca named her third daughter, Ann, born in 1772, for her sister. Finally, in naming Lucy Nelson Ambler, born in 1776, Rebecca linked the first name shared by her sister and her famous great-aunt with the surname of her guardian uncle.

The recollections of her daughters provide valuable glimpses of the fair Rebecca who enchanted Thomas Jefferson as a teenager and danced with him in the Apollo Room before declining his proposal of marriage. Rebecca's daughters heard her tell a favorite anecdote about the baron de Botetourt, Virginia's last popular royal governor. Botetourt was a frequent dinner guest at the Yorktown home of her guardian uncle, William Nelson. After returning to the Governor's Palace "from one of those visits," Botetourt had "sent down a Leaden Box containing a delicious double Gloster cheese to a Lady whom he had understood had a great fancy for it," Rebecca's daughters recalled in their correspondence. "This Lady was our good Mother, who had expressed a wish for a double Gloster cheese."[47]

Rebecca Burwell Ambler's daughters knew that their mother "was often disposed to gaiety" and that she "enjoyed the blessings of life" as well as imported cheddar. They admired the "natural sprightliness of her mind" and knew that she enjoyed "all the innocent gaieties of life." In their banter about courtships and flirtation, dances and ball gowns, they reflected glimpses of their mother's youthful experiences as well. Rebecca's daughters knew that she was a woman of resolution and faith who "considered cheerfulness as a Christian virtue," but also a woman of delicate nerves.[48]

A predisposition toward chronic depression apparently ran in Rebecca's family—a "dreadful nervous malady" that she and her daughters knew all too well.[49] The War of Independence sapped her strength. "Poverty and perplexity of every kind" shattered Rebecca's vulnerable nerves. Exacerbating "a nervous malady begun in early life," the trauma of war eclipsed the radiance that had caught Jefferson's eye and dazzled his heart.[50]

For Rebecca and her girls, the story of the Revolution began bravely in 1775 with "a British Ship threatening to fire on [Yorktown]" and "marvelous stories of Dunmore's outrages."[51] But their story turned tragic in the final year of the war. Yorktown's deep-water port sealed the village's fate in 1781 as Cornwallis and the British army arrived, having fought their way north through the Carolinas, seeking a place of rendezvous with the British fleet. When they encamped to await the arrival of the fleet, Yorktown's population was "forced to seek an asylum in a less exposed country." Rebecca's family "were amongst the first to fly."[52]

As a member of Jefferson's Council of State, Jaquelin Ambler and his wife felt especially vulnerable. It was "absolutely necessary for him to run no risques of falling into the hands of the enemy." Three times the Ambler family fled their Yorktown home before they found refuge northwest of Richmond in the forests of Hanover County. Ever alert to the danger of roving British soldiers, Jack Ambler slept "in the old coach every night with faithful old Sam as his guard," while Rebecca and their girls made themselves "as comfortable as we can in the Overseers tiny dwelling."[53]

There was, however, no escape from the war in the spring of 1781. Late one evening in May, as British raiders scoured the countryside around Richmond, the Amblers once again took flight, "this time thro' byways and brambles till we could get to the Main Road leading to Charlottesville." After traveling all night, Rebecca and the girls greeted the dawn in the empty house of a family friend while Jack pressed on toward Charlottesville, where the legislature was scheduled to convene. Just as Rebecca and the girls began "spreading pallets to rest [their] weary heads," however, a local resident arrived with word that Banastre Tarleton and his cavalry were riding hard to "catch the Governor before he could reach Charlottesville." Fortunately, Jack Ambler heard the clatter of Tarleton's horses in the quiet woods, eluded capture, and made his way back to his family. Then everyone trudged back to the tiny cottage in Hanover—"a spot," his daughter wrote, "that I defy the British or even the devel himself to find."[54]

The Amblers were not the only Virginia officeholders scrambling to escape Tarleton's cavalry in the spring of 1781. The legislature had convened in Charlottesville on May 28 just long enough to adjourn across the Blue Ridge to Staunton—prevented in their haste from electing a new executive. Governor Jefferson, whose second term was technically over, was Tarleton's prime target. At Monticello, after sending his family south through the woods to Ned Carter's Blenheim, Jefferson spent the morning securing the documents and papers of his office while monitoring through a telescope the movement of British redcoats near the village below. Finally, as Tarleton ascended toward Monticello from the north, Jefferson rode south across Carter's Mountain to Blenheim. From there he took his family to Poplar Forest, a farm eighty miles to the south in Bedford County that his wife inherited from her father.[55]

Central Virginia was quickly abuzz with tales of near misses and hasty retreats. At their sanctuary in Hanover, the Amblers compared notes with neighbors who had survived the crisis—and Rebecca's daughter recounted two stories that "made even my poor Mother smile." One was about a "neighbor P——'s escape just as the enemy entered the Town." The other was an "account we have of our illustrious G[overno]r who they say took neither rest or food for man or horse till he reached C[arte]r's Mountain."[56] Jefferson was a more prominent target for capture than Rebecca's husband, but the Ambler family's good-natured commentary recognized that as prominent leaders in the state government, neither man had any choice but escape.

The anecdote about Jefferson's flight from Monticello interested the Amblers not because Jefferson had once proposed to Rebecca but because the governor's experience was so very much like their own. Indeed, nothing in the Ambler family correspondence suggests that Rebecca regarded Jefferson as an old flame, and nothing hints of any personal animus toward him.[57] Jefferson's bungled courtship may have briefly flattered and puzzled Rebecca Burwell when she was young. Beyond that, there is no evidence that Jefferson mattered at all in her later life.

FOR THOMAS JEFFERSON, on the other hand, Rebecca Burwell's decision to marry Jaquelin Ambler was fraught with consequences. Regardless of whether he truly loved Rebecca Burwell in 1763 and 1764, Jefferson had given her a central place in his dreams for the future. At twenty, his soul was in ferment, his character undecided, his prospects uncertain—and he was lonely. "I do not like the ups and downs of a country life," he confessed to Fleming. "To day you are frolicking with a fine girl and tomorrow you are moping by yourself."[58]

The collapse of Jefferson's romantic dreams immediately disrupted his health. News of Rebecca Burwell's engagement to Jack Ambler triggered a "violent head ach" that lasted at least three days. It was the first of many excruciating headaches that would plague Jefferson on and off during the next forty-five years of his life.[59] Although they are often described as migraines, Jefferson himself never used that term (which was already three centuries old) or its contemporary synonyms. Recent scholarship suggests that he suffered not from migraines but rather from severe muscular-contraction headaches triggered by tension or stress.[60]

Jefferson's descriptions of his headaches, and their symptoms, are thoroughly consistent. When they struck, the headaches lasted for days or even weeks. Unlike migraines, these attacks were clearly linked to intensely stressful events in his private or political life.[61] Examples abound, but three will suffice. One of the few things we know about Jefferson's relationship with his mother is that in 1776 her death triggered six weeks of debilitating headaches. Jefferson described the onset of another headache atop Natural Bridge, the famous rock arch over Cedar Creek in Rockbridge County, in his *Notes on the State of Virginia*. "Few men have resolution to . . . look over into the abyss," he wrote. "You involuntarily fall on your hands and feet, creep to the parapet and peep over it" to the creek nearly three hundred feet below. "Looking down from this height about a minute," Jefferson wrote, "gave me a violent head ach." A third example occurred in March of 1807. For nearly three weeks Jefferson was "obliged to be shut up in a dark room from early in the forenoon till night, with a periodical head-ach." This time it coincided with the simultaneous collapse of pivotal treaty negotiations with Great Britain, the life-threatening illness of his son-in-law, and the impending treason trial of Aaron Burr. While Jefferson suffered severe recurrent headaches during moments of intense stress over a period of forty-five years—starting in March of 1764, when he learned of Rebecca Burwell's betrothal to Jack Ambler—he would have none at all in the seventeen years after he retired from the presidency in 1809.[62]

Headaches were one manifestation of Jefferson's reaction to Rebecca Burwell's betrothal. The other notable reaction expressed itself in male bravado, in his deepening mistrust of women and his more predatory demeanor toward them. Jefferson's male bluster surfaced immediately after he admitted that Rebecca had "totally frustrated" his dreams. "Well the lord bless her I say!" Friends like Fleming and Page still might wish to marry, but Jefferson's new stance was, "No, thank ye."[63] He was a rock. He was an island. He would mask his pain and henceforth would seek his own pleasure.

Responding to this emotional crisis in a new posture of bravado, Jefferson penned one of the more mysterious passages in all of his voluminous correspondence. It is a passage that warrants a close reading. As an inhabitant of Williamsburg, "and a young inhabitant too," Jefferson bragged to Fleming, "many and great are the comforts of a single state. . . . For St. Paul only says that it is better to be married than to burn." He continued, "Now I presume that if that apostle had known that providence would at an after day be so kind to any particular set of people as to furnish them with other means of extinguishing their fire than those of matrimony, [Saint Paul] would have earnestly recommended them [i.e., those "other means"] to their practice."[64]

Of all the biblical injunctions about marriage that might have come to mind as Rebecca Burwell prepared to marry someone else, Jefferson was drawn to Saint Paul's admonitions about the management of sexual passion. More puzzling, however, is Jefferson's contention that youthful residents of Williamsburg in the 1760s now possessed an alternative—some "other means of extinguishing their fire"—that Saint Paul might have recommended had it been known to him about A.D. 50.

Perhaps Jefferson had "bundling" in mind—a custom of overnight dating often associated with Pennsylvania and New England but evidently still practiced in England, Wales, Scotland, and Europe in the eighteenth century.[65] Perhaps Jefferson and Fleming were joshing about masturbation, which had not yet been transformed into the life-threatening horror of the Victorian era.[66] Perhaps they were musing about the attractions of indentured servant girls and milkmaids.[67] Williamsburg surely had a few prostitutes[68]—but Saint Paul would not have recommended them, nor would he have recommended dalliances with married women. Perhaps, although few spoke of it openly, Jefferson and Fleming were simply acknowledging the fact that female slaves on British plantations throughout the South and the Caribbean gave wealthy planters and their sons opportunities unknown to the apostle and not as readily available to men in New England or Great Britain.[69]

Because Will Fleming's thoughts about these "other means of extinguishing their fire" have not survived, we can only speculate about what

he and Jefferson had specifically in mind. Regardless of Saint Paul's
scruples, however, Jefferson had *something* in mind. His conduct did
change after his disappointment with Rebecca Burwell, and within a few
years he was repeatedly propositioning the wife of a neighbor and friend.

Because the sexual favors of a prostitute or a slave cannot be dismissed out of hand, two fragments of evidence must be considered. The
first is a cluster of four unusual entries in Jefferson's account books for
August, September, and October 1770. These entries, among the very
few that Jefferson took care to write in shorthand, may record sexual
liaisons with a married woman, Molly Dudley (at a cost of five or six
shillings each time), or a slave girl, Sukey.[70] The other fragment of evidence surfaces decades later, in 1815, when Jefferson's personal physician
was treating his symptoms of urinary obstruction. In the course of the
diagnosis, Dr. Thomas Watkins asked very discreetly "whether [Jeffer-
son] may have had early in life any continuance of gonorrhæa."[71] Jefferson's answer, if he gave one, is lost to history.

These fragments of historical evidence are inconclusive at best. On
the one hand, Jefferson's urinary problems at seventy-two could well
have been caused by an enlarged prostate, a common ailment among
older men, regardless of whether his medical history included venereal
disease.[72] On the other, even *if* Jefferson's carefully disguised account-
book entries were meant to record illicit sexual encounters, contracting
venereal disease was a possible but not *inevitable* consequence. The jux-
taposition of Dr. Watkins's question with these four rather secretive
account-book entries does sustain only one very limited inference.
Whether based on his general career experience with other Virginia
patients or his five years of familiarity with this patient, the good doctor
felt it necessary to ask Jefferson a delicate question about whether his
youthful conduct might have resulted in venereal disease. The question
conclusively proves only that Dr. Watkins thought it possible.

THE EVIDENCE for Jefferson's embrace of misogyny in the 1760s is
much more substantial.[73] Like many studious young men, Jefferson
began jotting memorable passages from his reading into notebooks
before he came to college. His teacher James Maury may well have recommended the practice of keeping a "commonplace book," as they were

called. The printing office in Williamsburg sold blank account books, but Jefferson's earliest literary notes were apparently copied into an empty notebook that had belonged to his father. Into this volume, which has come to be known as his *Literary Commonplace Book,* Jefferson copied passages from his reading from the late 1750s to about 1773. The notebook entries reflect the reading and the moods of a complex young man through his adolescence and early adulthood.[74]

In his various notebooks, Jefferson reflected his distress in the lonely years between his rejection by Rebecca Burwell and his marriage. Inscribed inside the cover of a 1770 memorandum book, for example, was a Latin verse apparently of his own composition that translates as:

> Entrust a ship to the winds, do not trust your heart to girls.
> For the surge of the sea is safer than a woman's loyalty:
> No woman is good: but if a good one has befallen anyone
> I know not by what fate an evil thing has become a good one.[75]

Passages expressing this kind of fear and hostility toward women abound among the entries in Jefferson's *Literary Commonplace Book* during and after his courtship with Rebecca Burwell. He quoted Virgil's general frustration: "A fickle and changeful thing is woman ever." From the works of playwrights both ancient and contemporary he copied other quotations that bristle with the virile consolation of sexual conquest. Gentle poets provided him with melancholy passages about the disappointments of tender love. "Let th'aspiring youth beware of love," warned one poet whose lines Jefferson admired, "for 'tis too late, when on his heart the torrent softness pours" and "wisdom prostrate lies."[76]

Still other verses copied from the same Scottish poet echoed Jefferson's late-night reveries—and perhaps his dreams of Rebecca Burwell—while his head and heart ached and the candle burned as low as his spirits:

> While the world,
> And all the sons of care, lie hush'd in sleep, . . .
> Sighing to the lonely taper, [he] pours
> His idly-tortur'd heart into the page, . . .

All night he tosses . . . till the grey morn
Lifts her pale lustre on the paler wretch,
Exanimate by love. . . .
Then a weak, wailing, lamentable cry
Is heard, and all in tears he wakes, again
To tread the circle of revolving woe.
These are the charming agonies of love.[77]

On a more bombastic note, Jefferson's outburst to Fleming after Rebecca Burwell's engagement to Jack Ambler had its emotional parallel in this passage that he copied from a play by Thomas Otway:

—Wed her!
No! were she all Desire could wish, as fair
As would the vainest of her Sex be thought,
With Wealth beyond what Woman's Pride could waste,
She should not cheat me of my Freedom. Marry!
When I am old and weary of the World,
I may grow desperate,
And take a Wife to mortify withal.[78]

Again, with the same masculine bluster that he exhibited in his letter to Fleming, Jefferson endorsed the aggressive virility of the playwright's farmyard metaphor as he copied another passage from *The Orphan; or, The Unhappy Marriage* into his notebook:

The lusty Bull ranges through all the Field,
And from the Herd singling his Female out,
Enjoys her, and abandons her at Will.[79]

When Jefferson's adolescent infatuation with Rebecca Burwell ended after his clumsy discussions of marriage in the autumn of 1763, his immediate and involuntary reaction to her subsequent engagement to Jack Ambler was the first of a series of excruciating headaches that recurred in moments of crisis during the next forty-five years of his life. The collapse of his idolized dream of married life with Rebecca Burwell also intensified Jefferson's private misogyny, or antipathy toward women. After 1764 both his attitudes and his behavior toward women were less adolescent and ultimately less sympathetic. We may never know what he and Will Fleming meant by "other means of extinguishing their fire," but the record is clear that during the lonely years before he found a wife of his own, Jefferson was both attracted to women and uncomfortable in their presence.

CHAPTER THREE

Elizabeth Moore Walker

Entrust a ship to the winds, do not trust your heart to girls.
For the surge of the sea is safer than a woman's loyalty.

—Thomas Jefferson, memorandum book, 1770

You will perceive that I plead guilty to one of their charges, that
when young and single I offered love to a handsome lady. I
acknolege its incorrectness; it is the only one, founded in truth,
among all their allegations against me.

—Thomas Jefferson to Robert Smith, July 1, 1805

JACK WALKER is engaged to Betsy Moore," Thomas Jefferson wrote
their friends in January 1764, when the groom-to-be wanted "all his
brethren [to] be made acquainted with his happiness."[1] From their
youth, John Walker and Thomas Jefferson had been schoolmates and
more than just neighbors. Their fathers, Peter Jefferson and the physician and explorer Dr. Thomas Walker, had worked closely together in
the exploration and mapping of Virginia from Albemarle west across the
mountains into Kentucky. As one of Peter Jefferson's executors, Dr.
Walker had encouraged Jefferson to attend the College of William and
Mary in 1760 and had sent his own son there a year later.

Soon after Jack Walker finished college he married Elizabeth Moore.
On Wednesday, June 6, 1764, Jefferson stood as a groomsman at Chelsea,
the bride's home overlooking the Mattaponi River in King William
County. The couple settled in Albemarle County after the wedding.
They resided first at Castle Hill, the Walker family plantation several
miles northeast of Monticello, then at nearby Belvoir, where they lived
happily together until their deaths in 1809.

Elizabeth Moore Walker was born about 1745 at Chelsea, the house that her father built overlooking the Mattaponi River in King William County.

Courtesy of the Library of Virginia.

Prior to his participation in the American Revolution, John Walker's only sustained absence from Belvoir and his wife was in 1768—an absence from July through November that was the direct consequence of his father's towering reputation as an expert on western lands and Indian diplomacy. On that occasion John Walker asked his boyhood friend to look after his wife, Elizabeth Moore Walker, and their infant daughter. Lonely and without any romantic attachments at the time, Thomas Jefferson was unable to control his carnal desire and carried that assignment a good deal further than his friend intended. Years later, long after he had devised means to control the women in his life, Jefferson's attempts to seduce Betsy Walker became public and he had to acknowledge that allegations of his youthful lapses were "founded in truth."[2]

BORN IN February 1744 at Castle Hill, a few miles east of Jefferson's birthplace at Shadwell, John Walker was a year younger than Jefferson. Their parents were neighbors and friends, and the boys virtually grew up together. Dr. Thomas Walker was not only a trusted physician and pioneering resident of Albemarle County; at midcentury he was one of Virginia's preeminent authorities on the diplomacy and politics of the western frontier. Although John Walker's father was not the first Virginian to venture past the Allegheny Mountains into Kentucky, his written account of a 1750 western expedition through "Cave Gap" was the one that brought attention to the famous trail that Daniel Boone would exploit two decades later. A steadfast Whig who admired the duke of Cumberland for his 1746 defeat of the Stuart pretender Bonnie Prince Charlie at Culloden Moor in Scotland, Dr. Walker was the man who gave his hero's name to the Cumberland Gap, the Cumberland River, and the Cumberland Mountains.[3]

Jack's father was Albemarle County's leading participant in the speculative venture of the Loyal Company. Organized in 1749 with Walker as its chief agent, the Loyal Company promoted its investors' claims to 800,000 acres of Virginia land west of the Blue Ridge Mountains. Its principal rival, the Ohio Company of Virginia, had been founded in 1747 by Thomas Lee of Stratford Hall. As one of Virginia's foremost western explorers, Dr. Walker had shared his knowledge of Kentucky geography with Joshua Fry and Peter Jefferson for the 1751 first edition of their famous *Map of Virginia*.[4] During Peter Jefferson's final illness in 1757, Dr. Walker, as the family physician, was a constant presence at Shadwell.

The death of Jefferson's father gave Dr. Walker a larger role in Jefferson's life, for Peter Jefferson had designated his friend and physician as one of his children's legal guardians.[5] Castle Hill stood about halfway between Shadwell and the Reverend Maury's school, where John Walker, Tom Jefferson, and Dabney Carr were classmates. When school was in session, the Walker house often served as a weekend home away from home for both Jefferson and Carr, whose parents lived in Louisa County. Carr and Walker both followed Jefferson to the College of William and Mary in 1761.

Like Jefferson, Jack Walker made friends readily in Williamsburg among the younger generation of Tidewater gentry. His prospects were not harmed by the likelihood that their parents had been speculating in western lands with his father for years. Jack also inherited his father's good humor. In addition to his love of snowball fights—in which he enlisted all the neighbor children—Dr. Walker was known as a frontier prankster. Tales were told of his fondness for rattlesnake meat, which he also served to guests. On one occasion, the story goes, Dr. Walker beheaded a rattlesnake and slipped it into a kettle of brewing coffee. After accepting his guests' compliments on the flavorful brew, he pulled the snake's carcass from the pot to their horror and his amusement. On another occasion, when a neighbor praised the quality of a fine mutton dinner, Walker announced that the roast had not been mutton at all but rather "a piece of 'Old Fowler,' a cur dog well known to the visitors of Castle Hill." Jack, who sometimes served as a physician's assistant to his busy father, applied the paternal sense of humor to the treatment of a hypochondriac neighbor. Assigned the task of preparing a batch of pills for his dubious array of aches and pains, Jack "picked up some lamb droppings, rolled them in flour," and presented them in a pillbox to the unsuspecting patient. "A few weeks later the man returned and asked for more," the story has it, "saying that they did him more good than any medicine he had ever taken."[6]

Caring little for pomp and pretense, Dr. Walker refused to purchase a carriage for his wife and daughters. They could learn to walk, he said, because he could never afford to marry them to wealthy husbands.[7] In fact, Dr. Walker's daughters all married into the Virginia gentry, and his eldest son, Jack, found the girl of his dreams at a splendid Tidewater mansion in King William County, just upriver from the Pages and Burwells of Gloucester. No portraits survive of Elizabeth Moore, but good looks apparently ran in her family. Her mother was regarded as "a great beauty," and Elizabeth was acknowledged to be a "handsome lady."[8] On her father's side, a joint portrait depicting her father with his sister Lucy portrays the latter, Elizabeth's aunt, as a tall, attractive, and exceptionally poised young woman.[9] The heiress to all these traits, Elizabeth and John Walker's only daughter, Milly, turned heads on the streets of Philadelphia when her father was a member of Congress.[10]

ELIZABETH MOORE was born at Chelsea, in King William County, about 1745.[11] Her wealthy grandfather Augustine Moore had settled in Tidewater Virginia about 1705 and established the family seat overlooking the Mattaponi River just before it meets the Pamunkey to form the York at West Point. At his death about 1743, the family's landholdings

Elizabeth Moore Walker's aunt Lucy Moore holds a Chelsea rose in her right hand.
Elizabeth Walker's father, Bernard Moore, was a teenager when this joint portrait
was painted by Charles Bridges, an artist active in Virginia from 1735 to 1743.

Courtesy of the Virginia Historical Society.

were scattered up the entire length of the Middle Peninsula, from Gloucester County on the Chesapeake Bay westward past King William to
Spotsylvania and Caroline Counties in the Piedmont.[12]

Elizabeth's father, Bernard Moore, was born about 1720. At age
twenty-one or so he married Ann Catherine "Kate" Spotswood, the
eldest daughter of Virginia's distinguished former governor Alexander
Spotswood.[13] Sixteen or seventeen years old when they married, Kate
Moore lived into her late seventies and was known for her good looks
and high spirits. One of Elizabeth's nieces remembered Kate Moore as
"a great beauty" attired "in a fawn-colored satin, square in the neck, over
a blue satin petticoat, with satin shoes and buckles to match on her very
small and beautifully shaped feet."[14] Another recalled her youthful fascination watching Elizabeth's mother "combing her white and silken hair."
The proud daughter of an able royal governor, Kate Moore expressed her

sympathy with the British during the American Revolution, in contrast to her patriot husband and children, by drinking contraband tea. According to family lore, Elizabeth's mother punished a plantation overseer who had offended her by having the slaves toss him in a blanket as she watched from an upper window at Chelsea. Another tale recounts Kate Moore's bravery in the face of a threatened Indian attack while her husband was away at Hanover Court House. She calmly rallied her children and slaves to launch a boat and retreat safely down the Mattaponi to West Point.[15] She died in 1802.

Governor Francis Fauquier described Elizabeth's father, Bernard Moore, as "a Gentleman of Note in this Colony for whom I have a great personal Regard."[16] Moore built the elegant brick mansion at Chelsea, with its fine paneling and Georgian staircase. The house was named for the London neighborhood of Henry VIII's chancellor, Sir Thomas More, who may have been Bernard's relative. Advancing on the industrial developments of his father-in-law, Governor Spotswood, whose enterprises had made eighteenth-century Virginia a leading iron producer in the thirteen colonies, Moore operated a forge and a gristmill in King and Queen County valued at £6,000.[17] In addition to his marital connection with the Spotswood family, Bernard Moore was fatefully close to the powerful Virginia statesman John Robinson, longtime Speaker of the House of Burgesses and treasurer of the colony.

Lucy Moore, Bernard's sister, was Speaker Robinson's second wife, but far more than family linked these two men to each other—and to Dr. Thomas Walker. Visible to their contemporaries was their connection as leaders and investors in the Loyal Company, with its speculative claims to huge tracts of western land. Hidden from public view, at least prior to Speaker Robinson's death in 1766, was a more complicated and ominous connection. As treasurer of the colony since 1738, Speaker Robinson was responsible for managing the paper money that Virginia issued during the French and Indian War. Specifically, Robinson was supposed to destroy the promissory notes, which circulated as currency, as they came to the government in payment of taxes. Instead of burning these notes, however, Robinson began lending them to friends. Although historians recognize that Robinson's illegal loans expanded available credit and probably benefited the Virginia economy in general, Robinson's friends were the immediate beneficiaries. In the short run, Robinson's kinsmen Bernard Moore and John Chiswell had benefited most of all.[18]

The fraudulent loans became a public scandal soon after Speaker Robinson died on May 11, 1766. "The late Speaker," a planter reported to his English business associates in August, "instead of Burning the Paper Currency as it came into the Treasury for Taxes suffered it to Re-circulate by lending it out to Particuler friends to the amount of £100,000."[19] About a fifth of the total had gone to his brothers-in-law. Two years after Elizabeth Moore married John Walker, the colony learned that her father was hopelessly in debt to John Robinson's estate. The intertwined settlements of Robinson's estate and of Moore's affairs would continue for decades after both men's deaths.

Dr. Thomas Walker was preeminent among the trustees who initially attempted to help Bernard Moore settle his debts through a series of lotteries that began in 1766. Kate Moore's dowry apparently had some protection from creditors, but the prizes offered in Bernard Moore's lottery included real estate valued at £14,010 as well as fifty slaves and two hundred head of livestock.[20] By 1770, when the lottery had failed to discharge all of his debts, trustees were designated to liquidate the rest of Bernard Moore's estate, including Chelsea and another hundred slaves, for the benefit of his creditors. The process continued long after Moore's own death in 1773—and notable among the five trustees in charge of it were Dr. Thomas Walker and the rising young attorney Thomas Jefferson.[21]

The visible collapse of Bernard Moore's fortune came two years *after* the marriage, however, and Elizabeth's father's financial troubles had had little apparent effect on her courtship with John Walker. Once the bride and groom had told their friends about their engagement in January 1764, the family conversations at Castle Hill and Chelsea addressed such matters as houses, dowries, and other parental contributions toward the couple's happiness. By spring the families reached an understanding about the properties their children would bring to the match. The financial details of their betrothal are unusual not because such arrangements were made, but because their fathers committed the terms to paper, and their letters survived to reveal details that often remained private. Both fathers explicitly recognized that Elizabeth's decision to marry Jack was hers alone.

Because both family situations were complex—and because Vir-

Bernard Moore's lottery announcement in Alexander Purdie and John Dixon's Virginia Gazette, December 1, 1768.

Courtesy of the Library of Virginia.

ginia's landed gentry always had difficulties translating land, slaves, and other property into ready cash—Dr. Walker and Colonel Moore gave each other what amounted to promissory notes in support of their children's marriage. The Walker family's solvency was never at issue, and it seems likely that Jack already had possession of Belvoir, where he and Elizabeth built their new house with a large garden behind it.[22] Although the public exposure of Colonel Moore's financial plight lay two years in the future, perhaps Dr. Walker had inklings that a prudent exchange of notes might in some way help guarantee the couple's interests.

Whatever the precise motives were, Dr. Walker wrote first on Sunday, May 27, 1764—ten days before the wedding. His note politely mentioned that his affairs were "in an uncertain state"—no surprise to anyone familiar with the business side of a colonial medical practice, the current market for tracts of land in Albemarle and the west, or the temporary restrictions that a complex inheritance placed on his property at Castle Hill.[23] Hoping that Jack's intentions were "agreeable to yourself, lady, and daughter," Dr. Walker promised Colonel Moore that he would give the couple £4,000 in three installments: £1,000 in 1765, £1,000 in 1766, and the balance as soon as possible, "all to be [conveyed] in money or lands and other effects at the option of my said son, John Walker."[24]

Colonel Moore penned his response on Monday. "Your son, Mr. John Walker, applied to me for leave to make his addresses to my daughter Elizabeth," he wrote. "I gave him leave, and told him at the same time that my affairs were in such a state that it was not in my power to pay him all the money this year that I intended to give my daughter, provided he succeeded." The colonel promised Dr. Walker that he would give the groom "five hundred pounds next spring, and five hundred pounds more as soon as I could raise or get this money."[25]

After their wedding the newlyweds probably resided briefly with Jack's parents at Castle Hill, the Walkers' spacious mansion several miles northeast of Shadwell, while they finished their new house a mile and a half to the northeast.[26] When Belvoir was complete, Jack and Betsy Walker settled into the comfortable life of a moderately wealthy Piedmont family. Their only child, Mildred, was born between 1765 and 1767. Milly was an infant in July of 1768 when the colony of Virginia dispatched her father and grandfather to the frontiers of western New York on an important mission.

ON WEDNESDAY, June 15, 1768, acting governor John Blair gathered six members of the Governor's Council around a large table in the council chamber on the second floor of the capitol in Williamsburg. Spread before them were urgent letters from England and New York. It was imperative, the various letters said, that Virginia send a representative to look after the colony's interests "relative to completing a Boundary Line between the several Provinces and the Indians."[27]

In the five years since the end of the French and Indian War in 1763, British policy makers had struggled to keep the peace on the frontier— not only between colonists and Native Americans but among rival groups of settlers and speculators greedy for lands west of the Appalachian Mountains. Sir William Johnson, the Crown official responsible for the northern colonies, and his southern counterpart, John Stuart, were attempting to draw a line from Georgia to upstate New York—of which "the Indian Boundary Line to the Westward of Virginia" was the most vexing and controversial. To complete their task, Johnson was convening representatives from the Iroquois nations and the colonies of New York, New Jersey, Pennsylvania, and Virginia so that "every thing will be so clearly stated as to leave no room for future disputes." To the south, meanwhile, Stuart was arranging for parallel negotiations with the Cherokees.[28]

From Virginia's perspective, the question to be determined was whether the Old Dominion could make good on its claims to all of the territory comprising the modern states of Kentucky and West Virginia. Virginia needed to send its best men, and its best were Dr. Thomas Walker and frontiersman Andrew Lewis. Accordingly, with less than six weeks' notice, the council ordered Walker and Lewis "to proceed on that Service as soon as they conveniently can," and to "meet Sir William Johnson and the Indians of the several Nations concerned [on] the 25th of July." Stuart wanted them to consult with the Cherokees as well but expected that "it will be the month of September before the Indians can be prevailed upon to set out upon that Business."[29] The negotiations were critical for Virginia's interests in western lands and for Walker's own speculative interests in the Loyal Company. The New York parley alone was sure to take months. Dr. Walker and Colonel Lewis needed a reliable clerk and assistant who could pack and leave immediately. Jack Walker was the natural choice.

Not surprisingly, Jack Walker counted on his neighbor and boyhood friend, Tom Jefferson, to look after Betsy and their infant daughter, Milly, during his absence. Before departing for Fort Stanwix (now Rome, New York), Jack drew up a will that named "Mr. Jefferson as my neighbor and fast friend . . . first among my executors."[30] As expected, the negotiations at Fort Stanwix dragged on for months—and for good reason. According to the *Virginia Gazette*, they included not only the Iroquois but "about three thousand two hundred Indians from the different tribes of the Mohawks, Oneidas, Onandagoes, Senecas, Cayugas, Tuscororas, Coghnowagos, Onoghguagoes, Tutuloes, Shawanee, Delawares, Mingoes of Ohio, Nanticokes, Conoys, Chughnuts, Schoras, and Oriscas."[31] The negotiations ended in the middle of November, and Dr. Walker and his son were back in Albemarle County by Saturday, November 26.[32] A few days later, on December 1, the *Virginia Gazette* celebrated the success of their mission: "The Six Nations and all their tributaries have granted a vast extent of country to his Majesty, . . . southward as far as the Cherokee river" (a reference to the Tennessee River as it flows into the Ohio at present-day Paducah, Kentucky).[33] The Treaty of Fort Stanwix revived the dreams of Virginia's speculators in western lands—but at a greater personal cost than John Walker realized at the time. During the long months of his absence, Thomas Jefferson had devoted more attention to Elizabeth Moore Walker than her husband and father-in-law knew.

BY THE summer of 1768, Jefferson's law practice was doing well. He was also devoting some of his time to tentative design sketches for the house that would eventually become Monticello. Slave laborers were at work leveling the site at the top of the mountain and hoped to finish by Christmas.[34] Jefferson's account books indicate that his law practice took him to county-court sessions as far away as Staunton and Amherst. He spent a total of almost three months in Williamsburg: most of April, most of June, and all of October. When not attending to business in the capital, he bought tickets to plays and concerts, he socialized in coffeehouses and taverns, and on Monday, April 11, he spent seven and a half cents (the price of a cup of coffee) "for seeing an elk." While in Williamsburg he visited friends in Gloucester County—John and Fanny Page at Rosewell, Frank and Elizabeth Willis at Whitehall, Lewis and Judy Burwell at Fairfield, and Warner and Mary Lewis at Warner Hall.[35] In December the freeholders of Albemarle County elected Jefferson to his first term in the House of Burgesses (as they reelected Dr. Walker to his seventh). For all this activity, however, only one personal letter from Jefferson survives for the year 1768, and it sheds no light on his personal life.[36]

Many years later, amid the partisan political strife of Jefferson's presidency, John Walker outlined the attempts to seduce his wife that began in the summer of 1768. Jefferson acknowledged Walker's accusation as "the only one, founded in truth, among all their allegations against me."[37]

"In [17]68 I was called to Fort Stanwix," John Walker recalled,

being secretary or clerk to the Virginia Commission at the treaty with the Indians there held by Sir W[illiam] Johnson which was composed of Gen'l A[ndrew] Lewis and my father.

I left my wife and infant daughter at home, relying on Mr. Jefferson as my neighbor and fast friend having in my will made before my departure, named him first among my executors.

When Walker returned in November after a four-month absence, Elizabeth Walker kept silent both about Jefferson's advances during that time and about his continuing propositions. But she did, as her husband recalled, express "her constant objection to my leaving Mr. J[efferson] my ex[e]c[u]t[or] telling me that she wondered why I could place such confidence in him."[38] Still, she waited nearly sixteen years before sharing with her husband the story of the harassment she endured while he was in New York.

Aside from the allegations that Jefferson acknowledged to be true, we have little evidence about Jefferson's thoughts and actions in the summer of 1768. His account books, however, tell us where he was during John Walker's absence. That evidence supports the Walkers' allegations about Jefferson's conduct in two significant respects. First, it shows that there was opportunity in June for John Walker to meet with Jefferson and confer about his will and the care of his wife and daughter. Second, it confirms that Jefferson was in residence at Shadwell, a short ride from Belvoir, for three months after John Walker left for New York.

Jefferson happened to be in Williamsburg on June 15 when the council designated Dr. Walker as one of Virginia's representatives to the negotiations at Fort Stanwix. If John Walker conferred with Jefferson about his will, it may have been in Williamsburg during the third week of June.[39] Then, except for a two-day trip to Amherst County early in July, Jefferson spent the entire summer at Shadwell, from June 26 through September 23. That autumn, during the remainder of John Walker's absence, Jefferson was either in Williamsburg (from the last week of September through the first week of November) or in Staunton (during the week prior to Walker's return to Albemarle on or before November 26).

Betsy Walker's new house at Belvoir was a pleasant seven-mile ride from Shadwell. Riding was one of Jefferson's favorite forms of recreation and exercise, and there were few parts of the Albemarle terrain that he knew more intimately than the trails linking his boyhood home with Dr. Walker's Castle Hill, John and Elizabeth Walker's place at Belvoir, and the vicinity of Maury's old school. Three entries in Jefferson's memorandum book (two gratuities paid to Michael, one of the Walkers' slaves, and a note about handling a lawsuit for her father) provide written evidence of visits to Elizabeth Walker at Belvoir on Friday, July 8, and again on Monday and Tuesday, September 12 and 13.[40] Unless accompanied by expenditures, however, other visits to Belvoir would not have been recorded in Jefferson's account books.

Five years earlier, at twenty, Jefferson had complained about "the ups and downs of a country life: to day you are frolicking with a fine girl and tomorrow you are moping by yourself."[41] Now he was twenty-five, a lonely young bachelor with no romantic prospects, moping by himself in the languorous heat of an Albemarle summer, with every day a sad tomorrow. How easy it could have been to transform a neighborly ride to look after Jack Walker's wife and toddler into an occasion for seduction and a frolic with a fine young woman. Shared loneliness can be a bittersweet aphrodisiac.

For his part, Jefferson would later admit that "when young and single [he] offered love to a handsome lady." It is only fair to ask whether, during the long months alone except for the company of her young daughter, Elizabeth Moore Walker might have accepted that offer. At least one historian (who turned out to be right about Sally Hemings when many were not) has imagined that Jefferson's advances might have been welcome, perhaps even invited. "When the circumstances of that long-ago summer of 1768 are recalled," E. M. Halliday writes,

> it is hard to believe that only Jefferson's youthful libido was involved. He may well have been stirred by Betsey's sexual allure for years, and lubriciously excited by the surprising opportunity—by the obligation, almost—of spending lots of time alone with her. . . . Betsey, having learned the pleasures of the marriage bed, and quite possibly caught up in a confusion of frustrated desire and resentment at her husband for having disappeared into the wilderness for such an unconscionable stretch of time, could easily have made the first move.[42]

It is *possible* to imagine Jefferson repeatedly galloping from Shadwell to Betsy Walker's arms during the summer of 1768. "Infidelity by a woman with one of her husband's good friends," Halliday observes, "has a very long history."[43] On the other hand, laying the blame for sexual harassment on the victim of that harassment also has a long and unfortunate history.

IF JEFFERSON and Mrs. Walker did embark on a love affair in the summer of 1768, it would be easy to suppose that she would have wanted it to end once her husband returned from New York late in November. On balance, however, it seems unlikely that Elizabeth Walker had *ever* welcomed Jefferson's attentions.[44] His continued attempts at seduction over several years tend to contradict the motives E. M. Halliday assigned to Elizabeth Walker in his speculative account of a passionate summer romance. According to the statement that Jefferson acknowledged as "founded in truth,"[45] he "renewed his caresses" toward Elizabeth Walker in the months after her husband's return from New York. And Jefferson's harassment apparently continued from time to time for an entire decade.[46]

When the Walkers visited Jefferson at Shadwell in 1769—"a visit common to us being neighbors and as [John Walker] felt true fr[ien]ds"—Jefferson tucked a piece of paper into the cuff of Betsy

Walker's sleeve. It was a note "tending to convince her of the innocence of promiscuous love"—which she "on first glance tore to pieces." On another occasion, at the house of "a mutual acquaintance and distant neighbor," Jefferson feigned illness after the ladies had retired to their rooms. Leaving Jack Walker and the other gentlemen downstairs, Jefferson stole into the Walkers' room, where Betsy was undressing for bed, "instead of going to bed as his sickness authorized a belief."[47]

Although Jefferson claimed that his misconduct had occurred when he was "young and single," John Walker asserted that Jefferson's adulterous advances toward Mrs. Walker continued even after his own marriage to Martha Wayles Skelton in 1772. In support of his contention that Jefferson "continued his efforts . . . until the latter end of the year [17]79," Walker described an incident when the Jeffersons were visiting them at Belvoir. Their "old house"—which they replaced with a larger one about 1790—"had a passage upstairs with private rooms on each side and opposite doors." The Jeffersons slept in one bedroom, and the Walkers in the other. "At one end of the passage was a small room used by my wife as her private apartment," John Walker explained. "Knowing her custom" of visiting that dressing room "early and late," one morning Jefferson "was found in his shirt ready to seize her on her way from her Chamber—indecent in manner."[48]

Jefferson's aggressive pursuit of Elizabeth Walker reflected a more predatory sexuality than the adolescent reverence that had characterized his tongue-tied obsession with Rebecca Burwell. No longer a student, he was making his way as a lawyer, sketching his dream house on the mountaintop, and beginning his political career—but he was clearly lonely. All his friends were married and starting their families. Jefferson, meanwhile, was attempting to seduce Elizabeth Moore and acting out a role from the angry texts in his notebooks—the playwright Thomas Otway's lusty bull ranging through the fields, singling his female out, and enjoying and abandoning her "at Will."[49]

It was not until October 1779 that "Mr. J[efferson] desisted in his attempts," John Walker concluded. "All this time I believed him to be my best frd and so felt and acted toward him"—and "all this time I held him first named in my will, as Ex[e]c[uto]r ignorant of every thing which had passed."[50]

Jefferson's place in John Walker's will was the thing that especially irritated Betsy Walker. Control of her own destiny was at stake. For nearly sixteen years—from her husband's return from New York in November of 1768 through Jefferson's departure for France in 1784—she voiced her "constant objection" to Jefferson's inclusion as an executor.[51] With both her father and her father-in-law relying on his legal counsel, Jefferson was already too involved in the affairs of her family. The very thought that Tom Jefferson might exercise any authority over her prospective widowhood was abhorrent—but for the time being she was, as the Tidewater saying goes, careful not to startle the horses. Unwilling to disclose the full reasons for her distress, Elizabeth Walker repeatedly expressed reservations about her husband's choice of Jefferson as his principal executor.

Not until after Jefferson had departed for France in July of 1784 did Betsy Walker reveal exactly why she wanted Jefferson's name expunged from her husband's will. "Soon after his sailing for France was known," John Walker explained, his wife again "recurred to my will and being as before asked her objections, she related to me these base transactions." She apologized "for her past silence," he concluded, "from her fear of its consequence which might have been fatal to me."[52] Betsy cared about her husband's pride and reputation, and there was always the chance that a confrontation might have led to a duel.[53] Jack apparently did write to Jefferson about his outrageous behavior, but his letters never reached Paris. Many of the letters that Jefferson's sister-in-law Elizabeth Wayles Eppes sent to Paris in this period went astray as well. The last of Walker's letters was evidently dated May 15, 1788, but if he kept a copy, it is no longer known to exist.[54]

JOHN WALKER did rewrite his will. In the new document, dated January 29, 1787, he designated Elizabeth his principal executor, along with his younger brother Francis Walker and their son-in-law, Francis Kinloch. The will left everything to his beloved wife (or, in the event that she died before him, to their granddaughter, Eliza Kinloch).[55] At long last, it seemed, Elizabeth Moore Walker could stop worrying about Thomas Jefferson. Twenty eventful years, and the entire American Revolution, separated her from the fateful summer of 1768.

John and Elizabeth Walker were ardent patriots during the Revolution. He had entered the House of Burgesses in 1771 and then participated in the revolutionary conventions leading to independence. As the war loomed, Virginia once again sent him and his father to meet with tribes on the western frontier in the hope of gaining their support (or neutrality) against the British. At Fort Pitt in 1775 John Walker demonstrated his own negotiating skills in a successful meeting with the Shawnees and other tribes. He and the Virginians were less effectual with the Cherokees in South Carolina a year later.[56]

In 1777, as Virginia sent more men and matériel to battle against the British in the northern states, the state government decided to dispatch "a Gentleman of discernment, discretion, Veracity, and inviolable Attachment to the American Cause" as a liaison to General Washington. John Walker of Albemarle County was their man. Serving as Virginia's direct link to the general for more than a year, he won Washington's lasting esteem as "a very respectable Gentleman."[57] Elizabeth, doubtless with help from her daughter, Milly, ran the plantation.

In the summer of 1778, Virginia once again dispatched John to meet with the Shawnees at Fort Pitt, but this time he declined "on account of the Indisposition of his Family." Something was wrong at home. His mother, who would die the following November, may have taken sick. Perhaps there was illness in the neighborhood that afflicted Elizabeth and Milly as well. Two years later, when John was attending Congress in Philadelphia, he happily wrote that his family had "perfectly recovered from the small-pox, . . . Mrs. Walker had only two pustules and Milly one for each of the United States."[58] Although victims of smallpox risked severe scarring or even death, Milly's and Elizabeth's complexions were unscathed by the disease. Indeed, it was in Philadelphia that Milly's beauty attracted a husband in South Carolina congressman Francis Kinloch. The family tradition says that he "met Mildred Walker on the street as she was returning from her hairdresser, and fell in love with her at first sight and afterwards married her."

In 1781 the congressman brought his courtship to Belvoir, where at breakfast in June he was captured by Banastre Tarleton and taken prisoner. After the war, they married, and soon Milly gave birth to the Walkers' only grandchild, Eliza. Then tragedy struck the family. In a letter to a mutual friend in September 1785, Jefferson reported from Paris that the Walkers had suffered "the loss of their only child" but that fate had "left them a grand-child for their solace." Kinloch retreated sadly to his rice plantation in South Carolina and eventually remarried there. Betsy and John Walker welcomed Eliza into their empty nest, raised her as their own, and lived to see her marry Hugh Nelson of Yorktown.[59]

John Walker's varied experiences during the Revolution seem to have awakened his ambitions. He studied law and opened a legal practice—which coexisted nicely with his family's management of a large plantation. In the last twenty years of the Walkers' life together, John accepted only one more assignment that took them away from Belvoir for any significant time. In March of 1790 he accepted the high honor of an appointment to the Senate of the United States to fill the vacancy caused by the death of William Grayson. Betsy doubtless accompanied him to New York for the duration of his term, which ended in November.[60] Perhaps it was during this absence that John and Betsy had their original house moved to another site so they could build a grander house on the property they loved, the scenic rolling countryside of northeastern Albemarle County.[61]

Every morning the sun rose over their spacious garden, which stretched from the new house at Belvoir to the tree line at the foot of the Southwest Mountains. At dusk it disappeared many miles to the west, behind the misty forested crest of the Blue Ridge Mountains. Senator and Mrs. Walker, now in their mid-forties, were nestled into a peaceful and comfortable existence—the life of a prosperous planter and lawyer's family. As the year 1790 drew to a close, Elizabeth and John Walker could reasonably have expected to enjoy a placid retirement together without interruption until their deaths in September and December 1809—except that their neighbor and former friend got himself elected president.

In September 1802, sixteen months after Thomas Jefferson's inauguration as president, the story of his attempted seduction of Elizabeth Moore Walker first came to public notice in a Richmond newspaper.[62] It was mixed with aspersions about his conduct as governor during the British invasion of 1781, scorn for his handling of certain financial transactions, ridicule of his religious beliefs, and rumors of a liaison with his slave Sally Hemings—a torrent of invective meant to serve the over-wrought partisan political disputes of the new republic.

The journalist who unleashed this flood, James Thomson Callender, was by all accounts a pitiful if not detestable human being. He got many details wrong. But much of what he printed was true. To the dismay of Elizabeth Walker and her husband, many American readers felt that of all the charges leveled at the president by Callender and echoed by other newspapers, the allegation about Jefferson's attempted seduction of Betsy Walker was the most believable and damnable.[63]

Precisely because Elizabeth Walker's story *was* credible, because she *was* innocent of any wrongdoing, and because her story *was* highly offensive to ordinary churchgoing American women and men—precisely for these reasons Jefferson's critics and adversaries found Eliza-beth Walker's story most useful. And precisely for these reasons Betsy and John Walker were fated to see their lives and reputations dragged into a whirl of nasty speculation. It was *her* story—the true story of her stalwart resistance to an attempted seduction. But once it hit the news-papers, Elizabeth Walker suffered anew simply because she had been the target, three decades earlier, of Jefferson's aggressive lust.

Despite the fresh anguish that Elizabeth Walker felt when her life became a political issue during Jefferson's presidency, at the distance of two centuries it is apparent that the newspaper squabbles said less about her than about the vicious political climate and prevailing code of male honor that circumscribed both John Walker's and Thomas Jefferson's responses to the controversy and to each other.

While Jefferson was able to rely on the unspoken conventions of southern honor to maintain public silence about interracial sex, in the case of adultery with the wife of another gentleman that same code of honor enforced its call for an apology with the threat of a duel. The more notorious the affront, the greater the social pressure upon the aggrieved gentleman to seek "satisfaction" at gunpoint on a field of honor. Accord-ingly, in person and through intermediaries, Jefferson and Walker took steps in 1803 to suppress the newspaper accounts and "consign this unfortunate matter to all the oblivion of which it is susceptible."[64]

In these public arguments, the rhetoric of both Jefferson's detractors and his defenders reflected blatantly patriarchal values, rooted in their code of male honor, that startle modern sensibilities with their cavalier indifference to the person of Elizabeth Walker. One Federalist writer revealed the dilemma that she faced—a contradiction that could threaten any respectable woman's reputation. In the space of just a few lines, the president's critic exalted Elizabeth Walker for "the purity of her character" while describing Jefferson's harassment of the innocent woman as an attempt "to ruin" her. In a similar reflection upon the vulnerability of a virtuous woman's reputation, another irate correspondent contrasted "the purity of her character" with Jefferson's "unpardonable, and unsuccessful attempt to *destroy* her."[65]

Male prerogative pervades even the private statement of Jefferson's offenses that John Walker dictated to Henry Lee in 1805. Compassion for Elizabeth Walker's reputation was eclipsed by a greater concern for her husband's honor. Early on, John Walker described Jefferson's attempts to seduce his wife as "efforts to destroy my peace." Several lines later, narrating the termination of his harassment, Walker originally stated that Jefferson "desisted in his attempts on her"—but then he crossed out "her" and replaced it with "my peace." The statement closed by emphasizing Jefferson's affronts to John's honor rather than his insults to Elizabeth's virtue: "My injury is before you. Let my redress be commensurate. It cannot be complete and therefore ought to be as full as possible."[66]

Once the male code of honor was brought to bear—in private and in the newspapers—Betsy Walker's feelings counted for little. "You must remember," her husband reminded Henry Lee, that "some mode was to be devised whereby it might be made known to the world, that satisfaction had been given to me."[67] With the Burr-Hamilton duel fresh in mind, no one needed to be reminded that *satisfaction* was a word that could lead to drawn pistols and sudden death.[68]

Sensing the blood in the water, Jefferson's adversaries in New England were relentless. Some Federalists were looking hard for evidence of an impeachable offense. Others may have hoped to prod Walker into issuing a formal challenge. None of the Federalists were unhappy about the embarrassment they were heaping on the hated president.

In 1805 the story came to the floor of the Massachusetts legislature. A Federalist named Hulbert, from Sheffield, assailed Jefferson's attempted seduction of Mrs. Walker, his liaison with Sally Hemings, and his response to Banastre Tarleton's raid of 1781 in a general attack on the president's character, religion, and policies. Mr. Hulbert's lengthy speech was published in New York and Boston and widely reprinted—all to the embarrassment both of the Walkers and of the president.[69]

Once again, considerations of political prudence and male honor dictated the subtle evasions of Jefferson's private apology, as well as the delicate footwork with which he and John Walker danced around the prospect of a duel. With the incendiary General Henry Lee acting as Walker's intermediary, Jefferson assuaged both the offended husband's honor and the concerns of his own political allies with private notes of apology—only the shorter of which has survived. Jefferson admitted that he had "offered love to a handsome lady," and then he hedged about the dates, duration, and extent of his misbehavior "when young and single."[70] By this gesture the president avoided the colossal public humiliation that he and his friends had forced upon Secretary of the Treasury Alexander Hamilton in the 1790s over Hamilton's adulterous affair with Mrs. James Reynolds. But Jefferson was not yet out of danger. As in Hamilton's case, the public face of the Jefferson-Walker scandal involved not only sex and honor but money, too.

After sleeping with the man's wife, Hamilton had been blackmailed by James Reynolds (probably with his wife's cooperation) and had paid Reynolds off to keep the matter quiet. But the lady's husband was greedy. He wanted more money, or perhaps a job in the Treasury Department. When Hamilton's opponents got wind of the situation, they surmised that the secretary had used Treasury funds to pay off the blackmailer. Hamilton had in fact paid Reynolds with his own money—but it was there that the peculiar values of the male honor code took over when James Monroe and others close to Jefferson confronted Hamilton privately with their suspicions. To clear himself of what he and his male critics regarded as the very serious charge of financial dishonesty, Hamilton published a lengthy and detailed pamphlet admitting to the world (and to his embarrassed wife and family) that he had been caught in adultery and had paid the woman and her husband to hush it up.[71]

In Jefferson's case, the financial aspect of the Walker affair was more oblique and unintended—having begun, by the standards of Jefferson's friends, innocently. After Jefferson and his family returned from France, his daughters had asked him why they no longer visited the Walkers at

Belvoir, "knowing [how] intimate they were before he went to F[rance]." Hiding the real reason from his girls, Jefferson said something vaguely to the effect that "some difference had arisen about money matters." That was a lie, but nothing came of it for years.

Then, probably at a family gathering early in Jefferson's presidency, Jefferson's daughters were "interrogated" about the Walkers by their uncle David Meade Randolph. A Federalist who had been federal marshal in Richmond during the Adams administration, Randolph had been supplanted by a Jeffersonian appointee in 1801. In response, he became one of Callender's informants about the private life of his distant presidential cousin. In answer to their uncle's prying questions, Jefferson's daughters had innocently but "incautiously" repeated their father's explanation about the cessation of their visits to Belvoir. "Thus," as Jefferson's longtime secretary, William Armistead Burwell, explained in his memoir, "an explanation intended to preserve the happiness and tranquility of his daughters, and *never* given elsewhere was made the basis of that charge against him . . . and attributed to the iniquity of his heart."[72] Lying to his daughters was acceptable—disparaging a gentleman's financial probity was not.

It was not true, as Jefferson's Federalist adversaries repeatedly claimed in print, "that in order to cover the real cause of the separation between Col. Walker and himself, he did FABRICATE A NOTE respecting an unsettled account which he said, had produced the schism."[73] It was true, however, that to cloak the real reason for coolness between himself and the Walkers—to avoid the admission that he had propositioned Elizabeth Walker many years before they were born—Thomas Jefferson lied to his daughters. Gauged by the contemporary standards of male honor, it was a little white lie "to preserve the[ir] happiness and tranquility." Jefferson's secretary, like many of the president's admirers, could regard that deception as harmless as long as it remained entirely private—as long as it was "*never* given elsewhere."[74] Once Jefferson's comment was repeated outside his immediate family, however, the president was ensnared by the same gentlemen's code that had prompted Alexander Hamilton to publish his account of an adulterous affair with Mrs. Reynolds. For Thomas Jefferson, as for his contemporaries, male pride and gentlemen's honor trumped female sensibilities and truth.

. . .

THE STORY of Elizabeth Moore Walker, John Walker, and Thomas Jefferson ended sadly in the autumn of 1809. "Our neighbor Mrs. Walker departed this life the 10th of the month," a distant cousin wrote in September, "and Mr. Walker left Belvoir immediately after for Philadelphia to try the skill of the faculty [of the medical college] there on his ulcerated face, from whence it is expected he will not return." John Walker died on Saturday, December 2, according to his obituary in the *Richmond Enquirer,* after "a long, acute and painful disease, which he bore with the greatest fortitude, yielding up his life with the greatest resignation."[75]

Elizabeth and John Walker had died within months of each other, as loving couples sometimes do. In wistful moments at Monticello, Jefferson may well have envied their long and happy life together as he reflected upon the ten short years of his own "unchequered happiness" with Martha Wayles Skelton Jefferson. Forced by circumstances to admit to his closest associates that in a youthful lapse of self-control he had "offered love to a handsome woman" who was another man's wife, Jefferson had ample time to regret that impulsive youthful behavior, which dragged his and the Walkers' private lives and reputations into the newspapers and disrupted the functioning of his presidency.

CHAPTER FOUR

Martha Wayles Skelton Jefferson

In every scheme of happiness she is placed in the foreground of the picture, as the principal figure. Take that away, and it is no picture for me.

—Thomas Jefferson to Robert Skipwith, August 3, 1771

Mrs. Jefferson has at last shaken off her tormenting pains by yielding to them, and has left our friend inconsolable. I . . . scarcely supposed that his grief would be so violent as to justify the circulating report of his swooning away whenever he sees his children.

—Edmund Randolph to James Madison, September 20, 1782

NEW YEAR'S DAY 1772, at the Forest in Charles City County, two dozen miles west of Williamsburg, was a joyful holiday for twenty-nine-year-old Thomas Jefferson and twenty-three-year-old Martha Wayles Skelton. On that wintry Wednesday they were married at the home of Martha's father, John Wayles, a wealthy English-born attorney, slave trader, and business agent for the Bristol-based tobacco-exporting firm of Farell & Jones. Jefferson's new father-in-law, who was also one of his legal clients, was known as "a most agreeable companion, full of pleasantry and good humor."[1] The wedding celebrations lasted at least three days, and the newlyweds stayed on for another two weeks at the Forest.[2]

On about January 18 the Jeffersons began their journey home, stopping first at Shirley plantation, on the James River a few miles southwest of the Forest, where Jefferson had arranged for a last-minute repair to his carriage.[3] Then they stayed a few days at Tuckahoe, west of Richmond, the home of his cousin and boyhood friend Thomas Mann Randolph and his wife, Anne Cary Randolph, where Jefferson and his family had resided many years earlier after the death of Randolph's father.[4] Finally, during the last weekend of January, Thomas Jefferson brought his new wife to their new home—such as it was. Jefferson had been sketching plans for Monticello for several years, but on the eve of his wedding the only habitable part of the new house was a small one-room brick structure, twenty feet square, that now comprises the South Pavilion of Monticello. He had moved into this temporary residence after his mother's house at Shadwell was destroyed by fire in February 1770. He had been living there and supervising the construction of the main house throughout the entire period of the courtship with Martha.[5]

Not only had their carriage broken down twice during the marriage trip from the Forest to Monticello, but the couple made the final leg of their journey in a severe winter storm. The snow piled deeper with every mile as they rolled into hilly Albemarle County. Stopping briefly at Blenheim late on the afternoon of January 26, they found no one home except Ned Carter's overseer. With only eight miles to go, they were "obliged to quit the carriage and proceed on horseback," pressing forward as the sun disappeared behind the Blue Ridge Mountains to the west. Finally, after riding for hours "through a mountain track rather than a road, in which the snow lay from eighteen inches to two feet deep," the Jeffersons arrived at Monticello. A blazing hearth, a hot meal, and cozy blankets might have transformed any cottage into a honeymoon sanctuary against the raging blizzard, but it was "late at night" and the newlyweds found "the fires all out and the servants retired to their own houses."[6]

Their new quarters were little more than a cabin at the edge of a raw and frozen construction site. At the intended location of the main house, only the basement foundation was visible in that snowy January of 1772. Martha's first impression of her husband's architectural project focused, as her eldest daughter wrote later, on "the horrible dreariness of such a house, at the end of such a journey." But the couple's first night at Monticello did not stay dreary for long. "Part of a bottle of wine, found on a shelf behind some books," was made to substitute "for both fire and supper." Then, as the story was told and retold to their children and friends,

Completed late in 1770 and known as the Honeymoon Cottage, the South Pavilion was the first part of Monticello that Jefferson built.

Courtesy of the Library of Virginia.

the young couple found "sources of diversion in these ludicrous *contre-temps* and the 'horrible dreariness' was lit up with song, and merriment and laughter."[7]

The decade that Jefferson shared with Martha was far and away the most creative period of his long and remarkable political career. His *Summary View of the Rights of British America*, published in Williamsburg in 1774, launched his reputation in Virginia. His Declaration of Independence, written in Philadelphia in 1776, established his subsequent fame throughout America and the world. In three years of labor revising Virginia's legal code, Jefferson between 1776 and 1779 wrote the Virginia Statute for Religious Freedom (adopted a decade later in 1786) and drafted the legislation that was ultimately passed in 1819 to create the University of Virginia. And finally, in the last years of their life together, Jefferson began the compilation of his only book, *Notes on the State of Virginia*. Despite the likelihood that his overtures toward Elizabeth Moore Walker continued for several years after his marriage, and despite the embarrassing denouement of his final days as governor of Virginia, Jefferson remembered his life with Martha Wayles Skelton as a period of "unchequered happiness."[8]

The marriage lasted for almost eleven years, from their wedding on New Year's Day 1772 to her death at Monticello on September 6, 1782, a few weeks short of her thirty-fourth birthday. Martha's mother had died when she was born, and Martha never regained her health following the birth of their youngest daughter, Lucy Elizabeth, who in turn died of whooping cough two and a half years later. Of the six children born to Martha and Thomas Jefferson, only two daughters survived to adulthood. Mary died in childbirth in her twenties, and only their eldest daughter, Martha, outlived her father.[9]

THOMAS JEFFERSON did not sit for a portrait until after his wife's death, and no likeness of Martha Wayles Skelton was ever put to canvas. "Mrs. Jefferson was small," recalled the Monticello slave Isaac Jefferson, and "a pretty lady."[10] Family members described her as "a little above medium height" and "slightly but exquisitely formed." She had auburn hair. "Her complexion was brilliant," and "her large expressive eyes [were] the richest shade of hazel." She moved with grace when she walked, or danced, or rode a horse—and there was a distinctly musical lilt to her charm. Martha sang beautifully and played the spinet piano and the harpsichord "with uncommon skill." She was "well read and intelligent." Genial in conversation, she exhibited both "excellent sense and a lively play of fancy." Her personality exhibited a "frank, warmhearted, and somewhat impulsive disposition."[11] She was "a favorite with her husband's sisters, with his family generally, and with her neighbours."[12] Had some artist been able to capture her lively temperament on canvas, however, deep and tragic shadows might have brooded in the background. For all her vivacity, death seemed to stalk Martha Wayles Skelton and her family.

Her father, John Wayles, had outlived three wives. Martha was born in October 1748, the only surviving child of his first marriage to Martha Eppes, who died a month later. Three stepsisters were the children of John Wayles's second wife. Then, after Wayles's third wife died without issue in 1761, about thirteen months after their wedding, the family history took an unusual turn. For the last dozen years of his life, John Wayles lived openly with one of his slaves, a mulatto woman named Betty Hemings, whose father was an English sea captain. They had six children together—many of whom were brought to Monticello as slaves after John Wayles died in 1773, the year that their youngest child, Sally Hemings, was born.[13]

THOMAS JEFFERSON made his first recorded visit to the Forest in the autumn of 1770, when Martha Wayles Skelton was a widow with a three-year-old son. Her first husband, Bathurst Skelton, had been a year younger than Jefferson and had also studied at the College of William and Mary. That marriage lasted twenty-two months, from their wedding on November 20, 1766, to Bathurst Skelton's death on September 30, 1768, after a sudden illness. Neither Bathurst Skelton nor Martha Wayles was mentioned among the circle of Jefferson's friends in Williamsburg, but it is possible that Jefferson met his future wife as early as October 1768, when he accepted her father as a legal client just a few weeks prior to her husband's death.[14]

As a young widow already possessed of some estate and with the prospect of more from her father, Martha Wayles Skelton attracted many suitors in a society that never frowned on an advantageous marriage. Jefferson wrote in his autobiography that Martha's portion of her father's estate "was about equal to my own patrimony, and consequently doubled the ease of our circumstances."[15] We know little about Jefferson's courtship of her beyond two anecdotes preserved by family tradition. The first recounts the story of two rival suitors who chanced to approach the front door of the Forest at the same time. Ushered into a sitting room, they heard Martha's harpsichord and soprano voice wafting through the house in harmony with Jefferson's violin and tenor. The rivals listened for a few minutes and then "took their hats and retired, to return no more on the same errand."[16]

The second story, confirmed by Jefferson's account books, tracks the deepening of his commitment. In December 1770, Jefferson decided to buy Martha Wayles Skelton a small clavichord. He wanted it to be "as light and portable as possible" and veneered with "the finest mahogany." Six months later in their courtship he decided that his fiancée should have a larger and more expensive pianoforte. Jefferson specified that his amended preference was for an instrument "of fine mahogany, solid, not vineered"—and of a quality "worthy [of] the acceptance of a lady for whom I intend it."[17]

Martha Wayles Skelton was beautiful, talented, and wealthy, but Jefferson also found her status as a widow attractive. "Intimate emotional engagement with women," historian Winthrop Jordan observed, "seemed to represent for [Jefferson] a gateway into a dangerous, potentially explosive world." In private life and in public policy, Jefferson was always more comfortable with married women than with their undomesticated sisters. Jordan was not the first to notice that "throughout his life after the Burwell affair, Jefferson seemed capable of attachment only to married women." Jefferson's first biographer, who had the unique advantage of direct conversations with his family and contemporaries, hinted in the same direction. "Last [but] not least," Henry S. Randall wrote in his list of Martha Wayles Skelton's appealing qualities, "she had already proved herself a true daughter of the Old Dominion in the department of house-wifery." Marriage, Jefferson wrote tersely in a notebook, "reverses the prerogative of sex."[18] Mary Deverell put the matter more clearly in an essay published near Philadelphia in 1792:

> To the moment of your marriage it is your reign, your lover is proud to oblige you, watches your smiles, is obedient to your commands, anxious to please you, and careful to avoid everything you disapprove; but you have no sooner pronounced that harsh word *obey*, than you give up the reins, and it is his turn to rule so long as you live.[19]

Once the vows of marriage had been spoken, husbands, Jefferson wrote, "expected to be pleased" by wives who were "sedulous to please."[20] Like many of his contemporaries, Jefferson regarded women's sexual appetites as equal to or even stronger than men's, and he felt a deep-seated fear of women as threatening both to his own self-control and to the proper ordering of society. As Winthrop Jordan perceptively observed,

Thomas Jefferson felt that "female passion must and could only be controlled by marriage."[21]

MARRIAGE, domesticity, and motherhood, in Jefferson's estimation, encompassed all the elements of a woman's destiny. "Sweetness of temper, affection to a husband, and attention to his interests," Jefferson wrote in an essay for his eldest daughter, Martha, "constitute the duties of a wife and form the basis of matrimonial felicity."[22] To the extent that his sentiments were merely conventional they were not without merit as fatherly advice for a young couple.[23] The intensity of his language, however, betrayed more than a settled opinion about the wife's duty to preserve the harmony of a marriage at all costs. Jefferson exhibited a deep distrust of women's capacity to disrupt their homes and his world.

Lamenting that married women often employed "charms of beauty" and "brilliancy of wit . . . more for the attraction of every body else than their husbands," Jefferson cautioned Martha that when she took a husband, "the pleasing of that one person [must] be a thought never absent from your conduct." There will be times, Jefferson warned, when a wife "must teach her husband to be at peace with himself." More ominous was Jefferson's acknowledgment that wives face "afflictions less easy to be endured: Those which a husband inflicts, and the best wives feel most severely."[24] There is no reason to suppose that Jefferson tolerated spousal violence, but no attorney could pretend that it did not happen in Virginia.[25] As an indication that he recognized the emotions that could lead to spousal abuse, his words speak for themselves.

In the patriarchal ideal that Jefferson outlined for his own daughters, even the responsibility for a husband's failings ultimately lay with his wife. A woman faced with difficulties in the marriage, Jefferson advised his daughter, must not "allways look for their cause in the injustice of her lord" because "they may proceed from many trifling errors in her own conduct." He wrote:

> Above all, let a wife beware of communicating to others any want of
> duty or tenderness, she may think she has perceived in her husband.
> This untwists, at once, those delicate cords, which preserve the unity

of the marriage engagement. And its sacredness is broken forever, if third parties are made witnesses of its failings.[26]

For his daughters—and for all wives—Jefferson expected complete subordination to the husband. "Your new condition will call for [an] abundance of little sacrifices," he had reminded his daughter Martha soon after her marriage, for "the happiness of your life depends now on continuing to please a single person."[27] Jefferson's advice matched Mary Deverell's observation that "the moment a woman enters into the nuptial state, she should look upon herself as a new being, or rather as being in a new kind of existence, . . . [for] the pleasing levitics, and agreeable fooleries of a girl, are particularly disgusting in a wife." A married woman, Deverell concluded, must "attend to seeming trifles, both on account of the unfavorable impressions her husband may receive on her neglect, and what constructions a busy world may put on it."[28]

Martha's younger sister, Mary, got the full Jeffersonian sermon in 1797 when she married John Wayles Eppes and settled with him at Eppington, on the Appomattox River in southern Chesterfield County. As it happened, Jefferson's own sister Mary lived nearby at Chestnut Grove with her alcoholic husband, John Bolling. Jefferson knew that his brother-in-law was "happy only with his glass in his hand," and he protested to Mary that his sister's plight (rather than the impending nuptials) provoked his tendency to "sermonize" on the general subject of marriage. However that may be, his advice to Mary was no different from what he had told Martha seven years earlier.[29]

"Harmony in the married state is the very first object to be aimed at," Jefferson advised his younger daughter. But again his advice was grounded in the belief that when necessary to preserve the harmony of a marriage, it was the wife's duty to yield. "How light in fact is the sacrifice of any other wish," he urged, "when weighed against the affections of one with whom we are to pass our whole life." In a difficult marriage like his sister Mary's, the cumulative effect of small acts of "opposition" between wife and husband led inexorably to "alienation" from each other. "A single instance will hardly of itself produce alienation," Jefferson admitted, but therein lay the danger. Imperceptibly small disagreements between wife and husband, allowed to pile up over months and years, could result in an estrangement so complete that "it would puzzle either to say why; because no one difference of opinion has been marked enough to produce a serious effect by itself."[30] Based on his awareness of his sister's problems with an alcoholic husband, Jefferson attempted to express this analysis of the sad progress from alienation to estrangement in essentially gender-neutral language.

As he turned his attention to remedies for these challenges, however, Jefferson again fell back into a conventional male perspective. If tensions arise because "*he* finds *his* affections wearied out by a constant stream of little checks and obstacles," Jefferson thought, then clearly the wife must yield. "Other sources of discontent," he told his daughter,

> are the little cross-purposes of husband and wife in common conversation, a disposition in either to criticise and question whatever the other says, a desire always to demonstrate and make *him* feel *himself* in the wrong, and especially in company. Nothing is so goading. Much better therefore, if our companion views a thing in a light different from what we do, to leave *him* in quiet possession of *his* view. What is the use of rectifying *him* if the thing be unimportant; and if important let it pass for the present, and wait a softer moment and more conciliatory occasion of revising the subject together.[31]

Perhaps if applied equally to both husbands and wives, some of this fatherly wisdom was sensible enough. Still, the intensely masculine prejudice of Jefferson's advice to his own daughters seems puzzling in light of his private opinion about the men they were likely to marry. "The chance that in marriage they will draw a blockhead," Jefferson commented to a French friend, "I calculate at about fourteen to one."[32]

To what extent did Jefferson's advice to his daughters reflect actual experiences with Martha Wayles Skelton during the decade of their marriage? Very likely there were moments that fell short of the "unchequered happiness" that Jefferson remembered in his autobiography decades later. Surely no two people, no matter how loving and thoughtful, could live together for ten years without *ever* stumbling over the "little cross-purposes" about which Jefferson warned his girls so knowingly.[33] On the other hand, his advice was also informed by perceptions of marriages other than his own.

MARTHA WAYLES JEFFERSON excelled in all the domestic duties that she and her husband accepted as her province—ably assisted by the pastry cook, washerwoman, and wet nurse, Ursula, as well as Betty Hemings and her daughters Betty Brown, Nance, Critta, and Sally. Ursula's son Isaac later recalled that "Mrs. Jefferson would come out . . . with a cookery book in her hand and read out of it to [his] mother how to make cakes, tarts, and so on." Their working relationship seems to have been respectful and affectionate. In January 1773, one year into their marriage, Martha had persuaded Jefferson to attend an estate auction fifty miles away in Cumberland County because she was "very desirous to get a favorite house woman of the name of Ursula." It seems likely that she had known Ursula and her husband at the Forest prior to the dispersal of slaves and other property in the settlement of her father's estate. Regardless of how Ursula had come to be Martha's "favorite," Jefferson bought her and her two sons for £210 on January 12, 1773. Soon thereafter he purchased her husband, Great George, from another planter in Cumberland for £130.[34] Betty Hemings and her daughters had even stronger connections with the Forest. Betty had been John Wayles's consort in the years before his death, and her daughters Sally and Critta were Martha Jefferson's half sisters.[35]

Of the few surviving documents written in Martha Wayles Jefferson's own hand, one is a small leather-bound volume of music. Another is a collection of recipes and notes that chronicle her daily management of the household at Monticello. Mrs. Jefferson was particularly adept at brewing. During her first year at Monticello she produced 170 gallons of small beer—enough for about five twelve-ounce servings a day. When a plantation mistress turned the energies of the slave women toward the manufacture of needed commodities, the quantities were rarely small. When Martha Wayles Jefferson directed the making of soap on June 20, 1774, the result was fifteen gallons of soft soap and fifty-four pounds of hard soap. When she made candles on March 13, 1774, she and her slaves finished twelve dozen.[36]

Throughout the year, Martha Jefferson had cattle, fowl, and sheep killed as needed for her table and the plantation as a whole. And whenever an animal was slaughtered, she had its fat and tallow quickly processed into candles and soap. Her day-to-day plantation management is evident in the entries from her household accounts for April 1775, a fairly typical month. Martha had "2 ducks killed" on Friday, April 7, and the first of three shoats killed on Sunday the ninth. Shoats are young pigs less than a year old but no longer suckling, which were harvested year-round for fresh pork. On Saturday, April 15, she slaughtered a cow, "sold one quarter" of the beef, and rendered fifteen pounds of tallow. On Monday the seventeenth she made eight dozen candles and killed another shoat. By Thursday the twentieth she had accumulated enough animal fat to make sixty-eight pounds of soft soap. Finally, on Sunday, April 30, she killed the third shoat that month.[37]

Butchering and curing adult hogs, however, was a seasonal industry on Virginia plantations. It required the crisp weather of January and February so the pork could be soaked in brine or cured in rock salt for several weeks before it was hung in the smokehouse until ready for the table. The labor necessary to bring ham and bacon to the table is startling to modern consumers—and the sheer quantities emphasize the difference between a self-sufficient eighteenth-century plantation and a modern American kitchen. In January and early February 1778, Martha Jefferson directed the butchering and preservation of twenty-two hogs "raised at Monticello," forty-two hogs "that came from [Poplar Forest in] Bedford," and twenty-eight hogs "that came from Elk Hill," the island plantation in the James River that she had inherited from her father. Once all that pork was salted away for curing, there were valuable by-products to preserve for the coming year. Although Martha Jefferson may not have used everything but the squeal, by mid-February 1778 she could tally "60 gallons leaf fat put in the cellar," fifty-two pounds of tallow "from Elk hill," and the manufacture of yet another "pot of soft soap."[38]

The two pages documenting Martha's management of the household at Monticello between January and June 1777 (shown at the right) warrant a close examination. The year began (at the upper left) with the slaughter of sixty-nine hogs on January 1, 9, and 27. By June, when her inventory reached the bottom of the facing page, she had butchered three beef cows, eight shoats, two sheep, a goose, two ducks, and a spring lamb. In Febru-

Martha Wayles Jefferson's household accounts, January to June 1777—one of the few surviving documents in her handwriting.

Courtesy of the Library of Congress, Manuscript Division.

ary she gathered tallow, and March saw the manufacture of soap and candles as well as an inventory of beds, bolsters, mattresses, pillows, and blankets. In April she took stock of her husband's shirts, listed a variety of other clothing for herself and their four-year-old daughter, Martha, who was called Patsy, and made more candles and soap. In May she planted vegetables—French beans on Monday the twelfth and "gadding peas" on Monday the nineteenth—and made forty more candles.[39]

These pages from Martha Jefferson's household accounts are also notable for the information they do not convey. At the beginning of 1777, twenty-eight-year-old Martha Jefferson was four months into her fourth pregnancy. On May 28—two days after butchering a spring lamb—she gave birth to a son, who died two weeks later. Martha's slow recovery from childbirth (and the third death of an infant) drastically altered the customary pattern of food preparation at Monticello.

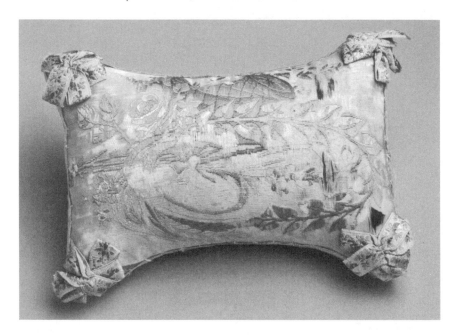

This embroidered pincushion made by Martha Wayles Jefferson is evidence of her mastery of domestic skills that her husband recommended to their daughters. "In the country life of America there are many moments when a woman can have recourse to nothing but her needle for employment. In a dull company and in dull weather for instance," Jefferson wrote, "the needle is then a valuable resource. Besides without knowing to use it herself, how can the mistress of a family direct the works of her servants?"

Courtesy of the Thomas Jefferson Memorial Foundation.

Throughout June and July 1777 the household relied on the purchase of forty-eight chickens, fourteen ducks, and four geese—and Martha noted that "all these were paid for with bacon."[40]

MARTHA JEFFERSON's accounts reveal that much of her day-to-day life at Monticello accorded with the conventional duties of planters' wives in eighteenth-century Virginia, but her role as Jefferson's loving partner transcended those mundane domestic responsibilities. In his marital advice to his daughters, Jefferson only hinted at the depth of romantic love and companionship that he enjoyed for ten years with Martha. "The office of wife includes the exertion of a friend," he told his eldest daughter, for "there are situations, where it will not be enough to love, to cherish, to obey: she must teach her husband to be . . . reconciled to the world, etc., etc."[41]

It is easy to suppose, especially in light of his unbearable grief when she died, that Thomas and Martha Jefferson probably were loving companions during their marriage—but no outsider's estimation can ever get beyond *probably*. Posterity can never know the inner dynamics of their marriage—or perhaps of any marriage. We scarcely comprehend the intimate relationships of our own neighbors, friends, and even siblings. We are often surprised when their relationships fail—and sometimes when they thrive. Our curiosity about the Jeffersons and many other eighteenth-century Americans, however, is further complicated by the frequent absence—and in this instance the conscious destruction—of private correspondence. Except for some poignant words on a slip of paper that he kept with a few strands of her hair until his own death, Jefferson destroyed any correspondence that might hint at the physical and emotional intimacy that he and Martha presumably shared. His purge was thorough. Only four documents in Martha's hand survive: a few pages of music, sixteen pages of household accounts, the *Tristram Shandy* passage found among Jefferson's possessions after his death, and a fund-raising letter that represents her only known venture into public life.

Martha Wayles Jefferson was five months pregnant in August of 1780 when she received a letter from Martha Washington soliciting her help, as wife of the governor of Virginia, in the work of a Ladies' Association that was raising money and making clothing for the soldiers of the Continental Army. She was not in good health, midway through her sixth pregnancy, but Martha Jefferson did all she could to encourage Virginia women to join their "sisters" of Pennsylvania and Maryland in the campaign to support the troops. She published an appeal for donations in the *Virginia Gazette*, explaining that collections would be gathered through the churches, where "sermons suited to the occasion will doubtless be preached by the several Ministers of the Gospel." Nationwide, the Ladies' Association campaign raised $300,000—enough, given the depreciation of Continental currency during the war, to supply Washington's army with 2,200 badly needed linen shirts. Martha Jefferson also enlisted the help of Eleanor Conway "Nelly" Madison, James Madison's mother, in a campaign for the relief of Virginia soldiers imprisoned at Charleston, South Carolina. Their project raised nearly $100,000 in paper money— as well as one diamond earring, a gold watch chain, and eight gold rings—but the British surrendered at Yorktown before the state put these resources to use. Martha Jefferson's letter to Nelly Madison remains one of the only four documents in her handwriting that survive.[42]

Thomas Jefferson was not alone in destroying all the remnants of private correspondence from courtship or the absences occasioned by wartime, business, or public office. Martha Washington similarly destroyed the weekly letters that she and George Washington had written to each other when they were apart.[43] Both families meticulously preserved public papers and general correspondence, but each surviving partner vigilantly destroyed every scrap of paper that might betray the details of their intimate lives. The melancholy act of destroying a departed lover's correspondence can be a cathartic ritual, a final communion that forever seals the mysterious chambers of a private relationship against the intrusion of nosy people. The only other person ever meant to share the sentiments expressed in those private letters was dead. By destroying their love letters, Thomas Jefferson and Martha Washington placed their marriages eternally beyond desecration. Posterity must simply accept that its best glimpses of their genuine intimacy are like the fleeting shadows of reality cast against the walls of Plato's cave. *Probably* is the best we can ever do—the rest is lost to history.

MARTHA and Thomas Jefferson's children were the most obvious evidence of their physical intimacy, but each birth took its toll on Martha's vitality. Any single childbirth can be a life-threatening event, but in eighteenth-century America the pattern of repeated pregnancies and births, commonly spaced about two years apart, sapped many women's strength. The prospect of repeated pregnancy instilled fear in many, too. If they lived long enough, many women regarded menopause as a welcome relief from the exhausting years of fertility, pregnancy, and childbirth. Unless death intervened, the average eighteenth-century Virginia woman had seven or eight full-term pregnancies during her childbearing years.[44] At one extreme, couples such as George and Martha Washington had no children together. At the other, a robust few such as Patrick

Henry's second wife, Dorothea, and the Jeffersons' eldest daughter, Martha, each raised eleven children to adulthood. In regard to health and childbearing, just as Rebecca Burwell Ambler apparently inherited a delicate constitution from her mother and passed it along to her daughter Mary Willis Ambler Marshall, Martha Wayles Skelton, in the Jefferson family's recollection of her, was "*slightly* but exquisitely formed," hinting at the frailty that she shared with her mother and her younger daughter, Mary, both of whom died young after childbirth.[45]

Martha apparently had only one pregnancy during her short marriage to Bathurst Skelton. They were wed in November 1766, and their son, John Skelton, was born in 1767. Bathurst Skelton died on September 30, 1768, and their son died in 1770. Martha was pregnant six times during her second marriage. She was pregnant during at least 54 of the 128 months of their married life. The conception of the Jeffersons' first child, Martha, occurred within days of their wedding on New Year's Day 1772.[46] Martha was born at Monticello on Sunday, September 27, 1772. She inherited her father's vigorous constitution and died sixty-four years later, in 1836, after bearing twelve children, eleven of whom lived to maturity.

The second daughter, Jane Randolph Jefferson, was conceived on about July 11, 1773, immediately after the Jeffersons returned from a visit at the Forest and almost ten months after Martha's birth. Jane was born at Monticello on April 3, 1774, and died seventeen months later in September 1775.

More than two years passed since Jane's birth—marked by momentous events of war and independence—before Thomas and Martha Jefferson's only son was conceived in Philadelphia on about August 27, 1776. Jefferson had been serving in Congress that summer (notably as the principal author of the Declaration of Independence), and Martha had joined him in Philadelphia in August. Their male child, sometimes identified as Thomas, was born at Monticello on May 28, 1777, but he lived only two weeks.

When Mary Jefferson was conceived on about November 8, 1777—just five months after the birth of their short-lived boy—the Jeffersons were in Williamsburg for the autumn session of the General Assembly. Mary was born at Monticello on August 1, 1778, and seems to have inherited her mother's physique—"low like her mother and longways the handsomest, pretty lady jist like her mother."[47] Mary, called Polly and later Maria, died in 1804 from complications of her second childbirth at the age of twenty-six.

Martha and Thomas Jefferson gave the name Lucy Elizabeth Jefferson, in turn, to their last two children. The first Lucy Elizabeth was conceived at Monticello on about March 9, 1780—nineteen months after Mary's birth—and was born there on November 30. She was not yet five months old when she died on April 15, 1781, six weeks before Banastre Tarleton's troop of British cavalry sent the family scrambling to Poplar Forest in Bedford County. The second Lucy Elizabeth was conceived at Poplar Forest on about August 14—eight and a half months after the birth of her namesake—and born at Monticello on May 8, 1782.

In a marriage that lasted almost eleven years, Martha Jefferson had been pregnant nearly half the time. Her husband's intermittent absences during the American Revolution probably occasioned the two long intervals between her pregnancies. During the 29.5 months from Jane Randolph's birth in April 1774 to their son's conception in September 1776, Jefferson's involvement in state and national affairs may have occasioned recurrent absences that coincided with Martha's ovulations and fertility. Similarly, the 19.5 months prior to the first Lucy's conception in March 1780 coincide with his tenure as governor of Virginia. The intervals between her other three births and subsequent conceptions averaged only 7.9 months. Contraceptive techniques were not unknown in eighteenth-century America but seem not to have been used. And Martha Jefferson's difficulty with breast-feeding denied to her the months of lactation that enabled other mothers to postpone conception and space their births at least two years apart.[48] For Martha, as for her mother and her daughter Mary, physical intimacy ultimately proved fatal.

THE SPRING of 1781, with Lucy's death in April and Tarleton's raid in June, was a dark period in Thomas Jefferson's life, but 1782 was even worse. Smarting from the insult of a legislative inquiry into his actions as governor during the British invasion, Jefferson also faced tragedy at home. In April the freeholders of Albemarle County elected Jefferson and Dr. Thomas Walker to the legislature—but within a month even that gesture of support promptly turned sour.

James Monroe was in Richmond on Monday, May 6, 1782, waiting for other members of the newly elected House of Delegates to achieve a quorum and begin their legislative session when he learned that William Short was in town on his way to Monticello. Monroe quickly dashed off a letter thanking Jefferson for some recent advice, expressing his joy "that a few days more will give us your aid in the House and society to your friends," and offering his "best respects to Mrs. Jefferson." We do not know when William Short arrived at Monticello, but perhaps if he rode hard and fast, Martha Jefferson got word of Monroe's good wishes before she went into labor.

Jefferson was terribly worried about his wife's health as she and Aunt Carr (Jefferson's sister Martha, Dabney Carr's widow) prepared for the birth of the second Lucy Elizabeth, which came on Wednesday. On the same Monday that Monroe was dispatching his letter to Monticello, Jefferson handed his old friend Dr. Thomas Walker a short letter to John Tyler, Speaker of the House of Delegates, "declin[ing] the office of delegate for this county to which I have been lately elected."[49] Jefferson gave Tyler no reason for his decision—not a word about his wife's frailty or the family's fears. Nor, it seems, did Dr. Walker betray to any of Jefferson's friends in Richmond his impressions of the domestic tragedy that was unfolding at Monticello.

Both Monroe and Tyler responded to Jefferson's resignation with expressions of stern disappointment that reflected the dissatisfaction being expressed in Richmond and Albemarle by Jefferson's colleagues and constituents. "Publick opinion," Monroe warned, held that one of "the fundamental maxims of a republican government" was that "you should not decline the service of your country."[50] Speaker Tyler wrote that he had presented Jefferson's letter to the House of Delegates but that "the Constitution in the Opinion of the Members will not warrant the acceptance of your resignation." Tyler admitted that he was willing to "suppose your reasons are weighty." Nevertheless, he suggested, "good and able Men had better govern than be govern'd, since 'tis possible . . . that if the able and good withdraw themselves from Society, the venal and ignorant will succeed."[51]

Monroe and Tyler were not grossly insensitive men. They were entirely unaware of Martha Jefferson's life-threatening situation. And the times were indeed perilous. Good and able men were sorely needed in

Richmond and elsewhere. Only seven months earlier, in October 1781, Cornwallis had surrendered his army at Yorktown, but no treaty negotiations had begun since then. "In times of Peace," Speaker Tyler reminded Jefferson, "men of moderate abilities perhaps might conduct the affairs of the State, but at this time when the Republic wants to be organized . . . I cannot but think the House may insist upon you to give attendance without incuring the Censure of being seized [by the sergeant at arms]."[52]

Jefferson responded to these warnings with a long letter that Monroe shared with other lawmakers in Richmond, justifying the legality and propriety of his retirement from office. "I might have comforted myself under the disapprobation of the well-meaning but uninformed people," he complained, "yet that of their representatives was a shock on which I had not calculated." Their ingratitude "inflicted a wound on my spirit which will only be cured by the all-healing grave." Finally, after reflecting on the fact that "public service and private misery [seemed] inseparably linked together," Jefferson closed his letter with this cryptic and ominous statement: "Mrs. Jefferson has added another daughter to our family. She has been ever since and still continues very dangerously ill."[53]

Martha Jefferson never regained her strength after giving birth to Lucy Elizabeth on May 8. As she was slowly dying, Jefferson was powerless to do more than keep her company and hope for her recovery. During the "four months that [Martha] lingered, he was never out of calling," his eldest daughter remembered. "When not at her bedside, he was writing in a small room which opened immediately at the head of her bed."[54]

Most of their conversations are lost to history, but throughout the summer Jefferson doubtless read to her from Laurence Sterne's *Tristram Shandy*, a novel they both admired. One day Martha found enough strength to commit a favorite passage to paper, but her energy failed before she could finish. "Time wastes too fast," Martha wrote:

> every letter I trace tells me with what rapidity life follows my pen. the days and hours of it are flying over our heads like clouds of windy day never to return more. every thing presses on—

Then her hand wavered. Jefferson took the pen and finished the passage: "and every time I kiss thy hand to bid adieu, every absence which follows it, are preludes to that eternal separation which we are shortly to make!"

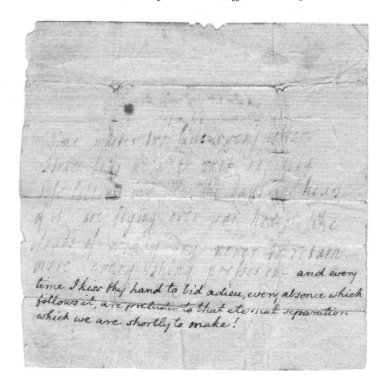

and every
time I kiss thy hand to bid adieu, every absence which
follows it, are preludes to that eternal separation
which we are shortly to make!

In the summer before her death on September 6, 1782, Martha Wayles Jefferson began to write a favorite passage from Laurence Sterne's Tristram Shandy *out. As her strength waned, Jefferson took the pen and finished the passage. He treasured this slip of paper for the rest of his life. His eldest daughter found it among his possessions, together with a lock of her mother's hair, after Jefferson died on July 4, 1826.*

Courtesy of the James Monroe Museum and Memorial Library,
Fredericksburg, Virginia.

Whether prompted by hope or by despair, Jefferson stopped the text just short of Sterne's next line: "Heaven have mercy on us both!"[55] Much later in life Jefferson expressed his hope for "an ecstatic meeting with the friends we have loved and lost and whom we shall still love and never lose again"—but for now he found no consolation in thoughts of heaven.[56]

By Friday, September 6, the family and household slaves sensed that Martha's death was only hours away. Jefferson shared his grim bedside vigil with Martha's sister Elizabeth Wayles Eppes, his own sister Martha Carr, and half a dozen of his wife's favorite household slaves. Ursula was there, as were Betty Hemings and her daughters Betty Brown, Nance,

Critta, and Sally—the two youngest being Martha's half sisters. As Jefferson sat by Martha's deathbed, these witnesses later recounted, "she gave him directions about a good many things that she wanted done" after her death. "When she came to the children," according to those present,

> she wept and could not speak for some time. Finally she held up her hand, and spreading out her four fingers, she told him she could not die happy if she thought her four children were ever to have a stepmother brought in over them. Holding her other hand in his, Mr. Jefferson promised her solemnly that he would never marry again.[57]

Just before Martha Wayles Jefferson died at 11:45 a.m. on Friday, September 6, 1782, her husband "was led from the room almost in a state of insensibility by his sister Mrs. Carr, who, with great difficulty, got him into his library where he fainted, and remained so long insensible that they feared he never would revive."[58] Two weeks after Martha's death, Edmund Randolph visited Monticello and found Jefferson "inconsolable." Cloistered away on his mountain, he was stricken with a grief "so violent as to justify the circulating report of his swooning away whenever he sees his children." Although James Madison was skeptical, contending that his friend's "philosophical temper render the circulating rumor . . . altogether incredible," Jefferson's eldest daughter, who was only ten years old, witnessed her father's uncontrolled grief (and complete disregard for the feelings and anxieties of his children) at first hand.[59]

Nearly half a century later, Martha Jefferson Randolph vividly recalled "the violence of his emotion, of his grief . . . [which] to this day I dare not trust myself to describe." Utterly without regard for anyone else, Jefferson withdrew to "his room for three weeks," she remembered, "and I was never a moment from his side. He walked almost incessantly night and day, only lying down occasionally when nature was completely exhausted, on a pallet that had been brought in during his long fainting fit." Jefferson's sister Martha and his sister-in-law Elizabeth "remained constantly with him for some weeks" until "at last he left his room." Then he spent most of October riding aimlessly about the plantation, accompanied only by his preadolescent daughter.[60]

"He was incessantly on horseback rambling about the mountain in the least frequented roads, and just as often through the woods," Martha recalled. "In those melancholy rambles I was his constant companion, a solitary witness to many a violent burst of grief, the remembrance of which has consecrated particular scenes of that lost home beyond the power of time to obliterate."[61]

In some measure, the intensity of Jefferson's grief bore testimony to his deep love for Martha Wayles. His friends were surprised, his family alarmed, and his daughters probably terrified by the utter failure of his self-control—but no more alarmed than Jefferson himself. Intellect and will had totally succumbed to emotion. Head had been conquered by heart. The man who had so recently "folded [him]self in the arms of retirement, and rested all prospects of future happiness on domestic and literary objects," had discovered instead that "a single event wiped away all my plans and left me a blank which I had not the spirits to fill up."[62] Proof again that women were dangerous.

After weeks of virtual solitude, by mid-October Jefferson began "emerging from that stupor of mind which had rendered me as dead to the world as was she whose loss occasioned it."[63] Then, on the twenty-fifth of November, a courier arrived with a letter from Philadelphia.[64] Congress wanted him to help negotiate the treaty that would end the American Revolution. Perhaps, his friends hoped, the appointment might assuage his grief and lure him back into public life. Under the cover of civic duty, he could escape from the gloomy mountain where he had watched Martha's lingering death, travel to France, and immerse himself in the comfortably masculine world of statecraft. His head once again would have firm control of his life.

CHAPTER FIVE

Maria Cosway

*The lady had . . . qualities and accomplishments, belonging to her
sex, which might form a chapter apart for her: such as music, modesty, beauty, and that softness of disposition which is the ornament
of her sex and charm of ours.*

—Thomas Jefferson to Maria Cosway, October 12, 1786

TWENTY-SIX-YEAR-OLD Maria Louisa Caterina Cecilia Hadfield Cosway was surely the most talented and fascinating woman Thomas Jefferson ever met. She captured his heart in a moment. Maria Cosway seemed to personify every attribute a gentleman could want. She was charming, beautiful, intelligent, artistic, and musical. Although Jefferson met her in the flirtatious years of her twenties, he sensed a depth of character that was deeply religious. Maria had been a devout Catholic as a young girl, and in later years she embraced her faith again and founded a convent in Italy. All in all, Maria Cosway's "qualities and accomplishments" seemed to surpass those of other women. Jefferson described her as "a chapter apart"—an assessment in which he was joined by dozens of smitten contemporaries in the capitals and byways of England and the Continent.

Maria Cosway was born in 1760 to expatriate English parents in Florence, the first city of the Renaissance. Barely escaping the fate of her four older siblings, who were murdered by a crazed nurse, Maria found refuge and nurture in a convent school. There she mastered five or six languages, contemplated embracing a life of chastity and obedience to God, and displayed exceptional talents in music and art. When she was ten the grand duke of Tuscany invited Maria to perform on the harpsi-chord at a concert in Florence. At eighteen, having studied painting and drawing with distinguished artists in Florence and Rome, this gifted

Maria Louisa Caterina Cecilia Hadfield Cosway, an eighteenth-century engraving by V. Green, from a self-portrait.

Collection of the author.

young woman was elected to membership in the Florence Academy of Fine Arts.

Maria's English mother, probably born in Shropshire, was Protestant. Her father, Charles Hadfield, was an Irish-born Catholic of liberal political sentiments. For thirty years, from 1747 until his death in 1777, they operated a famous hotel in Florence that catered to English nobility and artists traveling on the grand tour. Their guest register was a veritable who's who of elite British travelers, including the architects Robert Adam and Sir John Soane, the neoclassical sculptor Thomas Banks, and artists such as John Singleton Copley, George Romney, and Benjamin West. For Maria and her four younger siblings, Charles and Isabella Hadfield's "English Hotel" comprised an outpost and extension of elite

London society and culture. The Swiss-born painter Angelica Kauffmann, a founding member of the British Royal Academy and frequent collaborator with Robert Adam, treated Maria as a young protégée both in Italy and later in London.

Assisted by Kauffmann and Thomas Banks, in the spring of 1779 the ambitious widow Hadfield moved her family to London, where "the money which the father had gained in Florence was quickly spent . . . and the family were soon in some degree of distress."[1] Maria's mother swiftly arranged her marriage to the socially prominent artist Richard Cosway, an unusual man nearly twice her age who enjoyed lavish patronage from the rakish Prince of Wales (the future George IV). "Having refused better offers in her better days," one disappointed suitor wrote, "she from necessity married Cosway the miniature painter," who endeared himself to his new mother-in-law with a nuptial gift of £2,800. Maria's account of the marriage was circumspect: "I became acquainted with Mr. Cosway," she wrote many years later, "his offer was Accepted, my mother's wishes gratified, and I married tho' under Age."[2] Half a dozen rivals were disappointed. One sneered that Cosway "at that time adored her, though she always despised him." A more sympathetic voice observed that Maria's "capacity for the eccentric . . . made her a fitting wife for a husband who mingled not a little of charlatanism with very real gifts as an artist."[3]

Born at Tiverton in 1742 into a family of Devonshire woolen merchants, Richard Cosway demonstrated an early talent for miniature portraits. Assisted by local worthies who overcame the indifference of his parents (who conveniently died soon thereafter), Cosway at twelve boarded a coach for the three-day journey to London, 250 miles to the east. After winning first prize in a contest sponsored by the forerunner of the Royal Academy of Art, he studied first with Thomas Hudson, the capital's reigning miniaturist, then at William Shipley's prestigious drawing school in the Strand, and finally in the newly opened gallery of the duke of Richmond. Cosway's career blossomed as he exhibited both oil portraits and miniatures at major exhibitions in London—while on the side he did a lucrative private trade in "loose and amorous subjects" and "lascivious miniatures for snuff boxes." The first of Cosway's many commissions for the royal family was a miniature in 1764 of the two-year-old Prince of Wales, who later became Cosway's most important patron. Cosway's election to the Royal Academy in 1771, supported by the great Sir Joshua Reynolds, was a clear indication of the rising fame that caught the attention of Maria's mother.[4]

Despite his artistic genius and capacity for hard work, Richard Cosway's relentless ambition, his physical appearance and extravagant attire, and his sexual tastes were lightning rods for satire and ridicule. "Although a well-made little man," a friend recalled, Cosway was "certainly very like a monkey in the face."[5] Writing to a friend who was touring Europe, Cosway expressed his lust for Italian women with the vulgar bravado of a man seeking to proclaim his masculinity. Among the more exotic of Richard's close friends was the transvestite Charles Beaumont, chevaliere d'Éon, a former French diplomat notorious for demonstrating his fencing skills in exhibitions dressed as a woman.[6]

Rival artists fastened upon Cosway's "monkey face, apish figure, and his inane finicking dandyism" in caricature prints (now rare because their victim "purchased and destroyed every copy that he could lay his hands on"), depicting him as an insatiable monkey dressed in the costume of a dandy, or *macaroni*. A 1761 engraving by William Hogarth portrayed Cosway as a furry baboon dressed as a dilettante connoisseur. Another print stuck him for life with the derisive nickname "the Macaroni Miniature Painter." Even Cosway's friends admitted that he "was certainly the greatest fop of all." Contemporaries described him at court "in all the gay costume of the drawing-room, with pink heels to his shoes," or strutting through the royal apartments "on his scarlet heels, as important in his own estimation, as any newly created lord." John Thomas Smith, keeper of prints at the British Museum, recorded an encounter at a Christie's auction with Cosway, who was "full-dressed in his sword and bag, with a small three-cornered hat on the top of his powdered toupee, and a mulberry-silk coat, profusely embroidered with scarlet strawberries."[7]

After their wedding at St. George's Church in Hanover Square on January 18, 1781, the couple resided at 4 Berkeley Street, in London's fashionable West End, where Richard had lived since 1768. Richard Cosway immediately introduced his charming young wife to the social whirl of the city. Three years later they rented the central section of

Schomberg House at 81 Pall Mall, next door to the artist Thomas Gains-
borough, a fellow member of the Royal Academy and favorite of
George III, and a few blocks closer to St. James's Palace.

Richard Cosway decorated the twenty-six rooms of their four-story
town house in "so novel a character, as to surprise their new neighbors,
astonish their old friends, and furnish wonderment for the table-talk of
the town"—no small feat in light of the "over-flowing audiences" who
had frequented Schomberg House in its previous incarnation as "the
Temple of Health and Hymen" of the celebrated physician and sex ther-
apist James Graham. Where Graham had offered his "Celestial or
Magnetico-electrico bed" to barren couples for fifty pounds a night
(with the promise of "heavenly joys," "superior ecstasy," and "immediate
conception"), Maria now welcomed royalty, wealth, and celebrity to gala
musical evenings that caused traffic jams in the streets below. The
Cosways' guests were

> of all ranks and callings that had any pretensions to the elegant:—the
> writer of the last new poem, the speaker of the last best speech in the
> Commons; some rising star . . . in art; the man who made the last
> miraculous escape from shipwreck, or who had walked into the
> remotest latitudes; in short, all the lions of London were there, to see
> and be seen.[8]

Horace Walpole attended a "great concert at Mrs. Cosway's" featuring
an operatic performance by Giovanni Rubinelli. On other occasions
Maria might sing or perform on the harp or the pianoforte before intro-
ducing some touring musician to her guests, "while her odd little husband, dressed up in the very extreme of fashion, flitted about through his
gaily decorated rooms, ogling, flirting, and bowing . . . with the airs of a
Prince" as he showered attentions upon wealthy potential clients.[9]

According to the diary of American diplomat Gouverneur Morris,
some aristocratic Englishwomen regarded the Cosways' house as a place
"where, from the very mixed Companies which frequent it, dangerous
Connections may be formed"—a prospect that troubled Morris not at
all. A devotee of delicious gossip, good food, and convivial women, Morris was a frequent visitor at Schomberg House and an ardent admirer of
Maria Cosway. Dr. Samuel Johnson's famous biographer, James Boswell,

also enjoyed flirting with Maria, even if his affection took second place to the Corsican patriot General Pasquale Paoli. Exiled to London after the failure of his first attempt at Corsican independence in 1769, General Paoli had met Maria about 1783, probably at one of her concerts. Like her other admirers, Paoli was captivated by her beauty, talent, and charm, but he also shared Maria's affection for Italy and "understood the deeply pious and melancholy nature beneath her gay exterior."[10] Their ardent friendship surpassed all others in Maria Cosway's life and lasted until General Paoli's death in 1807.

IN THE SUMMER of 1786 a lucrative commission for a portrait of the duc d'Orleans and other projects brought Richard Cosway and his twenty-six-year-old wife to Paris. While visiting the capital they resided in rue Coq-Héron, on the Right Bank half a mile north of the Louvre. The official residence of the French kings until 1682, when the Sun King, Louis XIV, moved the royal court to Versailles, the Louvre now housed the Académie française and its departments for architecture, painting, sculpture, mineralogy, natural history, and agriculture. Biennial art exhibitions on the first floor presaged the building's subsequent transformation into a public museum, and the upper floors provided spacious apartments for favored artists and scientists. Among them was Jacques-Louis David, who had met the Cosways in London and appreciated both Maria's talent and her charm. David may have recommended the Cosways' lodgings in rue Coq-Héron, just past the ancient church of Saint-Eustache and the city grain market, or Halle au Blé, with its newly constructed dome.[11] There, in a chance encounter on Sunday morning, September 3, 1786, Maria Cosway enthralled the widowed American ambassador to the court of Louis XVI.

The Cosways were not the only artists from London who traveled to Paris in the summer of 1786. At the Hôtel de Langeac, Jefferson's residence at the western edge of the city, thirty-year-old John Trumbull was visiting Jefferson on recess from his studies with the great expatriate painter Benjamin West. Acclaimed for heroic canvases on grand historical themes, such as *The Death of General Wolfe* (1770), West enjoyed the patronage of George III and the friendship of Sir Joshua Reynolds. He had helped establish the Royal Academy of Arts and had welcomed

Richard Cosway into membership. Born in Pennsylvania, West had left for Italy about 1759 and then settled in London at the close of the Seven Years' War. Now, in the aftermath of another war that altered the fate of North America, his younger countryman John Trumbull aspired to apply West's epic style to the patriotic moments of the American Revolution. Tucked into his luggage as Trumbull arrived at the Hôtel de Langeac were preliminary portrait sketches of Jefferson and John Adams that found final expression on the canvas of *The Declaration of Independence* (1794).

THOMAS JEFFERSON loved domes. The architecture of Monticello and the Rotunda of the University of Virginia attest to a lifelong fascination. Even his design for the capitol of Virginia hid a dome beneath the classical roofline of a Roman temple. The Paris grain market, completed in 1767, was a huge circular structure. At the center was an open courtyard 450 feet in diameter surrounded by a second circle of arched colonnades. The splendid dome was built over the central space a dozen years later, and it made the entire structure one of the wonders of eighteenth-century Paris. An English visitor described the Halle au Blé in 1787 as "so well planned, and so admirably executed, that I know of no public building that exceeds it in either France or England." The structure was "a vast rotunda" constructed with the dome "entirely of wood, upon a new principle of carpentry, . . . as light as if suspended by fairies." Jefferson and Trumbull were eager to see it. Jefferson thought the construction technique might be adapted for a proposed market back in Richmond, which had recently supplanted Williamsburg as the capital of Virginia. The dome literally dazzled its visitors. Its architects had revived a sturdy but elegant construction technique originally developed by the Renaissance master Philibert Delorme. Twenty-five long windows radiating from a circular skylight at the crest of the dome flooded the interior of the circular building with daylight.[12]

The most direct route from Jefferson's house to the Halle au Blé was a scenic one-mile ride down the Champs-Elysées toward the Île de la Cité and the spires of Notre-Dame—roughly the same route a modern visitor might take from the Arc de Triomphe to Les Halles. At the place de la Concorde (then known as place de Louis XV), Jefferson's coach-

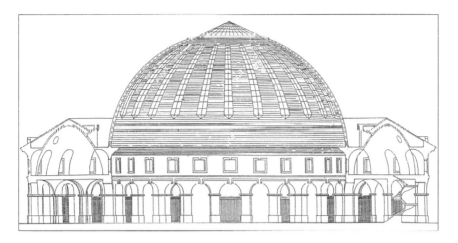

An eighteenth-century "Diagram of the Dome of the New Halle aux Blé." Jefferson's admiration for the Halle au Blé matched that of the English traveler Arthur Young, who in 1787 regarded the new grain market as "by far the finest thing I have yet seen in Paris. The gallery is 150 yards round. . . . In the ground area, wheat, pease, beans, lentils, are stored and sold. In the surrounding divisions, flour on wooden stands. . . . Stair-cases doubly winding within each other [lead up] to spacious apartments for rye, barley, oats, etc." Jefferson first met Maria Cosway in a chance encounter at the Halle au Blé on Sunday, September 3, 1786.

Collection of the author.

man wended left onto rue Royale, carrying Trumbull and Jefferson past the Hôtel de Coislin, where in 1778 Benjamin Franklin signed the treaty by which France recognized American independence and joined the war against Great Britain. Jefferson's mind was occupied with domes, arches, and bridges as Anselen turned right onto rue Saint-Honoré and drove past the Comédie-Française, the Palais Royal, and the Louvre. At last Jefferson and Trumbull had a clear view of the Halle au Blé, a block to the north. Along the south wall of the grain market they found the ancient column (still standing today) with narrow stairs spiraling to the top of the wall.[13] Erected in 1572 for Catherine de Médicis, who was said to have climbed it with her astrologer to consult the stars, the Medici column offered a perfect vantage for close examination of the magnificent dome. A "wonderful piece of architecture," Jefferson exclaimed after seeing the dome. "Oh! . . . the most superb thing on earth!"[14]

Jefferson had arrived with plenty of time to study the amazing structure and return home to dress for dinner that evening at the town house of the elderly noblewoman Louise-Élisabeth de La Rochefoucauld, duchesse d'Enville. As he and Trumbull reached the Medici column, however, they ran into Richard and Maria Cosway. Trumbull knew the Cosways from London and their paths had crossed in Paris, too. Now he made the proper introductions—and suddenly everything changed. By midafternoon Jefferson's heart was "dilating with [his] new acquaintances, and contriving how to prevent a separation from them," especially from Maria. The Cosways, Jefferson, and Trumbull all had evening commitments, from which they excused themselves by dispatching "lying messengers . . . into every quarter of the city."[15] Jefferson put off his dinner engagement with the duchesse de La Rochefoucauld d'Enville with a note pretending that a packet of urgent letters demanded his immediate attention. Off the foursome went for dinner in Saint-Cloud, a popular resort town midway between Paris and Versailles and the site of a château that Louis XVI had recently purchased for Marie Antoinette. After dinner the festive quartet headed for the pleasure gardens near Montmartre, where the Ruggieri family of Italian pyrotechnists were drawing enthusiastic crowds to their "lyric pantomimes in fireworks," including "The Salamander," "The Combat of Mars," and "The Forge of Vulcan." They closed the evening with a surprise visit to the composer and harpist Johann Baptist Krumpholtz.

Jefferson was utterly smitten. On this point his admiring biographer was entirely reliable. "A generally philosophical gentleman, hungrier for beauty and a woman than he realized," Dumas Malone wrote, "was quite swept off his supposedly well-planted feet."[16] For the next week or so Jefferson and Maria Cosway roamed Paris and its environs together, sometimes accompanied by Maria's husband, by Trumbull, or by Jefferson's secretary, William Short.

On Monday or Tuesday they visited the Royal Library (now the Bibliothèque Nationale),[17] where the sculptor Jean-Antoine Houdon had one of his studios. On Tuesday they traveled west to the ancient Château de Madrid in the Bois de Boulogne, the huge forest park in which Jefferson often walked. On Thursday they traveled to Saint-Germain, had a picnic at the royal retreat overlooking the Seine at Marly-le-Roi near Versailles, and toured the adjacent Pavillon de Musique at Louveciennes. On Friday evening Jefferson took Maria Cosway to a concert of Haydn symphonies at the Tuileries. On Saturday, while Trumbull set out for Frankfurt and Brussels on his return trip to London, Jefferson and Maria

Cosway viewed the crown jewels, tapestries, and objets d'art exhibited at the Hôtel du Garde-Meuble near the place de la Concorde.[18]

That evening Jefferson and his daughter Martha accompanied Maria Cosway to the Théâtre Italien, half a mile from the Cosways' lodgings. The program on Saturday, September 9, included the light opera *Richard Coeur-de-Lion* and a one-act *arlequinade*, or romantic farce in verse, entitled *Les Deux Billets*. Inevitably, as the widowed ambassador and his date watched the slapstick comedy about letters between the character Arlequin and his sweetheart, bits of dialogue struck close to home. A month later, after Maria Cosway returned to London, Jefferson promised to cherish her correspondence in the same spirit that "Arlequin in *Les Deux Billets* spelt the words *'je t'aime'* and wished that the whole alphabet had entered into their composition."[19]

Details are vague about whether Jefferson and Maria Cosway were together from Sunday through Wednesday, September 10 to 13, but his account book entries document excursions on Thursday and Friday into the countryside west of Paris. On Thursday, Jefferson paid three francs admission to a marvel from the reign of Louis XIV, the century-old "machine" that supplied water from the Seine to the fountains and gardens of Marly and Versailles.[20] On Friday they ventured farther west to the Désert de Retz, the ninety-acre retreat of the amateur architect François Racine de Monville. Among its eccentric structures were a temple of Pan in neoclassical style, a Chinese pavilion, the ruins of a Gothic chapel, and a pyramid-shaped icehouse. But Monville's showpiece was a five-story residence built to resemble the base of a huge broken column, forty-eight feet in diameter. Jefferson loved the spiral staircase at the center of the Broken Column house, and he later adapted a distinctive feature of its floor plan—oval rooms within a circular structure—for the Rotunda of the University of Virginia.[21]

THOMAS JEFFERSON's romantic outings with Maria Cosway ended painfully just two weeks after they met. Monday, September 18, was a pleasant autumn day with an afternoon temperature of 75 degrees Fahrenheit and cloudy skies. After a weekend at home, Martha had gone back to school at the Abbaye Royale de Panthémont. John Trumbull had left Paris a week earlier and had nearly reached Frankfurt. Jefferson's secretary and protégé, William Short, was probably at Saint-Germain with his lover, the unhappily married duchesse de La Rochefoucauld. And so it happened that Jefferson and Cosway were strolling in the riverside park of the Cours la Reine, near the Champs-Elysées and the place de la Concorde, when he impulsively attempted to vault a fence. Although Jefferson may have felt as youthful as his beautiful companion, his forty-three-year-old right wrist gave way.[22]

Whether Jefferson's wrist was broken or dislocated proved a moot point—the pain was excruciating and it continued for months. One surgeon was summoned but quickly dismissed as incompetent. The second surgeon was scarcely more helpful. Jefferson did not regain any use of his right hand until early November, and the wrist plagued him for the rest of his life. He kept the details of his accident to himself. "It was one of those follies," he assured a young acquaintance, "from which good cannot come but ill may." Years later Martha Jefferson recounted the accident as though it had happened not in the presence of Maria Cosway but during an earnest conversation with an unnamed male friend. Either Jefferson deliberately misled his eldest daughter about the circumstances of his injury (as he did when his girls asked about his estrangement from John and Elizabeth Walker), or Martha Jefferson subsequently deceived his biographer.[23]

The injury confined Jefferson to his house for two weeks. On September 27, in a letter written and signed by William Short, Jefferson excused himself from the dedication of a bust of Lafayette presented by the commonwealth of Virginia to the city of Paris, owing to "the consequences of a fall which confine me to my room."[24] Only the news that Richard and Maria Cosway were about to leave for London brought Jefferson out of his house on Wednesday, October 4—and the next morning he wrote a short and shaky note with his left hand. "I have passed the night in so much pain that I have not closed my eyes," he confessed to Maria.

> It is with infinite regret therefore that I must relinquish your charming company for that of a Surgeon whom I have sent for to examine the cause of this change. I am in hopes it is only the having rattled a little too freely over the pavement yesterday. If you do not go to day I shall still have the pleasure of seeing you again. If you do, god bless

you wherever you go. Present me in the most friendly terms to Mr. Cosway, and let me hear of your safe arrival in England. Addio Addio.

[PS:] Let me know if you do not go to day.[25]

Throughout his confinement, Maria had sent him notes hoping to visit, but her good intentions were always interrupted by her husband's schedule. "I am very, very sorry indeed," she now replied on Thursday afternoon, "for having been the Cause of your pains. . . . Why was I not more friendly to you and less to Myself by preventing your giving me the pleasure of your Company? . . . We shall go I believe this Morning, Nothing seems redy, but Mr. Cosway seems More dispos'd than I have seen him in all this time."

Perhaps Richard Cosway was indifferent to the depth of his wife's concern for Jefferson—or perhaps all too aware of it. And perhaps Jefferson's affection for Maria was deeper than her affection for him. "I beg you will think *us* sensible to your kindness," Maria wrote in closing. "With infinite pleasure I shall remember the charming days we have past together, and shall long for next spring."[26]

What was the true nature of the relationship between this forty-three-year-old widower and this flirtatious young woman trapped in a marriage of convenience? Was it love or just infatuation? Were they absorbed in each other? Or were they just carefree tourists enthralled together by the wonders of Paris? Answers to these riddles, if they can be found anywhere, require an examination of the denouement of their summer romance, beginning with the remarkable letter that Jefferson wrote to Maria Cosway on October 12, 1786, shortly after her husband abruptly ended their sojourn in Paris.

As it happened, packing for the return to London took longer than Richard Cosway had intended. On Friday, October 6, ignoring his pain as best he could, Jefferson accompanied the Cosways north to the little town of Saint-Denis, on the Seine, where they boarded a carriage headed for Antwerp en route home to London. Returning despondently to Paris, Jefferson had the company of his daughter Martha for the weekend. On Tuesday, in a brief letter, the second written with his left hand, he referred to the "dislocated wrist which for some time interrupted my attention to affairs." Although the injury surely did distract him from mundane business, so did a week of brooding after Maria's departure. Jefferson spent days sorting out his feelings toward Maria Cosway in the first draft of a 4,600-word essay—and then neatly copying it onto three fresh sheets of paper. All with his left hand.[27]

Before Jefferson dispatched his artfully composed dialogue to Maria, he also made a letterpress copy for his files—an act quite in contrast to his destruction of every shred of paper he had written to his late wife. As the text itself reveals, the dialogue was not really composed as a love letter for Maria Cosway. By retaining a file copy of his "Dialogue Between My Head and My Heart," Jefferson indicated that it expressed something other than deeply private romantic love. It became, rather, the record of a process by which Jefferson sorted out all the disorderly passions that had erupted as he and Maria Cosway rambled through Paris. By the bottom of the fourth page, Jefferson had tamed his adulterous longings for Maria Cosway, transforming his unruly emotions into lofty sentiments of friendship toward her *and her husband*. Then, for good measure, he diluted the intensity of those feelings in generalized reflections about humanity. Having reimposed a measure of self-control over his emotions through the vehicle of the dialogue, Jefferson made a copy of the document for himself and posted the original to Maria Cosway.

The opening scene of Jefferson's "Dialogue Between My Head and My Heart" described the Cosways' departure. "Having performed the last sad office of handing you into your carriage at the Pavillon de St. Denis, and seen the wheels get actually into motion," he wrote, "I turned on my heel and walked, more dead than alive, to the opposite door, where my own was awaiting me." After the long trip back to Paris, Jefferson portrayed himself "seated by [his] fire side, solitary and sad, [where] the following dialogue took place between my Head and my Heart."[28]

> HEAD. Well, friend, you seem to be in a pretty trim.
>
> HEART. I am indeed the most wretched of all earthly beings. Overwhelmed with grief, every fibre of my frame distended beyond its natural powers to bear. . . .
>
> HEAD. These are the eternal consequences of your warmth and precipitation. This is one of the scrapes into which you are ever lead-

ing us. You confess your follies indeed: but still you hug and cherish them.

The next section of Jefferson's dialogue recalled his first encounter with the Cosways at the Halle au Blé. "When our friend Trumbull [was] telling us of the merits and talents of these good people," Jefferson's Head complained, "I never ceased whispering to you that we had no occasion for new acquaintance."

"Sir," his Heart protested, "this acquaintance was not the consequence of my doings. It was one of your projects which threw us in the way of it. . . . I never trouble myself with domes nor arches. The Halle aux bleds might have rotted down before I should have gone to see it. . . . You then, Sir, and not I, have been the cause of the present distress." The reason for visiting the grain market, Jefferson's Head answered, was "public utility"—to determine whether its dome might be replicated for a new market in Richmond. "While I was occupied with these objects," however, "you were dilating with your new acquaintances, and contriving how to prevent a separation from them."

In the opening pages, Jefferson employed both his Head and his Heart to reminiscence about the places he and Mrs. Cosway had visited on the day they met. "Oh! my dear friend," his Heart exclaimed, "how you have revived me by recalling to my mind the transactions of that day! How well I remember them all." To which his Head replied, "Thou art the most incorrigible of all the beings that ever sinned! . . . You want nothing but the opportunity to act it over again."

Then, four pages into the twelve-page dialogue, Jefferson's pronouns began to reveal a subtle element of confusion, or indecision, that Maria could not have failed to notice. As Jefferson's Head and Heart turned their attention from the past to the future, *we* became *they*, the entire dialogue shifting to *us* and *them*.

After some scolding banter aimed at the Heart, the transition occurred on page four, in three successive sentences in the middle of a speech attributed to Jefferson's Head. First, employing a plural pronoun in reference to both Richard and Maria Cosway, Jefferson's Head admitted "that the persons indeed were of the greatest merit, possessing good sense, good humour, honest hearts, honest manners, and eminence in a lovely art." Then, focusing briefly on Maria alone, the Head confessed "that the lady had moreover qualities and accomplishments, belonging to her sex, which might form a chapter apart for her: such as music, modesty, beauty, and that softness of disposition which is the ornament of her sex and charm of ours." But finally, uniting Head and Heart under the pronoun *ours*, Jefferson addressed "the pang of separation" because "*their* stay here was to be short." By the time he reached this paragraph, the real debate between his Head and Heart was over. Jefferson had extricated himself from the romantic dilemma. Without abandoning the now-hollow rhetorical form of the dialogue, Jefferson's Head and Heart subsequently referred to themselves (his reunited self) as *us* and to the Cosways (equally united) as *they* or *them*.

"But *they* told me *they* would come back again the next year," his Heart feebly protested. "But in the meantime see what you suffer," his Head replied, "and *their* return too depends on so many circumstances that if you had a grain of prudence you would not count upon it. . . . You should abandon the idea of ever seeing *them* again."

HEART. May heaven abandon me if I do!

HEAD. Very well. Suppose then *they* come back [to Paris]—*they* are to stay two months, and when these are expired, what is to follow? Perhaps you flatter yourself *they* may come to America?

HEART. God only knows what is to happen. I see nothing impossible in that supposition. . . . Especially the lady, who paints landscapes so inimitably. She wants only subjects worthy of immortality to render her pencil immortal. The Falling spring, the Cascade of Niagara, the Passage of the Potowmac thro the Blue mountains, the Natural bridge. . . . And our own dear Monticello.

According to Julian Boyd, founding editor of the definitive edition of Jefferson's writings, the October 12 dialogue between Jefferson's Head and his Heart "is one of the most revealing in the entire body of TJ's correspondence, and one of the notable love letters in the English language." Revealing, yes. But the editor's exaggerated claim that twelve pages of eloquent indecision comprise a "notable love letter" suggests, instead, that Maria Cosway had swept Professor Boyd off *his* "supposedly well-planted feet." Historian Andrew Burstein's perspective is more accurate. "This stylish, evocative composition," Burstein writes, was created as "a testament to sentimental friendship" and serves posterity as "a window to the inner life of the man who fashioned it." And who can quibble with Dumas Malone's description of the Head and Heart dialogue as "a feat of ambidexterity, and . . . one of the most unusual tributes ever paid a pretty woman by a distinguished man."[29]

The only forthright declaration of love in the whole dialogue is in the final speech on page eleven, in which Jefferson's Heart expresses its love for both Maria and her husband. "I comfort myself with expectations of their promised return," it proclaims.

> Hope is sweeter than despair and they were too good to mean to deceive me. In the summer, said the gentleman; but in the spring, said the lady: and I should love her forever, were it only for that! Know then . . . that I have taken these good people into my bosom: that I have lodged them in the warmest cell I could find: that I love them, and will continue to love them through life: that if fortune should dispose them on one side the globe, and me on the other, my affections shall pervade its whole mass to reach them.

Jefferson's Heart at last promises his Head, "I will in like manner . . . do the like good turn for you with Condorcet, Rittenhouse, Madison, La Cretelle, or any other of those worthy sons of science whom you so justly prize."

The dialogue is a revealing window into Jefferson's psyche but hardly one of the most notable love letters in the English language. Surely it cannot be read as an impassioned plea for Maria to run off with Jefferson to America. Suppose, for the sake of argument, that immediately after her return to London, Maria Cosway had been sufficiently unhappy both with her husband and with London society to contemplate a future with Jefferson. What must have been her reaction upon reading Jefferson's twelve pages of impassioned ambivalence, much of it addressed to both her and her husband? Was she to infer from Jefferson's speculation about whether "*they* may come to America" that he was inviting *her* to come live with him at Monticello? How, exactly, would their relationship have worked there? Was Maria Cosway inclined to live on a Virginia plantation, brewing beer? Slaughtering hogs? Was she ready to spend days and nights directing the work of household slaves and field hands while awaiting her husband's return from the wider world, eager to wipe its cares from his furrowed brow? In the two weeks that they explored Paris together, did they talk about the duties that Jefferson had expected to be fulfilled by his late wife and had recommended to his daughters?

Surely not. "We were half days, and whole days together," Jefferson recalled two years later, "and I found this too little." Although John Trumbull misplaced the original pages of his diary for the week he spent with Jefferson and the Cosways in Paris, he "distinctly recollect[ed]," in his autobiography, "that this time was occupied . . . in examining and reviewing whatever relates to the arts, and that Mr. Jefferson joined our party almost daily, and here commenced his acquaintance with Mrs. Cosway, of whom very respectful mention is made in his published correspondence."[30]

WHAT WAS the nature of the relationship between Jefferson and Maria Cosway? Opinions vary from one historian or biographer to the next, depending on how each has interpreted the evidence available to them (see appendix C). Most do agree, first, that the relationship between Richard and Maria Cosway was unusual for a married couple, and, second, that a laissez-faire morality prevailed in Parisian society during the last years of the ancien régime. "Illicit love-making was generally condoned," Dumas Malone readily acknowledged, "and if [Jefferson] as a widower ever engaged in it, this was the time."[31]

If it were true that Jefferson and Cosway spent four weeks, or six weeks, or seven weeks together in Paris after their encounter at the Halle au Blé, it is easy to imagine their mutual attraction leading to a passionate love affair. And if they had become lovers, whether physically or not, then surely the Head and Heart dialogue *was* a love letter. But their time together touring the artistic, architectural, and cultural sites of Paris in the company of others occupied only ten or twelve days during a period of just two weeks—from the Sunday they met at the Halle au Blé to the Monday when Jefferson dislocated his wrist on the Cours la Reine. He saw them again only on October 4 and 6 as they were departing for London. In all, between September 3 and October 6, 1786, Jefferson and Mrs. Cosway spent, as he later complained, "half days, and whole days together" during a sustained period of only two weeks.[32] These outings had generally been in the company of John Trumbull, or William Short, or Maria's husband, or the author and antiquarian Pierre-François Hugues d'Hancarville. Yet another of Maria's admirers, d'Hancarville had secured for Richard and Maria Cosway an audience with Louis XVI and his queen, and when the Cosways left Paris on October 6, d'Hancarville accompanied them and Jefferson on the gloomy carriage ride to Saint-Denis.

The inescapable conclusion is that although Jefferson may have wanted it otherwise—that in fact he may have fallen "deeply in love," as Dumas Malone admitted[33]—the overall relationship between Jefferson and Maria Cosway was a flirtatious friendship enhanced by shared cultural interests rather than a passionately erotic affair. And this interpretation gains further support as we consider both their subsequent correspondence and the circumstances of the Cosways' second visit to Paris in 1787.

Jefferson, as we have seen, was reasserting control of his emotions by the fourth page of his Head and Heart dialogue—although he remained keenly aware that "when sins are dear to us we are but too prone to slide into them again."[34] He never had much chance for backsliding. Jefferson wrote fifteen letters to Maria Cosway in nearly four years between October 1786 and June 1790, when he congratulated her on the birth of her first and only child. Maria wrote Jefferson twenty-two letters in that same period. The imbalance in their correspondence was caused, in part, by Jefferson's reluctance to entrust any of his letters to the regular mail, where he knew they were routinely opened by French officials. After the summer of 1790 the correspondence between Jefferson and Cosway entirely lapsed for nearly five years. Then they exchanged a total of fifteen letters between the winter of 1794 and Jefferson's death in 1826. Maria Cosway was less concerned about secrecy. As a somewhat jealous American friend informed Jefferson, she had shared the Head and Heart dialogue with her acquaintances in London and "shews your letters to every body."[35]

Throughout the winter and into the summer of 1787, Jefferson was eager to have the Cosways return to Paris. "I am always thinking of you," he wrote on Christmas Eve. "If I cannot be with you in reality, I will in imagination. . . . You were to come in the spring, and here is winter. It is time therefore you should be making your arrangements, packing your baggage etc. unless you really mean to disappoint us."

In July he wrote again. "Come then, my dear Madam, and we will breakfast every day á l'Angloise, hie away to the Desert [de Retz], dine under the bowers of Marly, and forget that we are ever to part again." While Jefferson dreamt of spending days alone with Maria Cosway, she yearned for the company of friends. "If I come to Paris," she wrote, "there are but four people I could wish to pass all my time with. Is this too great a number?"[36]

Friendship, rather than romantic love, always characterized Maria Cosway's letters. "How I wish I could answer the dialogue!" she had written in October 1786. "But I honestly think my heart is invisible, and mute, . . . sensible of my loss at separating from the friends I left at Paris." Scolding him for not writing often enough, she described the happiness that accompanied letters from "persons whom we hold in esteem, . . . our happiness in being able to savor of their value, and . . . the pleasure which a sensitive soul feels in friendship." After two of his letters finally arrived, she worried that Jefferson would "be painted in future ages sitting solitary and sad, on the beautiful Monticello, tormented by the shadow of a woman." Then she begged him to write again and "to remember sometimes with friendship one who will be sensible and grateful of it."[37]

Had Mrs. Cosway been receptive to his attentions, perhaps their relationship might have deepened when she finally returned to Paris in August 1787. For Jefferson, however, her return visit could not have been more disappointing, even though it lasted until early December. Maria Cosway arrived on August 28, 1787, without her husband, who was immersed in projects for the Prince of Wales, but with a large retinue of servants. She stayed about three months, far from Jefferson's Hôtel de Langeac, as the houseguest of a displaced Polish princess, Aleksandra Lubomirska, whose admirers regarded her as "the most beautiful woman in Paris and Versailles." Maria spent most of her visit in the sparkling society of exiled Polish and Italian nobility—though she found time for outings with Pierre d'Hancarville and visits with the painter Jacques-Louis David and his wife. She saw little of Jefferson—and then only at crowded dinners and parties.[38]

"A fatality has attended my wishes," he reported in November to

Trumbull, who was in London. "Her and my endeavors to see one another more" had been unsuccessful. "She has happened to be from home several times when I have called on her, and I, when she has called on me." Jefferson attributed these near misses to "the meer effect of chance" and hoped "for better luck hereafter," preferring not to face the possibility that Maria Cosway was avoiding him.[39]

In stark contrast to his reporting of their excursions in September 1786, Jefferson recorded only three outings in his account books for the entire duration of Maria Cosway's return visit from August 28 through December 8, 1787. He attended the Théâtre des Variétés on Thursday, October 25, and he attended a concert on Thursday, November 1—neither of them necessarily in her company. Jefferson also arranged a large dinner party at his home on Sunday, December 2, just days before Maria Cosway returned to London. The evidence is fragmentary, but a few details about Jefferson's "great dinner" suggest that the evening may have had a retaliatory edge. The accounts for cuisine kept by his maître d'hôtel, Adrien Petit, show a threefold spike in expenditures immediately prior to the dinner party. Jefferson's guests were numerous. He invited many of the Polish émigrés with whom Maria Cosway had been spending so much of her time—Princess Lubomirska, Count Stanislas Potocki, and Julian Niemcewicz—as well as William Short and the ubiquitous Pierre d'Hancarville. The list was so extensive that it perplexed Mrs. Cosway, as perhaps it was meant to do. "Why will you make such a great dinner?" she asked. Her note implied that she had planned to visit Jefferson on Sunday along with her friend Princess Lubomirska—again dashing his hopes for more intimate conversation. Now, on "Saturday evening," she was accepting Jefferson's invitation for dinner "tomorrow" on behalf of herself, the princess, and several others. Did Jefferson contrive the "great dinner" as revenge for her months of inaccessibility? Was it a retaliation that left her, as she complained soon thereafter, "confused and distracted"?[10]

Already an emotional catastrophe for Jefferson, Maria Cosway's visit ended early in December on a particularly sour note. On Friday evening, December 7, the very eve of her return to London, Jefferson was finally able to engage her for the breakfast á l'anglaise he had suggested months earlier. Apparently on her initiative, their date was set for the next morning. Jefferson arrived on time, and Mrs. Cosway stood him up.

Late that evening, with everything packed for her departure, Maria Cosway had written Jefferson a terse, unsigned, undated note.

> I cannot breakfast with you to morrow; to bid you adieu once is sufficiently painful, for I leave you with very melancholy ideas . . . and I have the reflection that I cannot be useful to you; who have rendered me so many civilities.
>
> Friday night   [unsigned][41]

She rushed from Paris at dawn on Saturday, December 8, and her note did not reach Jefferson until hours later. Perhaps he was somehow spared the indignity of finding her note at the breakfast table or accepting it from a waiter. Based on their next few letters, however, probably not. The emotional details are reminiscent of Humphrey Bogart waiting for Ingrid Bergman at the train station in *Casablanca* or of Cary Grant pacing the observation deck of the Empire State Building in *An Affair to Remember*.

By Monday, Maria Cosway was at home in London writing an apology to Jefferson for having been "confused and distracted" on Friday evening and for her abrupt departure early Saturday. "You promised to come to breakfast with me the morning of my departure," she wrote. "Did you go?" Two weeks later, on Christmas Day, she wrote again and repeated her query. "You came to the invitation of my breakfast the morning of my departure! and what did you think of me?" she asked. "I did it to avoid the last taking leave, I went too early for anybody to see me. I cannot express how miserable I was in leaving Paris. How I regretted not having seen more of you."[42]

When Jefferson finally replied on January 31, he skipped lightly over the breakfast episode, addressing instead her unapproachable situation throughout the entire visit. "I went to breakfast with you according to promise," he wrote, "and you had gone off at 5 o'clock in the morning. This spared me indeed the pain of parting, but it deprives me of the comfort of recollecting that pain."

THE PROBLEM was that Jefferson had too many rivals for Maria's attention and affection. "You make everybody love you," he complained, while he was far more selective. He loved his friends "so dearly as to wish to enjoy their company in the only way it yields enjoyment, that is, in a small company." Her entourage, he complained, "was so numerous, and so imposing, that one could not approach you quite at their ease." Then, looking ahead rather than dwelling on his disappointment, Jefferson hoped that "when you come again, you must be nearer, and move more extempore."[43]

Jefferson repeated both his complaints and his hopes in April 1788. "When you come again," he lamented, "you will be somewhat nearer to me, but not near enough: and still surrounded by a numerous cortege, so that I shall see you only by scraps as I did when you were here last."[44]

But Maria Cosway and Thomas Jefferson never saw each other again—and a note of finality reverberates through their subsequent correspondence. By the autumn he was planning his return to Virginia, while Mrs. Cosway planned a trip to Italy.

In May of 1789, as the streets of Paris began to resound with the angry voices that would lead to revolution, Jefferson seems finally to have accepted the fact that Maria Cosway's affections would never be solely his. "Adieu, my very dear friend," he wrote. "Be our affections unchangeable, and if our little history is to last beyond the grave, be the longest chapter in it that which shall record their purity, warmth and duration." Mrs. Cosway replied in kind almost five months later. "It will be very flattering to me," she wrote from London on October 9, "if you think of me sometimes." She was, at that moment, two months pregnant.[45]

Jefferson learned of Maria Cosway's pregnancy in April 1790. "This Lady is with child for the first time," a mutual friend wrote from London. "She has been extremely ill, but is Now perfectly recovered and expects in a few months to Ly in."[46] Jefferson's reaction was noteworthy, for in the course of a short letter, he revealed the major peculiarities that we have noted in his attitudes toward women. "They tell me you are about to give birth," he wrote on June 23, 1790. "I congratulate you with all my heart. This will wean you from your harp and your pencil, by filling your heart with joys still more bewitching."

In Jefferson's estimation, motherhood entirely transcended the many artistic and musical qualities and accomplishments that had captured his attention in Paris. Motherhood also presented Jefferson with new and more urgent reasons to celebrate the virtues of America over Europe and of country over urban existence. "You may make children there," he wrote, "but this is the country to transplant them to. . . . All the distractions of your great cities are but feathers in the scale against the domestic enjoyments and rural occupations and neighborly societies we live amidst here."

Finally, with the Atlantic serving as a bulwark against temptation, Jefferson was at last able to close a letter to Maria Cosway, now safely domesticated by motherhood, with the candid declaration "*je vous aimerai toujours*"—I will always love you.[47] Nearly five years passed before he wrote her again.

DESPITE THE pleasures of London society, Maria Cosway never cared for its weather. "The climate did not agree with me," she wrote, and "in the middle of so much happiness [she] never enjoyed health." London's climate was "very bad, melancholy, and sad," she complained. "So much is the air darkened by the fog and smoke that it prevents the celestial inhabitants from penetrating with their gaze the human foibles of this island." Her difficult pregnancy and life-threatening childbirth only made things worse. "I only had one child," she wrote in an autobiographical letter. "I had a bad time and a worse confinement so that my life was in danger." After the arrival of her daughter, Louisa Paolina Angelica, on May 4, 1790, Maria's physicians recommended a "change of Air."[48]

By coincidence, Maria's brother George, an architect, had just won a prize to study in Rome, and her friend Lady Wright was planning to take her son to Italy for his health. Leaving her infant daughter behind in London, Maria set out for Italy with her brother, Lady Wright and her son, and one of her husband's nieces to recuperate from the ordeal of pregnancy and childbirth. Richard Cosway supported the plan and bought her a new carriage for the journey. The change of air, which was expected to restore Mrs. Cosway's health in a few months, lasted four and a half years. "Surely it is odd," gossipy Horace Walpole commented, "to drop a child and her husband and country all in a breath!"[49]

Walpole's opinion was tame compared with the rumors that circulated in London. The timing of Maria's departure, which happened to coincide with the return to Italy of Europe's leading castrato, renewed old gossip about a romantic liaison with Luigi Marchesi. She had described him to Jefferson as "the Most wonderfull Singer I ever heard," but the fact that she had painted his portrait and designed his costume for a new opera had set tongues wagging. "The charms of the fair Maria Cosway were so alluring in the eyes of Marchesi, on Saturday last at the Opera," London's *Morning Post* had declared, "that between the acts," in full view of the audience, "he went into the same box with the seductive artist, and remained there in tender homage till his theatrical duties call him again to the stage."[50]

Rumors about Richard Cosway's activities during his wife's long Italian vacation had more substance. "Her departure commenced the less satisfactory side of Cosway's career," the miniaturist's first biographer concluded. "Freed from Mrs. Cosway's restraint, the artist gave scope to his lower propensities." The truth behind this quaint Victorian language was that during his wife's absence, Richard Cosway embarked for six months with Mary Moser, a well-regarded painter of the day and member of the Royal Academy, on a highly visible "sketching tour" of England—and kept an illustrated journal of their escapade, replete with "lascivious statements about Miss Moser, and invidious comparisons between her and Mrs. Cosway."[51]

Embarrassing as they might have seemed, rumors of Richard Cosway's marital infidelity were less troubling to his wife than his growing involvement with Swedenborgian religious beliefs, Friedrich Anton Mesmer's theories of animal magnetism, and the occult. Cosway's principal companion in these visionary explorations (which also attracted William Blake) was his fellow academician and painter Philip de Loutherbourg, whose house at Hammersmith became a center for these fringe elements of Enlightenment religion and science. "The moment he gave himself to Hammersmith," Maria wrote later in reference to Loutherbourg's residence and co-enthusiasts, "began to lead him from me and from his home."[52]

Inspired by his visionary convictions, Richard Cosway became notorious for recounting his conversations with deceased luminaries such as James I, Charles I, and William Pitt, as well as with the Wandering Jew and, according to the essayist William Hazlitt, "more than one person of the Trinity." When one of his nieces admired an unfinished portrait of the Madonna in his studio, Cosway told her that "the Virgin Mary has sat to me in that chair several times for the study." Upon hearing his daughter's story, her father exclaimed, "I thought your Uncle Dick was only a drivelling coxcomb and a fool: but now I am satisfied the fellow is stark mad."[53]

Richard Cosway was nearly eighty when he died in London on July 4, 1821—exactly five years before Jefferson's death at Monticello on the fiftieth anniversary of the Declaration of Independence. Three days after her husband's funeral, Maria Cosway addressed a letter to Jefferson on black-edged mourning paper. "The Appearance of this letter will inform you," she began, "that I have been left a *widow*. Poor Mr. Cosway was suddenly taken by an Apoplectic fit—and being the *third* proved his *last*." After settling her husband's estate, she told Jefferson, "I shall retire from this bustling and *insignificant* world, to my favourite College at Lodi. . . . I wish *Monticello* was not *so far*!" Her letter concluded:

> I would pay you a visit if it was ever so much out of my way, but it is impossible—I long to hear from you—the remembrance of a person I so highly esteem and venerate, affords me the happiest consolation and your *Patriarcal* situation delights me. . . . I wish you may still enjoy many years and feel the happiness of the Nation which produces such Caracters.[54]

During the Cosways' first estrangement after Louisa's birth, the visionary circles at Hammersmith had drawn Richard away from his wife, while sunny Italy pulled Maria back toward the Roman Catholic faith of her youth. "I know 'twould be [her husband's] great wish I should be of his sentiments in point of religion," but "that is the only one [thing] I cannot do," she confided to a friend. "My father's last words to me were *fear God and preserve your religion*. I have had no reason or persuasion to change. My whole life has been *miraculously protected*. God is my all, heaven my only desire, a future happiness my only thought."[55]

Maria Cosway's change of air following the birth of her daughter also signaled the subsequent course of her life. "Madame Cosway in a convent!" Jefferson exclaimed in a 1793 letter to a mutual friend. "I knew that to much goodness of heart she joined enthusiasm and religion," he continued, "but I thought that very enthusiasm would have prevented her from shutting up her adoration of the God of the universe within the walls of a cloister."[56]

Louis XVI was beheaded in January 1793, and while revolutionary France waged war against its neighbors and the Terror raged within, Maria Cosway entered the Convent of the Visitation in Genoa on March 1, 1793. She had been there for more than eighteen months when news reached her that Richard Cosway had taken ill. Protected during her passage through France by her friendship with Jacques-Louis David, she returned to her husband and daughter in November 1794, a few months after the fall of Robespierre and the Jacobins.[57]

The Cosways' reconciliation did not last beyond their next tragedy. Upon her arrival in London, Maria wrote that she "had the happiness of finding Mr. C[osway] recovered . . . and a fine little girl to engage all my cares and occupations." For nearly two years she took delight in "seeing my child grow and profit of my education." And then came heartbreak. Louisa "was seized by a sore throat and in the sixth year of her age we lost her" on July 29, 1796, Maria wrote. "Our grief was great."[58]

Grief engulfed their marriage. Louisa's death gave Richard Cosway's private behavior another turn toward the weird. He had their daughter's body embalmed and placed in an elaborate stone sarcophagus that stood in their parlor for the rest of Maria's residence in London and until the very day of his own death twenty-five years later.[59] "The man Cosway does not seem to think that much of the loss belonged to him," Horace Walpole sneered. "He romanced with his usual vivacity." His wife, on the other hand, was "so afflicted for her only little girl, that she shut herself up in her chamber and would not be seen."[60]

In time Maria sought to assuage her sorrow by throwing her energies into new projects, which achieved some artistic success but brought little comfort. A full year passed before Jefferson, now vice president, heard news of her situation from one of the Polish émigrés they had known in Paris. "The loss of her daughter and the gloom into which that and other circumstances has thrown her," he informed a mutual friend, "has taken the hue of religion." She was devoting herself to religious exercises and education. "Our letters have been rare," he admitted, "but they have let me see that her gayety was gone and her mind entirely placed on the world to come."[61]

In October 1801 Maria Cosway left her husband in London and traveled first to Paris and then to Italy. In France she established a Catholic school for girls at Lyon under the patronage of Archbishop Joseph Fesch, Napoleon's uncle and ambassador to Rome. Then, with help from the duke of Lodi, who had been a guest at her soirées in London, she acquired an ancient convent south of Milan and established the Collegio delle Grazie at Lodi in 1812. Returning to London only to look after her husband during his last years, Maria Cosway dedicated the rest of her life to her "college for daughters of Catholic nobles and citizens." In 1830 she was made a baroness of the Austrian Empire by Francis I in recognition of her devotion to the education of young women. The seventy-eight-year-old Baroness Cosway died at Lodi on January 5, 1838. She was buried in the church of Santa Maria delle Grazie on the grounds of her beloved college, 130 miles northwest of Florence, the city of her birth.[62]

IN THE SPRING of 1787, midway between Maria Cosway's visits to Paris, Jefferson visited the ancient city of Nîmes on a tour through the south of France. There he saw with his own eyes the Maison Carrée, the Roman temple he had known only from engravings when he adapted its features for the design of a new state capitol in Richmond. "Here I am," Jefferson wrote to a friend in Paris in March 1787, "gazing whole hours at the Maison quarrée, like a lover at his mistress."[63] These were not words he could readily have written to anyone three years earlier, when he was still grieving the death of Martha Wayles Skelton Jefferson. Jefferson's sojourn in Paris, and his friendship with Maria Cosway, marked his slow recovery from both his political disappointments in Virginia at the close of the American Revolution and the personal tragedy of his wife's death.

On the eve of his departure for France in 1784, the grief Jefferson still felt over the loss of his wife had been readily apparent to a sharp-eyed Dutch traveler who met him while Congress was meeting in Annapolis. Jefferson had "retired from fashionable society," the Dutchman wrote, and had focused his attention on "affairs of public interest," with his "sole diversion being that offered by belles lettres." The perceptive visitor was not fooled by Jefferson's excuse that "poor health" kept him at home with his books. "Rather," the Dutchman observed, Jefferson was a man who had been "accustomed to the unalloyed pleasure of the society of a lovable wife" but who "since her loss" had become "impervious to the feeble attractions of common society."[64] The traveler's observations echoed Jefferson's own admissions to close friends: Martha's death had left him "dead to the world"—"a blank which I had not the spirits to fill up."[65]

Whatever else may have happened in their excursions together, Maria Cosway revived the capacity for love and friendship that Thomas Jefferson had denied himself after the death of his wife. Although at first Jefferson probably thought he was "deeply in love," as his biographer Dumas Malone suggested,[66] it was Maria Cosway who defined the terms of their relationship: a friendship enhanced by shared cultural passions rather than an erotic physical affair. During the early years of their friendship, Jefferson's behavior was notable both for the ways that it apparently differed from his earlier experiences with women and for a few similarities.

Jefferson's setbacks with Maria Cosway never resulted in the debilitating headaches that followed his disappointment by Rebecca Burwell.[67] He was able to enjoy Mrs. Cosway's company, so far as we know, without accosting her in her chamber or offending her with aggressive pursuit, as had happened with Elizabeth Moore Walker. The Head and Heart dialogue was a more considerate appeal for a married woman's affection than a "paper tending to convince her of the innocence of promiscuous love" slipped into the cuff of her gown.[68]

The parallels between Jefferson's conduct with Mrs. Cosway and his experiences with other women are also important. An appreciation for music and literature was one common characteristic of his relationships with Martha Wayles Jefferson and with Mrs. Cosway. Despite its obvious literary polish, however, the Head and Heart dialogue left its flesh-and-blood recipient without any clear sense of the relationship that Jefferson hoped for. In this respect, Jefferson's dialogue for Maria Cosway was as ambivalent as the well-rehearsed soliloquy at the Raleigh Tavern that collapsed before Rebecca Burwell into "broken sentences, uttered in great disorder, and interrupted with pauses of uncommon length."[69]

Finally, the Head and Heart dialogue points to the most important similarity among Jefferson's romantic relationships with women. The entire dialogue was as self-absorbed as Jefferson's correspondence with his buddies about Rebecca Burwell, his aggression toward Elizabeth Walker, or the responsibilities of wife and mother that he expected from

Martha Wayles Jefferson and their daughters. By 1786, as the dialogue demonstrates, Jefferson was capable of regaining his control over his emotions by the exercise of reason. The blunt facts remained, however, that three of the four women to whom Jefferson offered his Heart had rejected it, and the fourth had been taken from him by death. In light of these harsh truths, Jefferson allowed his Head to remind him that "this is not a world to live at random in." Henceforth in his relationships with women he would act with caution and with a balance in his hand, "put[ting] into one scale the pleasures which any object may offer; but put[ting] fairly into the other the pains which are to follow."[70] Thomas Jefferson's flirtation with Maria Cosway was the last time that any autonomous woman ensnared his Heart.

CHAPTER SIX

Sally Hemings

All Batchelors, or a large majority at least, keep as a substitute for a wife some individual of the[ir] own Slaves. In Virginia this damnable practice prevails as much as any where, and probably more, as Mr. Jefferson's example can be pleaded for its defense.

I can enumerate a score of such cases in our beloved An[cien]t Dominion. . . . Were they enumerated with the statistics of the State, they would be found by hundreds. Nor is it to be wondered at, when Mr. Jefferson's notorious example is considered.

—Diary of John Hartwell Cocke

O F ALL the women in Thomas Jefferson's life, Sally Hemings has been the most controversial ever since the angry journalist James Callender proclaimed in 1802 that "the man, whom it delighteth the people to honor, keeps, and for many years past has kept, as his concubine, one of his own slaves. Her name is SALLY."[1] The accuracy of Callender's assertion has been disputed ever since he printed it, and his veracity may never be determined with *absolute* certainty. Nevertheless, the available evidence now suggests that Callender was essentially correct about Jefferson's relationship with Sally Hemings. Thomas Jefferson fathered six children born to his slave Sally Hemings between 1795 and 1808.[2]

ON WEDNESDAY, January 26, 1785, in Paris, Thomas Jefferson was settling his bills for household furniture and wallpaper when a letter from America brought the sad news that his youngest daughter, Lucy Elizabeth, had died back in Virginia. Upon his departure for France six months earlier, Jefferson had reluctantly left Lucy and her sister Mary in the care of his sister-in-law Elizabeth Wayles Eppes at Eppington, her husband's estate on the Appomattox River south of Richmond in Chesterfield County. Francis and Elizabeth Eppes had two small children of their own. All four children fell ill when "the most horrible of all disorders, the whooping-cough," swept through the nursery at Eppington in the autumn of 1784. The two youngest, both named Lucy—Jefferson's two-and-a-half-year-old daughter and her cousin Lucy Eppes—died. Both the Eppeses' son, Bolling, and Jefferson's six-year-old daughter, Mary, or Polly, eventually survived the disease, though the boy was "reduced to a skeleton."[3]

Plans were soon afoot to retrieve Mary Jefferson from Virginia. Once she was reunited with her father in Paris, Polly would join her elder sister, Martha, or Patsy, at the Abbaye Royale de Panthémont, the convent school favored by English families in Paris. The logistics of transporting Polly safely across the Atlantic proved so daunting, however, that the reunion took more than two years to accomplish.

Jefferson wanted Polly to sail only in "April, May, June, or July . . . on account of the equinoxes" and the risk of late-summer storms. He also wanted to place her aboard the safest possible vessel—a ship neither so new as to be unproven nor "more than four or five years old." Then came the quest for the perfect escort. "Some good lady passing from America to France, or even England, would be most eligible," Jefferson thought. "But a careful gentleman who would be so kind as to superintend her would do. In this case some woman who has had the small pox must attend her." Finally, in the event that neither a good lady nor a sensible gentleman could be found, Jefferson ventured his opinion that "a careful negro woman, as Isabel for instance if she has had the small pox, would suffice under the patronage of a gentleman."[4]

Eager as he was to reunite his two surviving daughters, Jefferson brooded over the dangers of Polly's impending voyage. "My anxieties," he admitted to his brother-in-law, "would induce me to endless details, but your discretion and that of Mrs. Eppes saves me the necessity. I will only add that I would rather live a year longer without [Polly] than have her trusted to any but a good ship and a summer passage." With Isabel Hern firmly in mind as an acceptable escort, Jefferson focused his worries on the ship and the weather.

Almost thirty, Isabel Hern was an experienced and "careful negro woman" with several children of her own. Her husband, David Hern, was one of the skilled artisans at Monticello. Both were familiar to Jefferson and his sister-in-law, for they were among the slaves that Jefferson and his wife had inherited from the estate of John Wayles.[5]

Elizabeth and Francis Eppes followed Jefferson's advice to the letter in choosing a ship and booking Polly Jefferson's voyage to France in May of 1787. Isabel Hern, however, was unavailable as an escort. She was recovering from the recent birth of her daughter Edith, the fifth of her twelve children. Unable to send the "careful negro woman" Jefferson had requested, Elizabeth and Francis Eppes chose fourteen-year-old Sally Hemings as Polly's escort instead. It was a huge responsibility for any fourteen-year-old, but Sally must have earned their confidence. Presumably they explained their decision to Jefferson, perhaps in one of the several letters known to have gone astray between Eppington and Paris during these busy months. Like many other young slave girls in Virginia and the South, Sally Hemings probably had already had several years experience assisting in the care of Polly Jefferson. No doubt she had demonstrated some of the traits ascribed to her by an anonymous observer in 1802, who described her as "an industrious and orderly creature in her behavior."[6] The Eppeses' decision may also have been influenced by the fact that her brother James Hemings had accompanied Jefferson to Paris and was learning the secrets of French cuisine at the Hôtel de Langeac.

Polly Jefferson and Sally Hemings landed at London in June of 1787. They stayed several weeks in the home of John Adams, Jefferson's diplomatic counterpart in Britain, until Adrien Petit, Jefferson's butler, arrived to escort them across the Channel to Paris.

John Adams never mentioned the girls in his correspondence with Jefferson, but his wife, Abigail, promptly informed Jefferson of his daughter's safe arrival. "The old Nurse whom you expected to have attend her was sick and unable to come," Abigail reported in her first letter to Jefferson. Polly "has a Girl about 15 or 16 with her, the Sister of the Servant you have with you." The next day Abigail said a little more about Sally Hemings (without ever mentioning her name). "The Girl who is with [Polly]," Adams wrote, "is quite a child, and Captain Ramsey is of opinion will be of so little Service that he had better carry her back with him. But of this you will be the judge. She seems fond of the child and appears good naturd."[7]

JOHN AND Abigail Adams were completely unaware of other facts known to some people around Eppington and Monticello. Sally Hemings and her brother James were Polly Jefferson's aunt and uncle. Thomas Jefferson's father-in-law, John Wayles, had outlived three wives. Polly Jefferson's mother was the daughter of John Wayles and his first wife—but Sally and James Hemings were his children, too.

After John Wayles buried his third wife in 1761, he had lived with his mulatto slave Elizabeth Hemings. Betty, as she was known, was the daughter of an English sea captain named Hemings and a "full-blooded African" woman owned by Francis Eppes of Bermuda Hundred, in Chesterfield County. Born about 1735, eleven-year-old Betty Hemings had come to live at the Forest in 1746 when Wayles had married Martha Eppes, his first wife.

John Wayles's connection with Betty Hemings was far from unique in colonial Virginia. Relationships between prominent white planters and their female slaves were not uncommon, although the evidence about them is often sketchy.[8] The widower John Custis IV in 1744 had prevailed upon his colleagues of the Governor's Council "to free his Negro Boy Slave Christened John but commonly called Jack, born of the body of his Negro Wench Young Alice." Custis's generous provisions for the welfare of "his dear black boy Jack"—land, cattle, clothing, and even a portrait—clearly were the gifts of a doting father to his "Favorite Boy Jack." A decade earlier, the Eton- and Oxford-educated Mann Page— builder of Rosewell, member of the Governor's Council, and grandfather of Jefferson's classmate John Page—spent his dying hours in the exclusive company of his attorney and "a little Mulatto Boy of about eight years old," believed to have been his son.[9]

Judge George Wythe, Jefferson's mentor at the law, was plausibly believed to have "had a yellow woman by the name of Lydia who lived with him as wife and mistress" in Richmond after the death of his second wife in 1787. In Wythe's case the story was probably false. Nevertheless, as a Richmond physician recalled in the 1850s, slave mistresses were "quite common in this city fifty years ago with gentlemen of the older time."[10]

John Wayles and his son-in-law were among those gentlemen. "I can enumerate a score of such cases in our beloved An[cien]t Dominion," Jefferson's neighbor General John Hartwell Cocke noted in his diary. "It is too well known they are not few, nor far between. . . . Were they enumerated with the statistics of the State, they would be found by hundreds. Nor is it to be wondered at, when Mr. Jefferson's notorious example is considered." A prominent planter and statesman who worked closely with Jefferson to establish the University of Virginia, Cocke knew a great deal about "Mulatto Slave Mistress[es]" in Virginia and the South. "All Batchelors, or a large majority at least," he explained a few years later, "keep as a substitute for a wife some individual of the[ir] own Slaves. In Virginia this damnable practice prevails as much as any where, and probably more, as Mr. Jefferson's example can be pleaded for its defense."[11]

A Frenchman who visited Monticello in June of 1796 was startled to find slave children, probably Sally Hemings's nieces and nephews, "as white as I am."[12] Years later, when biographer Henry S. Randall visited the plantation, Jefferson's eldest grandson acknowledged the presence at Monticello of slave "children which resembled Mr. Jefferson so closely that it was plain that they had his blood in their veins." Born in 1792, Thomas Jefferson Randolph spoke from his direct personal observations: "He said in one case that the resemblance was so close, that at some distance or in the dusk that slave, dressed in the same way, might be taken for Mr. Jefferson." On another occasion, Randolph recalled,

> a gentleman dining with Mr. Jefferson looked so startled as he raised his eyes from [Jefferson] to the servant behind him, that his discovery of the resemblance was perfectly obvious to all. Sally He[m]ing[s] was a house servant and her children were brought up house servants—so that the likeness between master and slave was blazoned to all the multitudes who visited this political Mecca.

Unlike Jefferson's neighbor and associate John Hartwell Cocke, his grandson attributed the paternity of these light-skinned Hemingses to other men than his grandfather.[13] The presence at Monticello of light-skinned mulatto slaves who were somehow related to Jefferson's family, however, could not be denied.

JOHN WAYLES and Betty Hemings had six children together. Sally was the youngest, born in 1773. Sally Hemings's mother, Betty, was "a bright mulatto woman," recalled Isaac Jefferson, youngest son of Jefferson's trusted slaves George and Ursula. "Sally was mighty near white. Folks said that these Hemings'es was old Mr. Wayles' children. Sally was very handsome: long straight hair down her back."[14]

"Light colored and decidedly good looking," declared Thomas Jefferson Randolph about Sally and her sister Betsey.[15] Some thought they resembled their half sister and Jefferson's late wife, Martha Wayles.

Details about Sally Hemings's life are scant. She was living with her mother and siblings at John Wayles's Guinea plantation, in Cumberland County, when Wayles's estate was settled in January 1774.[16] Shortly thereafter, Betty Hemings and her children moved to the Elk Hill plantation in Goochland County, which Thomas and Martha Jefferson had inherited. Two-year-old Sally Hemings moved with her family to Monticello about 1775. Nine years later, in 1784, Sally probably accompanied his youngest daughters, Mary and Lucy, to Eppington when Jefferson took his eldest daughter, Martha, with him to Paris.[17] "Sally Hemings went to France with Maria Jefferson when she was a little girl," a former overseer remembered many years later. "They crossed the ocean alone. I have often heard her tell about it."[18]

During her two years in Paris, from July 1787 through September 1789, Sally Hemings may have resided intermittently at Jefferson's residence, the Hôtel de Langeac. More of her time was spent at the Abbaye Royale de Panthémont, however, where Patsy and Polly Jefferson were boarding students—and where Polly took the nickname Maria.[19] A few months after her arrival, Sally was inoculated for smallpox.[20] While in Paris, she was trained in needlework and the care of clothing, in accord with her responsibilities as lady's maid to Jefferson's daughters.[21] In 1788 and 1789, Jefferson occasionally paid Sally Hemings a monthly wage of twelve livres (about two dollars), half the amount that her brother received. Her training included a five-week sojourn with Jefferson's laundress in the spring of 1789, where she may also have benefited from an immersion in the language and culture. "She was just beginning to understand the French language well," according to her son's recollec-tions, when Jefferson and his household left Paris that autumn.[22]

When Patsy Jefferson began to participate in French society in the spring of 1789, Sally Hemings's role as her attendant was also reflected in the greater sums that Jefferson spent on clothing and accessories for his daughters and their servant.[23] Sally's domestic responsibilities were explicit in Jefferson's arrangements for their return voyage to America. "I shall have occasion for three master b[e]rths," Jefferson specified, "for [my]self and two daughters of 17 and 11 years of age, and b[e]rths for a man and woman servant, the latter convenient to that of my daughters."[24]

Once they had returned to Monticello, Sally Hemings worked there as a household servant for the rest of Jefferson's life. Nevertheless, as late as December of 1799—two years after Maria Jefferson had married John Wayles Eppes and moved with him to Eppington—Jefferson still referred to Sally as "Maria's maid."[25] Her son Madison later recalled that his mother's duties were "to take care of [Jefferson's] chamber and wardrobe, look after us children and do such light work as sewing, etc."[26] Looking after her own children was a luxury few other slaves enjoyed in eighteenth-century Virginia, but as overseer Edmund Bacon recalled of the Hemings women, "I was instructed to take no control of them. They had very little to do."[27]

UPON HER RETURN to Monticello from Paris, Sally Hemings probably lived with her elder sister Critta Hemings on Mulberry Row, the slave quarter closest to the main house, overlooking the vegetable gardens to the east. Critta lived in the stone house known as Weaver's Cottage. Four years later, Sally and Critta probably moved into one of the three new log cabins, twelve by fourteen feet in size, built on Mulberry Row in 1793.[28] Finally, sometime between 1803 and 1807, Sally Hemings moved into a masonry room near the eastern end of the "south dependency."[29] There is no subsequent evidence that Sally Hemings ever left Monticello until 1827, a year after Jefferson died.[30]

On many large Virginia plantations both the servants' quarters and service buildings such as stables, laundries, dairies, kitchens, smoke-houses, pantries, breweries, and icehouses dot the visible landscape. Jef-

West façade of Monticello. The windows of Jefferson's bedroom, study, and south piazza, or greenhouse, are visible at the right. About 1808, as he prepared to retire from the presidency, Jefferson installed louvered verandas, which he called "porticles," to deflect sunlight and increase the privacy of these rooms. His triple-sash windows opened onto the South Terrace with its Chinese Chippendale railings. The wooden "porticles" were removed about 1890 by a subsequent owner.

Courtesy of the Library of Virginia.

ferson's design for Monticello hid them all from view. He consolidated them into three long rows of masonry rooms, built at the basement level of the main house and arranged as three sides of a rectangle, tucked against the crest of the hill that forms the west lawn of Monticello. The roofs of the north and south dependencies support the terraces that define the edges of that lawn with crisp white railings in Chinese Chippendale style. Brick pillars supporting the outer edge of these terraces form a colonnade, or sheltered walkway, that connects with a stone-walled passageway that extends at cellar level beneath the entire width of the main house. Near the center of that passageway, or tunnel, narrow stairways connect the cellar with the first floor of the main house on either side of the entrance hall. Dumbwaiters, installed on either side of the dining room fireplace, also connect to the wine cellar. Jefferson's design gave these basement-level storage rooms and work areas, as well as the slaves who labored and slept in them, ready access to the living quarters and dining room used by his family and guests.[31]

In the 1850s, Jefferson's grandson Thomas Jefferson Randolph showed

Aerial view of Monticello from the north showing the main house, North and South Terraces, and North and South Pavilions. Jefferson designed Monticello to eliminate the outbuildings that cluttered the landscape of other Virginia plantations. Symmetrical terraces on either side of the main house defined the west lawn (to the right) and terminated in small buildings that he called pavilions. Beneath these terraces, at the basement level of the house, he placed rows of masonry rooms connected by a colonnade. Visible in the foreground is the North Terrace, which sheltered the icehouse (below the corner), stables, and carriage house. The South Terrace, on the opposite side of the west lawn, sheltered the kitchen, smokehouse, and rooms for slaves assigned to the household. Beneath the terraces linked to the main house is a passageway that provided access to the first floor of the residence by narrow stairways on either side of the entrance hall. Storage rooms for general commodities, wine, rum, and beer were situated along this passageway. The South Terrace connected Jefferson's library, study, piazza, and bedroom with the South Pavilion, or Honeymoon Cottage. Another small brick building (visible immediately above the South Pavilion) marks the far retaining wall of a large vegetable garden. Mulberry Row, with cabins and work areas for other slaves, paralleled the South Terrace and the vegetable garden on the south slope of Monticello.

Courtesy of the Thomas Jefferson Memorial Foundation.

a visitor "a smoke blackened and sooty room in one of the collonades"—
known today as the south dependency—"and informed [him that] it was
Sally He[m]ings' room." These servants' rooms, according to overseer
Edmund Bacon, "were very comfortable, warm in the winter and cool in
the summer."[32] There is no documentary evidence indicating that Sally
Hemings ever resided inside the main house at Monticello. The location
of her room, beneath the terrace outside the windows of Jefferson's study
and library, did permit ready access by stairs to the first floor of the main
house and Jefferson's private quarters.[33]

ONE OF MANY features at Monticello that fascinates modern visitors is
Jefferson's famous alcove bed, built into the wall between his bedroom
and his study in 1795, when he began an extensive renovation of the
entire house. Soon after the installation was complete, Jefferson recognized its limitations. The new alcove bed diminished both his comfort
and his privacy. The only fireplace in Jefferson's sleeping quarters was on
the far interior wall of the bedroom. Floor-to-ceiling windows with
multiple sashes comprised the exterior walls of the study and also func-
tioned as doorways to the South Terrace. On winter nights, drafts of
cold air blowing across his bed negated any minor convenience that Jefferson gained each morning from being able to step directly into either
room. The new design also exposed Jefferson's private quarters to view
from the outside.

To stop the drafts, in the autumn of 1795 Jefferson installed a glass-
paneled screen next to his bed on the side that faced his study, and it was
outfitted with a cloth curtain. When this contraption proved "heavy and
cumbersome," Jefferson replaced it with a "folding frame . . . covered
with paper on both sides." The result, as described by architectural historian Jack McLaughlin, "was a shoji screen, which cut off drafts—and
visibility—from the numerous windows in the study."[34]

As Jefferson's increasing fame brought hundreds of uninvited visitors
to Monticello during his presidency, even these measures proved insuffi-
cient in establishing his privacy. On too many occasions, Thomas Jefferson Randolph recalled, his grandfather was plagued by "parties of men
and women [who] would sometimes approach within a dozen yards, and
gaze at him point-blank until they had looked their fill, as they would

have gazed at a lion in a menagerie." Early in the new century Jefferson modified the greenhouse outside the south windows of his bedroom-library suite with louvered verandas, which he called "porticles," outside the east and west windows.[35] These wooden structures were removed about 1890 by a subsequent owner.

Although Jack McLaughlin explains the construction of these louvered verandas chiefly as a response to President Jefferson's rude and inquisitive visitors, "there are those," he warns, "who will view Jefferson's porticles as yet another strand in the web of circumstantial evidence linking him to Sally Hemings . . . constructed to conceal her presence in his bedroom and to allow her to slip more easily in and out of his sleeping quarters."

McLaughlin admitted "that the timing of their construction supports this allegation: they were designed, and certainly added, after the Sally Hemings scandal broke upon [Jefferson] in 1802." But, he countered, "a much more likely explanation for the timing . . . is the addition of the terrace walk [that created] a public promenade directly in front of [Jefferson's] bedroom-library suite."[36]

As we shall see, however, the timing of Jefferson's *earlier* expedient—the cumbersome glass-paneled screen rather than the porticles—might have some connection to the beginning of his relationship with Sally Hemings. It may only be a coincidence, but Jefferson made his first effort to shield his new alcove bed from view through the windows of his study in the autumn of 1795. It certainly cannot prove much, but Jefferson's notes for that first glass-paneled screen are part of a list dated October 20, 1795—two weeks after Sally Hemings had given birth to her first daughter on October 5.[37]

WHEN DID the sexual relationship between Jefferson and Hemings begin? When James Callender proclaimed in 1802 that Jefferson kept Sally Hemings as his "concubine," he also asserted that "the name of her eldest son is Tom."[38] Callender and others were probably wrong about "Tom," and wrong, too, about the timing of Sally Hemings's relationship with Jefferson. The oral traditions of the Hemings and Woodson families assert that Sally, then only sixteen, was pregnant in France by 1789. While she was in Paris, Madison Hemings explained, "my mother became Jefferson's concubine, and when he was called back home she was *enciente* by him. He desired to bring my mother back to Virginia with him but she demurred."

Because slavery was illegal in France (although not in its colonies), Madison Hemings believed that his mother could have claimed her freedom in Paris, but "if she returned to Virginia she would be reenslaved. So she refused to return with him." Jefferson, according to her son, "promised her extraordinary privileges, and made a solemn pledge that her children would be freed at the age of twenty-one years. In consequence of his promise . . . she returned with him to Virginia." It was "soon after their arrival," Madison Hemings continued, that "she gave birth to a child, of whom Thomas Jefferson was the father. It lived but a short time."[39]

Madison Hemings's narrative explains, perhaps too neatly, his mother's decision to return to Virginia rather than seek freedom under French law. Within four years of his return to America, Sally's adult brother James Hemings had been able to parlay his culinary skills into a formal act of emancipation, signed by Jefferson in 1793, upon the condition that he train another "good cook" for the kitchen at Monticello.[40] Madison Hemings's narrative may have extended the theme of Jefferson's ongoing negotiations with his uncle, first about returning to Virginia and then about training his replacement, to embrace his mother as well.

To be sure, James and Sally Hemings could have sued for their freedom while in Paris. Jefferson, in response to a question from a slaveholder who contemplated bringing a young slave with him to France in 1786, advised that "the laws of France give him freedom if he claims it, and that it will be difficult, if not impossible, [for the slaveholder] to interrupt the course of the law."[41] On the other hand, the legal process itself—hiring a lawyer, petitioning the French court of admiralty, and pressing a lawsuit—was neither simple nor inexpensive.[42] In this context, is it difficult to suppose that when twenty-four-year-old James Hemings decided in favor of returning to America, his sixteen-year-old sister might also have chosen to return to her home and family—even if, as was likely the case, she was *not* pregnant?

In Madison Hemings's narrative, his mother's first child by Jefferson "lived but a short time." Another family's tradition contends that the child lived and became known as Thomas Woodson. James Callender also contended that Sally Hemings had a child named Tom who was born about 1790. Whether a young man later known as Tom Woodson had any connection to Sally Hemings or Monticello is a question that historians have debated for many years.[43] It is one of the questions that was answered with certainty by DNA testing in 1998. There is no genetic connection between the Woodson and Jefferson or Hemings families. According to Thomas Turner, who lived in Virginia, it was "well known to many" that Beverley Hemings (born in 1798) was Sally's "eldest son."[44]

IF SALLY HEMINGS was not pregnant at sixteen when she returned from Paris, when did her relationship with Jefferson begin? Two plausible answers are October of 1793 (when Jefferson was back at Monticello for the first time in more than a year) or January of 1795 (nine months prior to the birth of Sally Hemings's first known child, Harriet, on October 5, 1795).

As secretary of state in President George Washington's first cabinet, Jefferson had spent the better part of three years, from March 1790 through December 1793, in Philadelphia or New York. He was busy with critically important work, helping Washington breathe life into the new government created by the Constitution of 1787, while contending against the aggressive policies of his chief rival in the cabinet, Treasury Secretary Alexander Hamilton. Between his appointment and his resignation as secretary of state, Jefferson found time for only three visits to Virginia. A few days in October 1791, a few weeks late in the summer of 1792, and almost a month in October 1793. During the third visit, Jefferson knew that his days in government were numbered. He had informed the president of his intention to resign from the cabinet and retire from public office at the end of the year.[45]

Jefferson was exhausted—"worn down with labours from morning to night, and day to day." He was concerned about his health, and wary of the fact that at fifty he had already lived longer than his father. While visiting with John and Abigail Adams in 1784, Jefferson had told Abigail that "he expects not to live above a Dozen [more] years." Now, almost a decade later, Jefferson confessed to his friend James Madison that "the motion of my blood no longer keeps time with the tumult of the world. It leads me to seek for happiness in the lap and love of my family, in the society of my neighbors and my books, [and] in the wholesome occupations of my farm."[46]

True to his word, on December 31, 1793, the secretary of state submitted his resignation and returned to Monticello with the intention of retiring forever from public life. "The little spice of ambition I had in my younger days has long since evaporated," he explained to James Madison. "My health is entirely broken down," he lamented, and "my age requires that I should place my affairs in a clear state."[47] We know that he lived three more decades, but Jefferson apparently felt he had only a few more years remaining.

Prior to this retirement from politics (which he intended to be permanent), Jefferson had always been careful to avoid linking his public image with the most repulsive aspects of the slave system, especially the buying and selling of human beings. Having decided in 1792 to sell eleven slaves from his Bedford plantations, for example, Jefferson had cloaked his actions from public view by having his overseer at Poplar Forest "carry them to some other sale of slaves in that part of the country" so the newspaper advertisements would make no reference to him. In the guarded language of his private letter stipulating the arrangements for the sale, Jefferson was explicit about his motives: "I do not (while in public life) like to have my name annexed to the sale of property." When his overseer remitted the balance from these sales—$184.26 after other farm expenses had been deducted—the cryptic entry in Jefferson's account book left no clue that the income may have derived from the sale of *human* property.[48]

Freed at last early in 1794 from the constraints of public life—firm in his "resolution never to permit myself to think of the office, or to be thought of for it"—Jefferson devoted himself to his crops, his new nail-making business, and a new round of remodeling and renovation at Monticello.[49] Although Jefferson's withdrawal from public life was cut short after three years, it had been his persistent dream since the final years of his marriage. After leaving the governor's office, Jefferson had "folded [him]self in the arms of retirement, and rested all prospects of future happiness on domestic and literary objects." That idyllic dream had been shattered by the death of his wife in 1782.[50] A dozen years later, he meant to make it happen anew—and without regard for public opinion. "Insinuations in the public papers, while I was in office," no longer mattered.[51] Retirement afforded him "an entire freedom of rest or motion, of thought or incogitancy, owing account to myself alone of my hours and actions."[52]

IN PARIS, at the Medici column near the brilliant dome of the Halle au Blé, a chance encounter with Maria Cosway had stirred Thomas Jefferson's grieving heart. She had reawakened his appreciation for the company of a beautiful woman. And then she, too, was gone. As Jefferson, began to contemplate a new dome for Monticello in the autumn of 1793 or January of 1794, apparently he found another woman who was "very handsome" and "decidedly good looking."[53] She spoke some French, and she had seen more of the world than most women in America, regardless of their status or station. Something about Sally Hemings may have reminded Jefferson of the young widow he had courted at the Forest and then lost—her half sister.

This time, Jefferson's encounter with the opposite sex was different than ever before—and he was acutely aware of the full and lascivious potential of his ownership of Sally Hemings. "The whole commerce between master and slave," he had written a dozen years earlier, "is a perpetual exercise of the most boisterous passions, the most unremitting despotism on the one part, and degrading submissions on the other. . . . The man must be a prodigy who can retain his manners and morals undepraved by such circumstances."[54] In all his dealings with women, from Rebecca Burwell to Maria Cosway, and even in the outpouring of grief after the death of his wife, Jefferson had always put himself and his needs first. With Sally Hemings, his possession, his control, and her submission were complete.

As Jefferson attained the age of fifty, his anxieties about declining health and impending mortality gave him a new and compelling need for the discreet sexual relationship he probably initiated between October 1793 and January 1795. Sally Hemings represented one facet of Jefferson's retirement plan to fend off the effects of old age and regain control of his life through diet, exercise, and regular sex. Among Jefferson's guides in these matters were the writings of the Swiss medical theorist Samuel Auguste David Tissot, whose complete works Jefferson owned in the original French.

First translated into English in the 1760s, Tissot's books of advice about health and medicine went through many editions in both languages. The two that Jefferson found especially pertinent in the mid-1790s were Tissot's *Essay on Diseases Incident to Literary and Sedentary Persons* and his more notorious *Onanism; or, A Treatise upon the Disorders Produced by Masturbation*, which Jefferson also owned in an English translation.

Jefferson's and Tissot's ideas about human biology were primitive by modern standards, but they agreed upon the benefits of sleep, exercise, fresh air, and moderation in food and drink. To the extent that common sense supported healthy practices, the intricacies of outdated medical science need not concern us. Jefferson was well served by his almost vegetarian diet, his refusal to use tobacco, his moderate consumption of cider and diluted wine, and perhaps even his practice of bathing his feet in cold water every morning. All were practices endorsed by Tissot. Jefferson's withdrawal from public life also embodied the Swiss doctor's advice to "exhausted" intellectuals and statesmen. "Old men consult their glory no less than their health," Tissot wrote, "by retiring" and "giving themselves up to leisure, chearfulness, and country pleasures." As historian Andrew Burstein has thoroughly demonstrated, the state of medical knowledge in Jefferson's day—an intuitive mix of classical lore and the first glimmers of modern biology—helps to explain many events in his adult life.[55]

Good health was often attributed to the proper balance of humors (blood, phlegm, yellow bile, and black bile) described long ago by Aristotle and Galen. Illness, according to these venerable theories, came as the result of imbalances that could be remedied by bloodletting, purging, blistering, and other "heroic" procedures. Jefferson instinctively shunned bloodletting, but that lingering theory carried George Washington to an early grave. Ignorance about the role of bacteria in the transmission of disease after childbirth also may have contributed to the deaths of Jefferson's wife and his daughter Maria.

Human reproduction, the mind, and the nervous system were realms of mystery and misinformation. Dutch scientists first examined human sperm under their microscopes in the 1670s, but the cutting edge of medical knowledge in Jefferson's day still regarded "seminal fluid" as a "vivifying liquor" that somehow connected the functions of the brain, the nervous system, and the testicles. "There is so close a connection between the brain and the testicles," Tissot's authorities proclaimed, "because these two organs [secrete] from the blood the most subtle and exquisite lympha which is destined to give strength and motion to the parts [of the body] and to assist even the functions of the soul." Human sperm, according to a physician whom Tissot quoted with approbation, "is the most perfect and important of all the animal liquors, and . . . like them derives its origin from the most perfect humours."[56]

By emphasizing the proper balance of bodily humors and fluids as the basis of health and sanity, Tissot's *Onanism* (and its scurrilous predecessor entitled *Onania; or, The Heinous Sin of Self-Pollution*) precipitated the Victorian-era hysteria about masturbation and madness. Among young men, masturbation was thought to be ruinous because it threatened "the Essential Oil of the animal liquors" with a "dissipation [that] leaves the other humours weak."[57]

For workaholic intellectuals of the Enlightenment, however, maintaining the body's proper balance of fluids and humors had converse implications. The perceived dangers of seminal dissipation went back to Galen's time, but so did perceptions (voiced in medical debates about the celibacy of monks and priests) about the dangers of seminal retention. "M. Tissot relates as many examples of illness due to retention as due to emission," Voltaire observed. "There is no stronger argument against the bold vows of chastity." Dr. Nicholas Robinson warned that "overlong Retention of this *Balsamum humani generis*" was "apt to fire the Blood, and disorder all Nature, if not timely evacuated." Married men were fairly safe. But if semen comprised a refined and intensified form of blood, and if equilibrium was essential for good health—as the medical science of Jefferson's day suggested—then a healthy widower needed to find a dependable therapy to prevent the excessive retention of semen. "If one indiscreetly wastes it, it can kill you," Voltaire declared, but "if one retains it, it can still kill you."[58] The French thinkers Diderot and Rousseau went so far as to endorse masturbation. Tissot and other experts recommended sexual intercourse with a healthy woman. Since his advice was aimed at elite men, is it any surprise that Tissot believed that "correspondence with a handsome women does not exhaust so much as with an ugly woman"?[59]

Sally Hemings was Thomas Jefferson's perfect remedy for wholesome sexual release. By all accounts she was physically attractive. She was young, healthy, and safely unattached. To the extent that emotion might come into play, Jefferson faced no risk of rejection. Hemings was sure to outlive him, and she could never leave him. He owned her entire family. Certain that his public career had ended with his retirement from Washington's cabinet, Jefferson had every reason to suppose that his private life at Monticello was of scant interest beyond his plantation.

THERE WERE, of course, other females among the approximately one hundred slaves who lived at Monticello in the 1790s, but it is unlikely that Jefferson cast his eye beyond the Hemings family. Sally's elder sisters already had partners and children. It mattered to Jefferson that Sally Hemings was "mighty near white" with "long straight hair down her back." It mattered that she was "light colored and decidedly good looking."[60] Jefferson's racism was the final consideration that elevated Sally Hemings—who was twenty years old in 1793—above any other potential candidates for his attention.

With remarkable and disgusting candor, Jefferson had explained his perceptions of black Americans in *Notes on the State of Virginia*, using language that reflected both his own extreme prejudices and the ancient humoral theories that Tissot had applied to the mysteries of human reproduction, diet, and health. "Whether the black of the negro . . . proceeds from the colour of the blood, the colour of the bile, or from . . . some other secretion," Jefferson wrote, "the difference is fixed in nature." Skin color, he insisted, was the initial "foundation of a greater or less share of beauty in the two races." Jefferson admired the "flowing hair," the "elegant symmetry of form," and the "fine mixtures of red and white" he saw in the faces of white women. He was utterly disgusted by the "eternal monotony" he saw in the faces of his Negro slaves, an "immoveable veil of black which covers all the emotions." Blacks, he believed, "secrete less by the kidnies, and more by the glands of the skin, which gives them a very strong and disagreeable odour."[61]

Ugly as these opening sentiments are, Jefferson's racism went much, much further. Blacks might be "equal to the whites" in their capacity for memory, he admitted, but their aptitude for reason was "much inferior" and their imagination was "dull, tasteless, and anomalous." In love they were "ardent," he thought, "but it kindles the senses only, not the imagination." Jefferson acknowledged the stark chasm of privilege and education that divided free whites from black slaves in Virginia, but he insisted nevertheless that the failings he perceived were rooted in nature rather than circumstance. "The improvement of the blacks in body and mind, in the first instance of their mixture with the whites," Jefferson contended, "proves that their inferiority is not the effect merely of their condition of life."[62]

From Thomas Jefferson's perspective in the 1790s, the light complexions and obvious talents of the Hemings family set them apart from the other slaves at Monticello and confirmed the virulent bigotry he had expressed in *Notes on the State of Virginia*. Within the framework of Jefferson's scientific racism, Sally Hemings's credentials for the role of consort, or "concubine," were enhanced by the fact that three of her four grandparents had been white, one of them Jefferson's own father-in-law.

THE EXISTENCE of Sally Hemings's children is posterity's clearest evidence for the duration of a relationship with Jefferson that began about 1795 and apparently continued until his death in 1826. Aside from the physical intimacy that resulted in six known pregnancies, however, details about the nature of their relationship remain elusive. Like other southern gentlemen, Jefferson complied with "the rules" that historian Bertram Wyatt-Brown described in his definitive study of southern honor. "Miscegenation between a white male and black female posed almost no ethical problems for the antebellum Southern community," Wyatt-Brown wrote,

> so long as the rules . . . were discreetly observed. First, the relationship, even if long-standing, had to seem to be a casual one in which the disparity of rank and race between the partners was quite clear to any observer. Second, the concubine had to be sexually attractive in white men's eyes. The lighter the skin, the more comely the shape, the more satisfactory the arrangement appeared to be. Third, the pairing could not be part of a general pattern of dissoluteness.

Finally, a southern gentleman would "never acknowledge in mixed company his illicit liaison with a woman, black *or* white."[63] Aside from ownership, Jefferson never explicitly acknowledged (or denied) any relationship with Sally Hemings—although some inferences can be drawn from his account books and the arrangements he made for Sally and her children.

Sally Hemings enjoyed much the same level of material privilege at Monticello that Jefferson extended to other members of her family. As domestic servants rather than field hands, all the Hemings women were spared the backbreaking labor of the annual harvest. Their clothing, too, was superior to the plain osnaburg fabric provided for Jefferson's other slaves. They wore knitted cotton hosiery instead of the woven stockings supplied to the others, and they received Irish linen, flannels, and calico instead of coarse woolens. Sally Hemings's quarters adjacent to the main house were doubtless more comfortable than the slave cabins near the fields below Monticello and on Jefferson's outlying farms.[64]

The emotional aspects of the relationship remain even more obscure. There is no evidence that Jefferson's physical relations with Sally Hemings involved violence or coercion beyond the obvious reality that no female slave could meaningfully grant or withhold her consent to a master's advances. None of the evidence from Monticello suggests anything like the sexually predatory behavior of the eighteenth-century Jamaican slaveholder Thomas Thistlewood, whose diary documents 3,852 acts of sexual intercourse with 138 women over thirty-seven years.[65] At the other extreme, romantic love of the sort that Jefferson had felt toward his wife or for Maria Cosway can only be a matter of sentimental speculation.

Sally Hemings's children regarded Jefferson as emotionally "very undemonstrative"—"affectionate toward his white grandchildren," as Sally's son Madison recalled, "but not in the habit of showing partiality or fatherly affection to us." On the other hand, Madison and his siblings "were permitted to stay about the 'great house,' and only required to do such light work as going on errands." Far more significant, they "were free from the dread of having to be slaves all our lives long. . . . We were always permitted to be with our mother, who was well used."

For many Americans, the fate of Sally Hemings's children remains the most revealing evidence about her status at Monticello and the nature of her relationship with Jefferson.[66] *All* of Sally Hemings's children attained their freedom either before Jefferson died or by the final codicil to his will.

Sally's eldest child, Harriet Hemings, was conceived in January 1795, a year after Jefferson resigned from Washington's cabinet and retired to Monticello. Harriet was born on October 5, 1795, and died about two years later, in December 1797.[67] In the months after Harriet's birth, as Jefferson plunged into the remodeling of Monticello, he was unaware that friends among the Democratic-Republicans were promoting his candidacy as successor to President Washington.[68] That autumn his friends successfully brought Jefferson's three-year retirement to an end. He was elected vice president on December 5, 1796, and inaugurated in Philadelphia on March 4, 1797.

Sally Hemings's second child, William Beverley Hemings, was conceived in July 1797 during Jefferson's extended vacation from national politics and the preparations for Maria Jefferson's marriage to John Wayles Eppes on October 13. Beverley was born on April 1, 1798; in his early twenties he ran away from Monticello. He was "white enough to pass for white," according to Jefferson's granddaughter Ellen Randolph Coolidge, but in doing so he lost touch with his family at Monticello. According to his younger brother Madison, Beverley Hemings "married a white woman in Maryland, and their only child, a daughter, was not known by the white folks to have any colored blood coursing in her veins."[69]

Sally's third child was an unnamed daughter born early in December 1799 who died in infancy. Her conception early in March 1799 corresponded with Vice President Jefferson's return to Monticello from Philadelphia after Congress had adjourned. Her fourth child was conceived in August 1800 while Jefferson was enjoying the summer's bountiful wheat harvest at Monticello and preparing his *Manual of Parliamentary Practice*. Harriet was born in May 1801 and given the name of Sally's first daughter, who had died. Overseer Edmund Bacon described Harriet as "nearly as white as anybody and very beautiful."

At Monticello, Harriet worked as a spinner until her twenty-first birthday, when she left at about the same time that her brother Beverley did. "By Mr. Jefferson's direction," Bacon recalled, "I paid her stage fare to Philadelphia and gave her fifty dollars." By the 1860s, when Madison Hemings lost touch with her, she had "married a white man in good standing in Washington City" and raised a family. "She thought it to her interest," her brother said, "to assume the role of a white woman, and by her dress and conduct" surrender her former "identity as Harriet Hemings of Monticello." The place and date of her death are unknown.[70]

Sally Hemings's fifth child, James Madison Hemings, was conceived at Monticello late in April 1804. Alarmed about the health of his daughter Maria Jefferson Eppes, the president had hurried home from Washington after the first session of the Eighth Congress adjourned on March 27. Arriving at Monticello on April 5, he witnessed Maria's death on the seventeenth and stayed nearly a month before returning to the White House on May 11. Madison Hemings lived at Monticello until Jefferson's death and was freed by the terms of his will in 1826. He married Mary Hughes McCoy, a free woman of mixed race, in 1831, and they had nine children together. After his mother died, he moved his family to Pike County, Ohio, where he made his living as a carpenter. By 1865 he had been able to purchase a sixty-six-acre farm in nearby Ross County. Interviewed by the editor of the *Pike County Republican* in 1873, Madison Hemings described himself as the son of Thomas Jefferson and his "concubine" Sally Hemings. He died in November 1878 with an estate valued at one thousand dollars.

Sally Hemings was thirty-four when her sixth and final child, Thomas Eston Hemings, was conceived late in August 1807. President Jefferson had left Washington at the beginning of August, and he returned in October for a special session of Congress in the aftermath of the diplomatic crisis precipitated by the British capture of the American frigate *Chesapeake*. Eston Hemings was born on May 21, 1808, and was effectively freed along with his brother by the terms of Jefferson's will. Because Eston was only eighteen when Jefferson died, Martha Jefferson Randolph saw that he was "given his time" until he turned twenty-one (a common practice of informal emancipation devised to avoid the legal stipulation that required freed slaves to leave the state within a year of their emancipation). In 1832 Eston Hemings married Julia Ann Isaacs, daughter of a Jewish merchant and his mixed-race wife. Eston and Julia Hemings moved to Chillicothe, Ohio, after Sally Hemings died in 1835. Barred from voting or participating in local government by virtue of his "light bronze color," Eston moved his family to Madison, Wisconsin, in 1852. There he changed his surname to Jefferson, compressed his mother's surname into the middle initial *H.*, and passed for white. Eston H[emings] Jefferson's career as a musician and cabinetmaker ended with his death in January 1856. He was buried in Forest Hill Cemetery in Madison.

JEFFERSON COULD not have been surprised by the escapes of Beverley and Harriet Hemings into white society in 1822, or by Eston Hemings's acceptance as a white man in Wisconsin in the 1850s. By his calculations (and by a Virginia statute enacted shortly before his liaison with Sally Hemings began and which remained in effect until 1910),[71] any children Jefferson fathered with Sally Hemings would legally be white. "Our Canon," Jefferson explained to a Boston scientist in 1815, "considers two crosses with [a] pure white [parent], and a third with [a parent of] any degree of mixture, however small, as clearing the issue of the negro blood."[72]

In Sally Hemings's case, the first "cross" had occurred between a white British sea captain and Sally's maternal grandmother. The second had been between John Wayles and her mother, Betty Hemings (a mulatto by the applicable Virginia statute of 1792 and a "half-blood" according to Jefferson's explanation). If Betty Hemings's daughters bore a child by a white father, according to Jefferson's explication of racial heredity and Virginia law the third "cross" resulted in a child with "less than ¼ . . . of pure negro blood, to wit ⅛ only, [who was] no longer a mulatto." Because Virginia law did not embrace the more intricate racial categories common to Louisiana and the Caribbean, Jefferson wrote that the "third cross clears the blood." Jefferson's children by Sally Hemings—as well as Mary Hemings's children by her common-law husband, Thomas Bell, a Charlottesville merchant—were legally white.[73]

But not free. "Freedom," Jefferson quickly added, "depends on the condition of the mother." Sally Hemings's children were born as slaves—but Jefferson recognized that if one of her sons were to be emancipated, "he becomes a free *white* man, and a citizen of the U.S. to all intents and purposes."[74] No matter how much interracial sex occurred on the plantations of the Old Dominion, according to Jefferson's calculations the commonwealth of free white men retained its ascendancy over the weaker sex and subordinate races. The duc de La Rochefoucauld-Liancourt commented on this legal paradox after he visited Monticello in June of 1796. "I have even seen," the French nobleman wrote, "and particularly at Mr. Jefferson's, slaves who have neither in their color nor features a single trace of their [African] origins, but they are sons of slave mothers and consequently slaves."[75]

CONCUBINE WAS the term that Madison Hemings, Israel Jefferson, and James Callender all used to describe Sally Hemings's relationship with Thomas Jefferson—less in the technical sense of a common-law marriage of equals (as in Roman law) than in reference to familiar Old Testament descriptions of the patriarchs and their consorts.[76] Whatever degree of affection Jefferson and Hemings may have felt for each other, her ultimate fate and the fate of her children testify to promises made and kept.

After Jefferson's death on July 4, 1826, his eldest daughter, Martha Jefferson Randolph, shouldered the delicate responsibility of fulfilling, without openly acknowledging, the unspoken assurances that her father had offered Sally Hemings and her children. Twice in her youth Martha's father had lied to her about his relationships with women— with Maria Cosway and with Elizabeth Moore Walker. In Paris, after he had dislocated his wrist while strolling near the Seine with Maria Cosway, Jefferson had suggested that the accident happened in the presence of some unnamed male companion. Back in Virginia, when his girls asked about the icy rift between their family and the Walkers, Jefferson had invented a comforting fib about some vague financial misunderstanding—a lie that seemed less innocent when it exploded in the newspapers.

Despite persistent accusations in the newspapers, and despite family resemblances that startled visitors at Monticello, Martha Jefferson Randolph never openly acknowledged her father's relationship with Sally Hemings. Year after year, with unexpressed anguish, she protected his secret—her family's open secret—with the timeless discretion of a southern lady. "We live surrounded by prostitutes," another slaveholding matriarch complained a few decades later.

Like the patriarchs of old our men live all in one house with their wives and their concubines, and the mulattoes one sees in every family exactly resemble the white children—and every lady tells you who is the father of all the mulatto children in everybody [else]'s household, but those in her own she seems to think drop from the clouds, or pretends so to think.[77]

Martha Jefferson Randolph clouded her private insights from visitors and family alike. She kept up the pretense as well as any southern woman. "Daughters," explained that southern matriarch, "are supposed to never dream of what is as plain before their eyes as sunlight, and they play their parts of unsuspecting angels to the letter."[78] Jefferson's eldest daughter even coached her own children with plausible half-truths so that they, too, could dismiss the persistent rumors and deny the reality they saw with their own eyes unto the next generation. Martha Jefferson Randolph kept the secret, but she also kept her father's promises, even in the face of his virtual bankruptcy.

On Thursday, March 16, 1826—fifteen weeks before he died—Thomas Jefferson composed and signed his will. Jefferson's skills as an attorney are evident in the carefully drafted provisions that complied with the patriarchal doctrine of coverture, which placed control of married women's property in the hands of their husbands, while protecting the inheritance of his eldest surviving daughter both from her husband's increasing dementia and his own creditors. In effect, Jefferson created a legal trust that benefited, in different ways, all his surviving children. (Maria Jefferson and her husband had already died, and their only surviving son had inherited their estate.)[79] Jefferson's will consigned "what will remain of my property" to three male trustees "to be held and administered by them, in trust, for the sole and separate use and behoof of my dear daughter Martha Randolph, and her heirs."[80]

The next day he prepared a two-page codicil, or addendum, that gave his "gold-mounted walking staff of animal horn" to his longtime friend James Madison and gold watches to each of Martha's children. The codicil also emancipated five slaves, all of them members of the Hemings family, who were the only slaves that Jefferson freed at his death.[81]

The codicil granted Jefferson's "good, affectionate, and faithful servant Burwell [Colbert], his freedom, and the sum of three hundred dollars, to buy necessaries to commence his trade of glazier." Jefferson's trusted valet, Burwell Colbert, at forty-three, was Sally Hemings's nephew (the son of her sister Betty Brown Hemings). To John Hemings and Joe Fossett he bequeathed "their freedom at the end of one year after my death; and . . . all the tools of their respective shops or callings."[82] John Hemings, fifty, was Sally's younger brother. Joe Fossett, forty-six, was her nephew (the son of her eldest sister, Mary Hemings). In addition to their obvious value and utility, the bequests of these tools and money demonstrated, if ever it were necessary, that all three men were capable of providing for themselves after emancipation.[83] Finally, Jefferson gave "to John Hemings the service of his two apprentices Madison and Eston Hemings"—Sally's youngest sons—"until their respective ages of twenty-one years, at which period respectively, I give them their freedom."[84]

The codicil did not mention Sally Hemings by name, but in the context of a very complicated estate burdened with debt, its brilliantly crafted provisions did protect her future. "I humbly and earnestly request [from] the legislature of Virginia," Jefferson wrote, "a confirmation of the bequest of freedom to these servants, with permission to remain in this State, *where their families and connections are,* as an additional instance of the favor . . . for which I now give them my last, solemn, and dutiful thanks."[85] Sally Hemings was fifty-three and (unless "supported and maintained" by Jefferson or his estate) technically ineligible for emancipation under the terms of Virginia law that were meant to protect aging slaves from being cruelly abandoned in their declining years.[86] In addition, Jefferson had been forced to evade the implications of coverture by placing Martha's inheritance in the care of trustees who were directed to comply with her independent judgment as though she were a widow capable of acting as a *femme sole.*[87]

Taken as a whole, the shrewdly drawn provisions of Jefferson's will and its codicil enabled Sally to live out her life as a virtually free woman in the physical care of her two youngest sons. To accomplish that goal, Jefferson retained her legal status as slave property—but "property placed under the exclusive control of my daughter and her independent will, as if [Martha Jefferson Randolph] were a *feme sole.*"[88]

Years later, Madison Hemings told the *Pike County Republican* that when Jefferson died he and his brother "rented a house [in Charlottesville] and took mother to live with us, till her death, which event occurred in 1835." In an 1833 census, Sally Hemings was listed as a free person of color living with Madison Hemings.[89] Acting upon verbal instructions that could only have come from her father,[90] Martha Jefferson Randolph had given Sally Hemings, her niece Betty Hemings, and her nephew Wormley (Hemings) Hughes "their time," because "if liberated they would be obliged to leave the state of Virginia."[91]

To settle the debts of his estate, the auction of Jefferson's personal property at Monticello began on Monday, January 15, 1827, and continued for five days. Along with horses, mules, cattle, carriages, wagons, and farm equipment—as well as "household furniture, many valuable historical and portrait paintings, busts of marble and plaister, [and] . . . various other articles curious and useful"—one hundred enslaved men, women, and children were sold that week for more than $48,000. Parents were separated from children. Jefferson's executor compared the wretched scene of the dispersal sale at Monticello to "a captured village in ancient times when all were sold as slaves."[92]

In many ways Thomas Jefferson's relationship with Sally Hemings had always been exploitive and selfish—an extreme version perhaps of his attitudes toward women in general. We know nothing about the emotional character of the relationship between the master of Monticello and his "concubine." With his daughter's help, Jefferson finally rescued Sally Hemings and all their surviving children from slavery. Against some formidable obstacles—through thoughtful actions that implied respect, gratitude, and some measure of affection—their story ended in a way that suggests that promises had been made and were kept.

CHAPTER SEVEN

Amazons and Angels

Recollect the women of this capital [Paris], some on foot, some on horses, and some in carriages hunting pleasure in the streets, in routs and assemblies, and forgetting that they have left it behind them in their nurseries; compare them with our own country-women occupied in the tender and tranquil amusements of domestic life, and confess that it is a comparison of Amazons and Angels.

—Thomas Jefferson to Anne Willing Bingham, May 9, 1788

Thomas Jefferson's personal relationships—his rejected proposal of marriage to Rebecca Burwell, his adulterous pursuit of Elizabeth Moore Walker, his marriage to Martha Wayles Skelton Jefferson, his infatuation with Maria Cosway, and his ownership of Sally Hemings—all reinforced his conventional patriarchal attitudes toward women. The bumbling adolescent courtship of his student days in Williamsburg had been followed by the wary misogyny of his twenties and his aggression toward the safely married wife of a boyhood friend. Jefferson had tasted the daily happiness of loving companionship with a dutiful wife—and the desolate grief that followed her death. In Paris his brief flirtation with another man's wife had rekindled his capacity for romantic friendship, even as her abrupt departure forced him first to confront and then to control his emotions. Finally, in the safe haven of Monticello, with Sally Hemings his dominion was complete. In his relationships with these five women, as in his relationships with his daughters, Thomas Jefferson had always put himself and his own needs first. Unsettling as some of his emotional interactions with these women may have been, none of them posed any challenge to Jefferson's ideas about women's place in marriage or society.

During the American Revolution, Jefferson was indifferent to women's hopes for an expanded role in public life and the reform of patriarchal laws. At the court of Louis XVI and in the salons and streets of Paris, he began to see women in a new and harsher light. When he returned from France, he was convinced that women in general posed a dangerous threat to republican government and the cause of liberty.

REMEMBER THE LADIES

THE ONE PERSON in Thomas Jefferson's entire life who confronted him with a direct challenge to his general disregard for women was Abigail Adams. She was too close a friend for Jefferson to ignore, and her arguments on behalf of women's rights and women's education were too thoroughly grounded in the rhetoric of the Revolution to be dismissed out of hand, whether by her husband or his friends.

Born in November 1744 a dozen miles south of Boston in the parsonage of the Congregational church of Weymouth, Massachusetts, Abigail was nineteen months younger than Jefferson and nine years younger than her husband. From her mother, a scion of the prominent Quincy family, she learned the domestic arts thought suitable for eighteenth-century women, while her Harvard-educated father indulged and encouraged her passion for reading. Commenting on her keen intellect and flair for argument, a girlhood friend forecast that she would "either make a very bad, or a very good woman."[1]

Scarcely five feet tall, with dark hair, piercing eyes, and a vigorous temperament, Abigail Smith was nineteen when she married John Adams in October 1764. Their love was grounded in a passionate friendship, and their union was more nearly a partnership of equals than most marriages of their day. During the span of two decades before, during, and after the War of Independence, Abigail Adams managed their household and the farm (as did many other wives whose husbands were absent during the war) without ever regarding these domestic responsibilities as the sole realm of her competence. Abigail's life demonstrated, as she told an old friend, that "a well-informed woman" was more capable "of engaging and retaining the affections of a man of understanding, than one whose intellectual endowments rise not above the common level."[2] Throughout his career John Adams relied on her for news and advice, and he proudly shared her informative letters with his colleagues in Congress. "I think you shine as a Stateswoman," he declared, "as well as a Farmeress."[3]

Jefferson and John Adams had first become friends in May 1776 when Jefferson arrived in Philadelphia for his first term as one of Virginia's representatives to the Continental Congress. Among many other shared experiences, they worked together on the committee responsible for drafting the Declaration of Independence. Through the momentous events of the Revolution, Jefferson and Abigail surely learned a great deal about each other from John Adams, but eight years passed before they had occasion to meet in person.

Abigail Adams and Thomas Jefferson first met in Boston on Saturday, June 19, 1784. Recently appointed to join her husband and Benjamin Franklin as the nation's diplomatic representatives in Europe, Jefferson had decided to tour New England before he sailed for Paris in July. While in Boston he stopped to invite Abigail to join his entourage for the voyage to France. Abigail had already booked passage, however, and she and her daughter were sailing the next day. Once they resumed their conversations weeks later in France, a close friendship blossomed and lasted for several years.

Jefferson ultimately disagreed with Abigail Adams about women's rights and many other things, and in the heated political atmosphere of the 1790s their friendship ended. Nevertheless, during the ten months that Jefferson and her husband worked together in Paris in 1784–85, Abigail came to regard the widowed Virginian as a dear friend. He was a frequent guest at the Adamses' house in the village of Auteuil during his first year in Paris—and unlike their obligatory guests, Jefferson was singled out by Abigail as one "who visits us in the Social friendly way."[4] Before John Adams's appointment as ambassador to Great Britain took Abigail and her family to London in May 1785, she clearly had enjoyed many opportunities to express her views in conversation with Jefferson. "I shall realy regreet to leave Mr. Jefferson," she informed her sister when word came of the appointment to London. "He is one of the choice ones of the earth."[5] Upon her arrival in London, her first letter to Jefferson lamented that their reassignment interrupted "the increasing pleasure, and intimacy which a longer acquaintance with a respected Friend promised," having left "behind me the only person with whom my Companion could associate with perfect freedom, and unreserve."[6]

Jefferson's affection and respect for Abigail Adams are evident on every page of the correspondence they maintained across the English Channel in the 1780s. "When writing to you, I fancy myself at Auteuil," Jefferson wrote, "and chatter on till the last page of my paper awakes me from my reverie." Abigail missed their freewheeling conversations as well. When Mather Brown finished a portrait of Jefferson, she was delighted to hang it in their London home, "tho it is but a poor substitute for those pleasures which we enjoy'd some months past."[7]

Evidence of Jefferson's firsthand acquaintance with Abigail's views about women's rights stands out in the very first letter he wrote her after the Adamses moved to London. As they compared their respective impressions of Britain and France, Jefferson wrote of the French "that I do love this *people* with all my heart"—and he underlined the word *people.* "I pray you to observe," he told Abigail, "that I have used the term *people* and that this is a noun of the masculine as well as feminine gender."[8]

While the single word *people* may not seem very significant at first glance, this letter to Abigail Adams represents the only time in all of his voluminous writings that Jefferson used gender-inclusive language. Abigail might not have been able to change Jefferson's mind about women and their place in society, but he obviously had listened carefully to the arguments that she voiced to him—as she had to her husband a decade earlier.

IN THE spring of 1776, just before Jefferson and John Adams teamed up on the committee to draft the Declaration of Independence, Abigail Adams had formulated her sentiments on behalf of women in a letter to her husband. She and John readily agreed about the importance of *education* for women.[9] With independence looming on the horizon, Abigail also hoped for more ambitious reforms. "In the new Code of Laws which I suppose it will be necessary," she wrote, "I desire you would Remember the Ladies, and be more generous and favourable to them than your ancestors. Do not put such unlimited power into the hands of Husbands. Remember all Men would be tyrants if they could." She went on to warn, "If perticuliar care and attention is not paid to the Laidies, we are determined to foment a Rebelion, and will not hold ourselves bound by any Laws in which we have no voice, or Representation."[10]

John and Abigail Adams agreed about the necessity of education for women, but on the eve of independence she was pressing for more. "That your Sex are Naturally Tyrannical is a Truth so thoroughly established as to admit of no dispute," Abigail contended. Why not, she asked, empower women against vicious and cruel husbands and fathers? She wanted Congress to alter the provisions of the common law that gave "such unlimited power to the Husband" and to enact "some Laws in our favour upon just and Liberal principals."[11]

Perhaps understandably, immersed as John Adams was in the congressional quest for unanimity on the paramount issue of independence, his immediate response was flippant. "I cannot but laugh," he wrote. "We know better than to repeal our Masculine systems." In fact, as his correspondence with a Bay State legislator demonstrated, John Adams recognized that his wife was raising serious issues about political consent and the inequities of the common law—dangerous issues that could unleash "Controversy and Altercation" and ultimately tend "to confound and destroy all Distinctions, and prostrate all Ranks, to one common Levell."[12]

Soon after she received John's reply, Abigail described it to her confidante Mercy Otis Warren, who was still publishing her plays and satires under a male pseudonym. John was "very sausy to me in return for a List of Female Grievances which I transmitted to him," Abigail reported. He had heard complaints that the principles of the Revolution were loosening "the bands of Government" and fueling rebellious spirits among children, apprentices, students, and slaves, she wrote, "but my Letter was the first intimation that another Tribe more numerous and powerfull than all the rest were grown discontented." By raising her voice on behalf of womankind, Abigail Adams felt she had taken a small step that "help'd the Sex abundantly" in matters that must eventually change. For the moment, though, she intended to tell John Adams only that she had tested "the Disintresstedness of his Virtue, and when weigh'd in the balance have found it wanting."[13]

· · ·

THE THOUGHTFUL candor that Abigail Adams demonstrated in all her correspondence with Jefferson reinforces the inference, based on his comment about *people,* that she had challenged in private conversations his attitudes toward women. In the four years from 1785 through Jefferson's departure from Paris in 1789, he exchanged 140 letters with John Adams and 38 with Abigail. In roughly the same period, Jefferson and Maria Cosway exchanged a total of 38 letters, but Jefferson's correspondence with Abigail Adams comprised an epistolary conversation. He wrote 18 times to her 20, while Maria Cosway's notes outnumbered Jefferson's by a ratio of 2 to 1.[14] The letters between Jefferson and Mrs. Adams were longer and more substantive than those he exchanged with Mrs. Cosway. There was something exotic and wistful about Jefferson's desired friendship with Maria Cosway. In Abigail Adams he found a genuine friendship rooted in common interests, shared republican values, the fiction of Laurence Sterne,[15] and real-world experiences including parenthood, child rearing, and shopping. Their friendship deepened, as well, when Abigail took charge of Jefferson's daughter Polly in 1787 upon her arrival from Virginia with Sally Hemings.

Jefferson and Abigail Adams bought fabrics and tableware and clothing for each other. He bought French lace, gloves, shoes, and objets d'art for Abigail Adams. She bought a dozen Irish linen shirts, damask tablecloths and napkins, and a pair of nutcrackers for Jefferson. They compared notes about plays and operas, and they counseled together about which household expenditures they could properly assign to the public accounts. John Adams was content to have Abigail keep Jefferson apprised of the social dimensions of diplomacy in London, while Jefferson reported on the doings of mutual acquaintances and notable personages in Paris. In short, they gossiped.

Jefferson occasionally flirted, as when he explained his choices for the figurines of mythical divinities that Abigail had asked him to purchase for her. "I could only find three of those you named," he wrote. "These were Minerva, Diana, and Appollo. I was obliged to add a fourth, unguided by your choice. They offered me a fine Venus; but I thought it out of taste to have two at table at the same time. . . . Beauty is jealous, and illy bears the presence of a rival." He continued, "At length, a fine

Mars was offered, calm, bold, his [sword] not drawn, but ready to be drawn. This will do, thinks I, for the table of the American Minister in London."

"I am totally foild at that . . . Compliment," Abigail replied.

> Surely the air of France conspired with the Native politeness . . . of the writer to usher into the World such an assemblage of fine things. I shall value the warrior Diety the more for having been your choise, and he cannot fail being in taste in a Nation which has given us such proofs of their Hostility.[16]

AFTER JEFFERSON and the Adamses had returned home to America and immersed themselves in their familiar circles, the correspondence between Jefferson and Abigail Adams lapsed. At first, when Abigail's husband was Washington's vice president and Jefferson was secretary of state in the early 1790s, their paths crossed at social events in the temporary capital. As partisan conflict between Federalists and Democratic-Republicans turned vicious in the mid-1790s, the once-friendly personal relationship between then President Adams and Vice President Jefferson, titular leaders of the rival political parties, was increasingly strained. By the time Jefferson defeated Adams in the election of 1800, the breach was complete.

Abigail Adams never forgave Jefferson for his role in the vicious newspaper attacks on her husband—or for displacing her son, John Quincy Adams, from a federal appointment he had held during his father's presidency. Nevertheless, having recently experienced the death of her adult son Charles in 1800 after losing two daughters in infancy, Abigail could not remain silent when she heard the news of Maria Jefferson's death on April 17, 1804. Unbeknownst to her husband, she sent a compassionate letter of sympathy to her former friend. "Had you been no other than the private inhabitant of Monticello," she began,

> I should e'er this time have addresst you. . . . But reasons of various kinds withheld my pen, untill the powerfull feelings of my heart have burst through the restraint, and called upon me to shed the tear of

sorrow over the departed remains of your beloved and deserving daughter, an event which I most sincerely mourn.

She recounted tender memories of nine-year-old Maria's arrival in London, her "strong sensibility," and "the attachment I formed for her."[17]

It had been a long time since Abigail Adams had remembered any "feelings of mutual sympathy" toward Jefferson. But she knew the cords of love that bound "a parents heart, . . . and when snapped assunder, how agonizing the pangs of seperation." Despite their estrangement, Abigail closed her letter with a bittersweet dose of the honesty that had always characterized her exchanges with Jefferson:

> I have tasted the bitter cup, and bow with reverence and humility before the great dispenser of it. That you may derive comfort and consolation in this day of your sorrow and affliction, from that only source calculated to heal the wounded heart—a firm belief in the Being, perfection and attributes of God, is the sincere and ardent wish of her, who once took pleasure in subscribing Herself your Friend.
>
> ABIGAIL ADAMS[18]

With these heartfelt sentiments, Abigail Adams opened a brief but remarkable exchange of letters with Jefferson—three each over the next five months.

Jefferson was touched. He thanked Abigail again for all that she had done for Maria and then expressed his "regret that circumstances should have arisen which have seemed to draw a line of separation between us." He might have stopped there, but the opportunity to justify his own conduct in Abigail's eyes—to open "myself to you without reserve" and "feel relief from being unbosomed"—was too great a temptation. Jefferson claimed that he never allowed his esteem for Abigail or her husband to have "been lessened for a single moment." Even the "different conclusions we had drawn from our political reading and reflections," he ventured, "were not permitted to lessen mutual esteem, each party being conscious they were the result of an honest conviction in the other." Warming to the occasion, he plunged ahead.

I can say with truth that one act of Mr. Adams's life, and one only, ever gave me a moment's personal displeasure. I did consider his last appointments to office as personally unkind. They were from among my most ardent political enemies, . . . and laid me under the embarrasment of acting thro' men whose views were to defeat mine.

But in time, Jefferson pretended, he had ascribed the midnight appointments that Adams made during the last hours of his presidency "to the influence of others." After "brooding over it for some little time," Jefferson claimed, he "forgave it cordially, and returned to the same state of esteem and respect for him which had so long subsisted."[19]

But Abigail was not looking for Jefferson's forgiveness. Had his letter "contained no other sentiments and opinions than those which my Letter of condolence could have excited," she replied, "our correspondence would have terminated here: but you have been pleased to enter upon some subjects which call for a reply." She justified her husband's final appointments as following the precedent set by President Washington, who left "not an office . . . vacant for his successor to fill."[20]

By opening these subjects to discussion, Abigail wrote, Jefferson had "taken off the Shackles I should otherways have found myself embarrassed with." Abigail unbound was a formidable adversary: "Now Sir I will freely disclose to you what has severed the bonds of former Friendship." She castigated Jefferson for hiring partisan journalists such as James Thomson Callender to slander Adams and his administration. For liberating the "vipers" who had been convicted under the Alien and Sedition Acts. For remitting Callender's fine, and for paying him "your reward of 50 dollars." Then, alluding to Callender's more recent reports about the Jefferson-Walker affair and "Dusky Sally," Abigail wrote smugly that "the serpent you cherished and warmed, bit the hand that nourished him, and gave you sufficient Specimens of his talents, his gratitude, his justice, and his truth." And finally, there was "one other act of [his] administration which [she] considered as personally unkind," but which she declined to mention.[21]

Jefferson's reply attempted to put his "charities to Callendar" in a more favorable light by disavowing his real part in promoting the partisan-newspaper controversies of the 1790s. But he was genuinely puzzled by her cryptic reference to that "one other act of [his] administration."[22]

Somewhat mollified by Jefferson's explanation of his dealings with Callender, Abigail explained that when Jefferson came into office and displaced her son, John Quincy Adams, from a district judgeship in Massachusetts, it "looked so particularly pointed" that even Jefferson's political allies in Boston expressed "their regret that you had done so."[23] To this accusation Jefferson honestly, and convincingly, explained that he had been unaware that her son had held the office to which Jefferson appointed another Federalist. "Had I known," he suggested, "it would have been a real pleasure to me to have preferred [John Quincy Adams] to some who were named in Boston in what were deemed the same line of politics."[24]

In her final letter, Abigail Adams acknowleged Jefferson's assurance that his failure to reappoint her son had not been intended as a personal insult, although she regarded his portrayal of the appointment process as "what the Gentlemen of the Law would term a quibble—as such I pass it." The final question she wanted to ask Jefferson was

> whether in your ardent zeal, and desire to rectify the mistakes and abuses as you may consider them, of the former administrations, you are not led into measures still more fatal to the constitution, and more derogatory to your honour, and independence of Character? Pardon me Sir if I say, that I fear you are.

"I will not Sir any more intrude upon your Time," Abigail concluded,

> but close this correspondence, by my sincere wishes, that you may be directed to that path which may terminate in the prosperity and happiness of the people over whom you are placed, by administering the Government with a just and impartial hand. Be assured Sir that no one will more rejoice in your success than
>
> ABIGAIL ADAMS[25]

With that, two extraordinary Americans parted company once again.

Years later, Jefferson confided to Benjamin Rush (who was attempting a reconciliation between Jefferson and John Adams) that by "yielding to an intimation in her last letter, I ceased from further explanation."[26] Perhaps so, but clearly Abigail Adams enjoyed the last word. In this remarkable exchange of letters, she politely but firmly challenged Jefferson to account for his conduct in the years since he had left Washington's cabinet. Can there be any doubt, cryptic as it may seem, that Thomas Jefferson's use of "the term *people* . . . [as] a noun of the masculine as well as feminine gender"[27] indicates that he had listened carefully to Abigail Adams's sentiments about female education and women's rights during their conversations in Paris? She could not change his mind about women and their place in society, but she had nudged him in that direction. If anyone ever presented a serious feminist challenge to Jefferson's general disregard for women, that person was Abigail Adams.

GAY AND THOUGHTLESS PARIS

DURING THEIR first weeks in Paris together, Abigail Adams and Thomas Jefferson had similar initial impressions of elite French women. At a dinner held by Ben Franklin, John and Abigail Adams were introduced to one of his dearest friends, the aging comtesse de Ligniville d'Autricourt, the widow of the philosopher Claude Adrien Helvétius and former hostess, or *salonnière,* of one of the leading salons of the Enlightenment. Franklin regarded her as "one of the best women in the world"—"wholy free from affectation or stifness of behaviour." Abigail was surprised when the comtesse arrived in soiled garments. She was aghast at dinner. Seated between Franklin and John Adams, the comtesse dominated the conversation and was constantly "spreading her Arms upon the Backs of both Gentlemans Chairs, then throwing her Arm carelessly upon [Franklin's] Neck." She had brought along her lapdog, "and when he wet the floor she wiped it up with her chimise." Abigail was astonished and, as she confided to her sister, "highly disgusted."[28]

After her encounter with one of Dr. Franklin's "most intimate friends," Abigail resolved "to find among the French Ladies manners more consistent with my Ideas of decency, or I shall be a mere recluse." The Adamses were far from reclusive in Paris, but John's diplomatic reassignment cut short his wife's opportunity to master the spoken language and participate more fully in conversation. "My acquaintance with French Ladies is rather small," Abigail wrote shortly before their departure for London—and the only one she admired was Marie Adrienne de Noailles, wife of the marquis de Lafayette. "A well bred French Lady has the most ease in her manners that you can possibly conceive of," Abigail Adams wrote, but the marquise de Lafayette had other virtues as well. She was "fond of her Children; and very attentive to them," and she was in love with and faithful to her own husband—qualities that Abigail Adams felt were "not the General Character of Ladies of high rank in Europe."[29]

Jefferson shared Abigail Adams's enchantment with the marquise de Lafayette for essentially the same reasons, but his more varied experiences during five years in Paris gave him a more complex perspective about Parisian and European women. Transatlantic visitors frequently contrasted the standards of marital fidelity that prevailed in America and France. "Almost all marriages here are happy," the French visitor Jacques-Pierre Brissot de Warville wrote of America in 1788, "and, being happy, are pure." American women were "entirely devoted to their households," Brissot reported, and cared "about nothing but making their husbands happy and about bringing up their children well."[30]

American perceptions of French society drew similar contrasts between "the voluptuary dress and arts of the European women" and the "chaste affections and simplicity" of American women. The French, Jefferson wrote, "consider fidelity to the marriage bed as an ungentlemanly practice and inconsistent with happiness." From the safety of her convent school, Jefferson's daughter Martha reported the news of a Frenchman who had killed himself because he thought his wife of ten years did not love him. "I believe that if every husband in Paris was to do as much," Martha wrote, "there would be nothing but widows left."[31] Abigail Adams perhaps exaggerated the number of prostitutes in Paris when she recounted a French priest's contention that the city had "52 thousand licenced unmarried women . . . so lost to a sense of shame, and virtue, as publickly to enter their Names at the police, for abandoned purposes." On the other hand, her reservations about the attitudes toward marriage that prevailed among the nobility came straight from a private conversation with the marquise de Lafayette. "I was married," the marquise told Abigail Adams, "before I was capable of Love." She was fortunate that her family had chosen well, because her love for her husband made her happier "than many others of my sex and country" who "seek their pleasures in dissapation and amusement" and "have no resource in Domestick life."[32]

EARLY IN the 1780s, Benjamin Franklin introduced Jefferson and the Adamses to the aging comtesse d'Houdetot and the "circle of literati" who gathered at her home at Sannois for occasional conversation. Once a friend of Rousseau and other departed philosophes, d'Houdetot now presided over the fading glory of a Parisian salon. Established in the 1630s when a few aristocratic women—the *salonnières*—opened their homes for serious conversation away from the royal court at Versailles, the salons of Paris became venues for conversations about the arts, literature, and philosophy that shaped and disseminated the ideas of the Enlightenment. The salons of seventeenth- and eighteenth-century Paris had comprised a "vast engine of power, an organ of public opinion." In their heyday, the philosophes and encyclopedists had attended salons on Tuesdays at the home of Franklin's friend the comtesse de Ligniville d'Autricourt in Passy, on Mondays or Wednesdays at the home of Marie-Thérèse Geoffrin in rue Saint-Honoré, and on Sundays or Thursdays at that of the baron d'Holbach. The salon of Suzanne Curchod Necker in rue Michel-le-Comte, on Fridays, was "the last great salon of the *ancien régime*."[33]

By the 1780s, however, Jefferson was too late to witness the grand salons of the Enlightenment. The preeminent *salonnières* and the famous philosophes who had attended them had already passed from the scene. Rousseau and Voltaire had died in 1778. Étienne Bonnot de Condillac, the leading French proponent of John Locke's ideas, had died in 1780, and the economist Anne-Robert-Jacques Turgot in 1781. Jean le Rond d'Alembert had died in 1783, and his co-editor of the great *Encyclopédie*, Denis Diderot, died in Paris on July 30, 1784, a week before Jefferson's arrival. Of the preeminent eighteenth-century philosophes, only the marquis de Condorcet was alive to welcome Jefferson at the Hôtel de La Rochefoucauld on the Left Bank near the Sorbonne.[34]

Jefferson did meet a few of Franklin's old friends from the heyday of the Enlightenment salons, and he met Condorcet and other Parisian men of letters through his friendship with the marquis de Lafayette. With the passing of Voltaire's generation, however, Jefferson was witnessing the domestication of the Enlightenment as it "passed into the hands of nonentities . . . lost its fire and became a mere tranquil diffusion of light, a comfortable ascent toward progress."[35] In the centuries since Jefferson served as America's envoy to France on the eve of its great revolution, his situation has repeated itself in capitals great and small throughout the developed and developing world. A foreign ambassador's basic job of representing his nation's interests to the prevailing regime naturally immerses the visitor in the social life of the elite. The society Jefferson met in these circles no longer represented the intellectual fervor that was brewing in Paris in the years immediately prior to the fall of the Bastille in July 1789. Jefferson traveled in the circles of privilege and culture, of men and women who took Voltaire's Enlightenment for granted. It was a polite world that was swept away when they proved themselves incapable of holding the reins of power in the French Revolution.

By the mid-1780s the preferred subjects of conversation in the Parisian drawing rooms that Jefferson frequented had slipped from the Enlightenment's exploration of philosophy and science, and its political and moral implications, toward more conventional banter about literature, art, music, and gardening. After spending an evening among the "circle of literati" who gathered at the home of the comtesse d'Houdetot, Jefferson's only comment was that he lost eighteen sous playing lotto.[36]

In the parlors of Lafayette's friends, Jefferson met society women who were less interested in political ideas than in the political fortunes of their friends and relatives. He knew that the comtesse d'Houdetot had lobbied successfully on behalf of Michel-Guillaume-Jean de Crèvecoeur, author of the *Letters from an American Farmer* (1782), for an appointment as consul to New York. Madame de Tessé, aunt of Lafayette and recipient of Jefferson's famous account of his gazing at the Roman temple at Nîmes "like a lover at his mistress," used her influence with the minister of war to advance a friend's military career. The marquise de Créquy was said to hold sway in decisions about appointments to the Académie française.[37] At the parties he attended, French noblewomen meddling in affairs of state aroused all of Jefferson's misogynist fears.

JEFFERSON WAS appalled, as Montesquieu and Rousseau had been, by the political influence exercised by French women, both in the streets and in the salons of Paris.[38] "Our good ladies," he purred to Anne Willing Bingham of Philadelphia, "have been too wise to wrinkle their foreheads with politics." The women of Jefferson's republic were "contented to soothe and calm the minds of their husbands returning ruffled from political debate" because "they have the good sense to value domestic happiness above all other."[39]

Jefferson painted a stark contrast between monstrous Parisian women "hunting pleasure in the streets . . . and forgetting that they have left it behind them in their nurseries" and "our own countrywomen occupied in the tender and tranquil amusements of domestic life." The contrast, he told Anne Bingham, was "a comparison of Amazons and Angels."[40] Even in this comparison, however, Jefferson's celebration of angelic Americans had a prescriptive edge that cut against women. This sermon-ette for Anne Willing Bingham, after all, was addressed to the poised, intelligent, and wealthy woman who soon created and presided over the foremost salon at the seat of American government in the 1790s—Philadelphia's so-called Republican Court.

A few months after Jefferson posted his letter to Anne Bingham, the financial plight of the French monarchy forced Louis XVI to summon the Estates-General into legislative session for the first time since 1614. Taking note of the many female participants in the public demonstra-tions that preceded the fall of the Bastille, Jefferson adopted a more joc-ular tone in a letter to David Humphreys at Mount Vernon. Formerly one of Jefferson's aides in Paris, Humphreys had returned to America in 1787 and rejoined Washington in the role of assistant and secretary that he had enjoyed during the American Revolution. Jefferson's message was no less censorious than it had been in his letter to Anne Willing Bingham. Revolutionary fervor among "all the handsome young women" of Paris, Jefferson advised Humphreys, constituted "an army more pow-erful in France than the 200,000 men of the king."[41] The *salonnières* of Paris were a powerful army. French women in the streets of Paris were Amazons. American women, so long as they attended to their nurseries, their kitchens, and their husbands' ruffled minds, were Angels.

The winter of 1788–89 was harsh. Food and fuel were scarce in Paris and throughout the provinces. As Europe waited for the Estates-General to convene in May 1789, however, Jefferson was generally opti-mistic. "I think the present disquiet will end well," he informed George Washington shortly before his election as the first president of the United States under the new Constitution. Frenchmen have "been awakened by our revolution, they feel their strength, they are enlightened," he wrote. Jefferson had extensive contacts among the liberal statesmen of Paris, and he was able to present Washington with a detailed analysis of French politics on the eve of the French Revolution.[42]

Remarkably, however, Jefferson's report to Washington expressed only one concern about the potential obstacles to the reform movement in prerevolutionary France. "How far they can proceed . . . towards a thorough reformation of abuse, cannot be foreseen," he wrote, because the men of France were not aware of the dangers posed by "a kind of influence, which none of their plans of reform take into account." According to Jefferson, French women were capable of undermining all of his male friends' hopes for reform.

Jefferson's eight-page letter to Washington devoted five pages to the prospects of constitutional reform in France in the months before the fall of the Bastille and three pages to the status of international negotiations about whale oil and fisheries. Between these reports Jefferson interjected an astonishing twelve-line outburst about French women.[43] Ostensibly he was addressing the question of whether the reformers' constitutional goals could be accomplished, but surely the outburst must have seemed as peculiar to George Washington (who never mentioned it in his reply) as it does to any modern reader. "In my opinion," Jefferson advised Washington,

> a kind of influence, which none of their plans of reform take into account, will elude them all; I mean the influence of women in the government. The manners of the nation allow [women] to visit, alone, all persons in office, to sollicit the affairs of the husband, family, or friends, and their sollicitations bid defiance to laws and regulations.

Jefferson recognized that "this obstacle may seem less to those who, like our countrymen, are in the precious habit of considering Right as a barrier against" influence peddling. He also admitted that "without the evidence of his own eyes" it might be difficult to "believe in the desperate state to which things are reduced in this country from the omnipotence" of French women. Finally—and again contrasting his view of France and America—Jefferson gave thanks that only the French women were exercising "an influence which, fortunately for the happiness of the sex itself, does not endeavor to extend itself *in our country* beyond the domestic line."[44]

The emotional intensity of this outburst raises the question of whether some element of Jefferson's personal life may have colored his immediate mood. His relationship with Maria Cosway had been cooling steadily for months. The letter to Washington was written between his April 1788 complaint that she had been "surrounded by a numerous cortege" during her second visit to Paris and his May 1789 recognition that her affections could never be his alone.[45] His disappointment was real, but not the force behind his misogynist outburst to Washington.

Although Jefferson's general attitudes toward women were shaped by his personal experience, the paranoia evident in his letter to Washington was rooted in a highly gendered perception of public events that he developed in France. Throughout the American Revolution, Jefferson more or less ignored women and their claims to a greater role in public life. In France, however, he began to perceive women as active threats to the cause of liberty and republicanism everywhere. Jefferson viewed the hapless Louis XVI and his government as the victims of female extremists. At one extreme, angry working-class women demanding food and fuel in the streets of Paris raised the specter of anarchy and violence. At the other, Jefferson blamed Queen Marie Antoinette for unleashing the French Revolution. She "plunged the world into crimes and calamities which will forever stain the pages of modern history," Jefferson wrote in his autobiography. "I have ever believed that had there been no queen, there would have been no revolution."[46] Between these extremes lay the delicate political territory in which Jefferson's friends of the patriot party were attempting to achieve reform without unleashing disaster. Yet it was in that precarious middle ground that Jefferson feared that his friends' efforts would be undermined by the female influence peddling that he decried in his letter to Washington.

Back in 1776, when Congress was debating independence, Abigail Adams had asked her husband and his revolutionary colleagues to remember the ladies. Now, as his French friends contemplated extensive reforms on the eve of their revolution, Jefferson turned Abigail Adams's values on their head. As he summarized the political situation in France and the prospects for "a thorough reformation of abuse," meddlesome women comprised the only threat to successful reform that Jefferson felt worthy of mentioning to the incoming president of the United States. Exciting political reforms were developing on both sides of the Atlantic. George Washington was about to become the first president of the United States under its new Constitution, and French patriots were poised to reform their ancien régime. For both countries Jefferson's attitude toward women was consistent. Women had to be kept on their side of "the domestic line."[47]

PÊLE-MÊLE

THOMAS JEFFERSON's 1788 letter to Anne Willing Bingham about the conduct of Parisian women on the eve of the French Revolution was not the first exchange on the subject that Jefferson had with the wealthy and influential beauty from Philadelphia. Her father had been mayor of the city. Her merchant and banker husband, William Bingham, was a political confidant of Alexander Hamilton and reputed to be the wealthiest man in America. Between 1784 and 1786 the Binghams had spent time in Paris and London, touring Europe and moving in many of the same circles of high society that greeted the American ambassador. Early in 1787, a year after the Binghams had returned to Philadelphia, Jefferson wrote Anne a chatty letter contrasting "the tranquil pleasures" of American women with "the empty bustle" of their counterparts in Paris. With his letter he enclosed some fashion magazines "to let you see that Paris is not changed in its pursuits since it was honored with your presence."[48]

Only a week earlier, in a confidential and partially encrypted letter to James Madison, Jefferson had expressed his condescending opinion of the Binghams more bluntly. William Bingham "will make you believe he was on the most intimate footing with the first characters in Europe and versed in the secrets of every cabinet," Jefferson warned, because he aspired to a diplomatic appointment. "Not a word of this is true," Jefferson declared. Bingham "had a rage for being presented to great men and had no modesty in the methods by which" he contrived to meet them. Once Bingham had been introduced, however, "if he obtained access afterwards, it was [only] with such as were susceptible of impression from the beauty of his wife."[49]

Jefferson enjoyed Anne Willing Bingham's charm and beauty, too, but his superficial admiration cloaked more than just antipathy toward her wealthy husband's politics. Jefferson sensed a dangerous aptitude behind her pretty face—and her reply in June of 1787 confirmed his fears. "The Candor with which you express your sentiments," she began, "merits a sincere declaration of mine." Anne Bingham heartily disagreed with Jefferson's "overcharged" depiction of frivolous Parisian ladies. "You have thrown a strong light upon all that is ridiculous in their Characters," she admonished him, but "you have buried their good Qualities in the Shade." She admitted that "the Women of France interfere in the politics of the Country and often give a decided Turn to the Fate of Empires." But what was wrong with that? "Either by the gentle Arts of persuasion, or by the commanding force of superior Attractions and Address," she continued, French women

> have obtained the Rank and Consideration in society, which the Sex are intitled to, and which they in vain contend for in other Countries. We [American women] are therefore bound in Gratitude to admire and revere them, for asserting our Privileges, as much as the Friends of the Liberties of Mankind reverence the successful Struggles of the American Patriots.[50]

Jefferson did not reply until May of 1788. Then he sent her another packet of fashion magazines along with his observations about Amazons and Angels and his expectation that "you will change your opinion, my dear madam, and come over to mine in the end."[51]

Far from converting to Jefferson's opinion, Anne Willing Bingham and her husband built a magnificent three-story home, modeled on the duke of Manchester's London town house, a few blocks from Independence Hall in Philadelphia. Built for entertaining, Mansion House at Spruce and Third Streets impressed Boston architect Charles Bulfinch as one that "would be esteemed splendid even in the most luxurious part of Europe." An English visitor exclaimed that he had "never seen any private house more admirably adapted for the reception of company." At Mansion House—much to Jefferson's dismay—Anne and William Bingham tailored the manners of the salons of Paris and London to the social and political capital of the early American republic.[52]

They were not alone in their social aspirations. When the new government was launched in Philadelphia in 1790, the Washingtons' res-

idence opened a second venue for capital society—senators, congressmen, diplomats, and distinguished visitors—at 190 Market Street, a few
blocks from the Binghams' mansion. Men attended the president's formal weekly levees on Tuesday afternoons and state dinners every Thursday (where Martha Washington was often the only woman present). For
his Tuesday levees the president donned a powdered wig and dressed in
black velvet with knee and shoe buckles, gloves, and a long sword. He
carried his hat as he circled the room greeting visitors by name, exchang-
ing bows and a few words with each guest, but shaking no hands, "even
with his most near friends, that no distinction might be made."

Martha Washington's levees, or "Drawing-Rooms," on Friday evenings were mixed gatherings, which the president regarded as social
rather than political. Clad usually in white with modest jewelry, the
hostess sat on a sofa on a slightly raised platform to greet her guests.
When introduced, the ladies curtseyed and then stepped to the side.
Often as not the president approached and spoke a few words "with a
grace, dignity, and ease that leaves royal George far behind him."
Refreshments in an adjoining room afforded a focus for continued conversation and sociability. Abigail Adams, who continued these levees
when her husband was president, wrote of her first visit to Martha
Washington's that "the room became full before I left it, and the circle
very brilliant. How could it be otherwise, when the dazzling Mrs. Bingham and her beautiful sisters were there; the Misses Allen and Misses
Chew; in short a constellation of beauties?" Others admired the wives of
French and Austrian ministers "blazing with diamonds," or elegant
Philadelphia girls "clad to the tip of the French fashions, of which they
were remarkably fond."[53]

Jefferson was aghast—as were the journalists he encouraged and supported. In 1792, Jefferson's paper, the *National Gazette*, spent six months
attacking Martha Washington's levees. Another paper placed "Levees!"
high in a list of the warning signs of resurgent monarchy. Martha Washington's drawing rooms were denounced as aristocratic "paraphernalia of
the courts." Her raised platform and her custom of greeting her guests
while seated were "too queenly." After the ratification of the controversial Jay Treaty, both the *Gazette of the United States* and the *Philadelphia
Aurora* sneered at "the President's levee of Tuesday last" as a "pageantry
of monarchy" demonstrating only that "the just resentment of an injured

and deeply insulted people had not yet reached the purview of Saint Washington." The "pageantry of courts," others declared, was "unsuited to infant republics."[54]

Jefferson perceived the social protocols of the Washington and Adams administrations—and women's participation in them—as reactionary and dangerous threats to republican government. Just as he thought he had witnessed the undermining of liberty and reform in France by "the influence of women in the government," Jefferson saw the insidious specter of female intrigue moving dangerously close to the heart of the republic at Martha Washington's and Abigail Adams's weekly receptions. When President Jefferson got his chance to set the tone of capital society, he fixed the date of his inauguration—March 4, 1801—as a day that "buried levees, birthdays, royal parades, and the arrogation of precedence in society by certain self-stiled friends of order," whom he regarded rather as "friends of privileged orders." Not surprisingly, when the new president banished vestiges of privileged precedence from state dinners in his White House—replacing them with manners he described as "pêle mêle" or "next the door"—the greater part of his ire fell upon a stylish, articulate, and threatening woman.[55]

TALL, WEALTHY, and very English, Elizabeth Leathes Merry, the elegant and outspoken wife of the British minister to the United States, embodied nearly everything that President Jefferson feared in women. Although born the daughter of a Suffolk farmer, she had married into the county gentry. Then, as a wealthy widow, she had met her career-diplomat husband in Paris and married him only months before he was posted to the United States. As if to compensate for her common birth, Elizabeth Merry carried herself with a hauteur that Americans readily mistook for aristocratic bearing. She became an irresistible target for the president. Soon after the Merrys arrived in Washington in November 1803, Jefferson flaunted his disdain for her (and for meddlesome women in general) with a series of deliberate public insults.

At the small dinners that were Jefferson's social forte in the new White House, as at Monticello, women participated as guests. Their very presence at Jefferson's table proclaimed their dependence upon their husbands. Public diplomatic receptions, on the other hand, presented

Elizabeth Leathes Merry by Gilbert Stuart, 1805.

Courtesy of the Museo Lázaro Galdiano, Madrid.

Jefferson with complications as he attempted to supplant time-honored formulas of international protocol, "especially those which savoured of anti-republicanism," with less formal and more democratic alternatives. "The principal of society with us," Jefferson wrote, "is the equal rights of all; and if there be an occasion where this equality ought to prevail pre-eminently, it is in social circles collected for conviviality. Nobody shall be above you, nor you above anybody, pêle mêle is our law."[56]

In the autumn of 1803, George III's minister to the United States and his wife caught the full brunt of Jefferson's republican zeal.

Jefferson's relaxation of diplomatic protocol had actually begun two years earlier, at a moment when the British consulate was between min-isterial appointments and being manned only by its secretary. For the first two years of Jefferson's presidency, the tiny diplomatic corps in Washington consisted only of representatives from France, Spain, and Denmark, none of whom had been terribly insistent upon the social rigors of diplomatic protocol in the new capital. The Spanish envoy's expectations were tempered by the soothing counsel of his Philadelphia-born wife, Sally McKean Yrujo. In short, until the new British minister arrived in Washington, the relative ranks of the resident diplomats had not mattered that much—but such things mattered a great deal to Anthony Merry and his wife. And in 1803 the situation was further complicated by world events: the Spanish having objected to the Louisiana Purchase, and the British and the French having resumed open warfare in Europe.

Jefferson's initial affronts to the new representative of George III occurred on two occasions—the first in private with Anthony Merry and the second in public with his wife. On Tuesday morning, November 27, Secretary of State James Madison accompanied Anthony Merry to the White House so that he could present his official letters of appointment to the president. Merry was dressed in full diplomatic regalia: "a deep blue coat with black velvet trim and gold braid, white breeches, silk stockings, ornate buckled shoes, plumed hat, and a sword." A colleague described him as "bespeckled with the spangles of our gaudiest court dress."[57] Jefferson greeted Merry in his "usual morning-attire." The president was "not merely in an undress," Merry later complained, "but *actually standing in slippers down at the heels,* and both pantaloons, coat, and under-clothes indicative of utter slovenliness and indifference to appearances and in a state of negligence actually studied."[58] They sat down to a conversation that was pleasant enough—except for Merry's astonishment as Jefferson idly dangled a well-worn slipper from his foot as they spoke, tossed it repeatedly into the air, and caught it with the tips of his toes.[59]

On the following Friday, still uncertain about whether the president had intended to insult him or his nation, Anthony and Elizabeth Leathes Merry arrived at the White House for their first state dinner. According to diplomatic etiquette as it had been practiced by Washington and Adams, this was an occasion at which the new minister and his wife could expect to be treated as the president's honored guests. Their first shock was the unexpected presence of the French chargé d'affaires, Louis André Pichon. With Britain and France at war, traditional diplomatic etiquette would have spared either party the social and political discomfiture of the other's presence. In fact, however, the French diplomat's presence was no accident. Jefferson had specifically urged Pichon to rush back from a business engagement in Baltimore so that he could attend the banquet at the White House.[60]

Pichon's presence was just a warm-up. Jefferson's new "pêle mêle" etiquette targeted Elizabeth Leathes Merry and her husband with a more direct and personal indignity. When dinner was announced in the antechamber, everyone expected the president, as host, to escort the wife of the British ambassador to the table in the dining room and seat her at his right hand. Instead, Jefferson took the arm of the woman standing closest to him, who happened to be Dolley Madison, and escorted her to dinner—despite her whispered plea to "take Mrs. Merry." Dolley's husband, the secretary of state, cushioned the shock slightly by leading Elizabeth Merry to the table. That left her stunned husband scrambling for a seat with the other guests. Jefferson declined to intervene when an eager congressman grabbed the remaining well-placed chair next to Sally McKean Yrujo. "This will be the cause of war!" she worried aloud.[61]

A week later, when James and Dolley Madison invited the Merrys to a private dinner in their home, circumstances impelled Madison and Albert Gallatin, members of the cabinet, to follow the president's example. Rather than being honored, as the wife of a newly arrived minister could reasonably have expected, Elizabeth Merry was left standing by herself as Madison bypassed her and escorted Hannah Nicholson Gallatin to the table. As the rest of the guests swept by them, Anthony Merry accompanied his own wife to the head of the table—where Hannah Gallatin gave up her seat without a word of thanks from Elizabeth Merry. Once again, as soon as the dinner was over, the Merrys called for their carriage and departed.[62]

Although creeping royalism was the ostensible target of Jefferson's pell-mell canons of etiquette, his deliberate insults were also skirmishes in a battle of the sexes. Elizabeth Merry gave the appearance of an articulate European woman thoroughly practiced in what Jefferson had described in his reports from abroad as "the spirit of female intrigue" and the corrupting "influence of women in the government."[63] She was herself a dangerous challenge to republican simplicity. Jefferson was not eager for American women to emulate her dazzling wardrobe. To a dinner at the home of Robert and Margaret Bayard Smith she wore a "brilliant and fantastic" white satin dress with a long train, "open at one side"

166 · MR. JEFFERSON'S WOMEN

and with an overskirt of white and dark blue crepe "so thickly covered with silver bangles that it appeared to be a brilliant silver tissue." Around her head she wore a matching blue crepe shawl that swept to the floor, held in place by a headband "with a diamond crescent before and a diamond comb behind." The entire ensemble was accentuated with "diamond ear-rings and necklace, displayed on a bare bosom."[64] More ominously, Jefferson did not want American women emulating her poise and independence.

"A woman of fine understanding," Margaret Bayard Smith wrote of Elizabeth Merry, "she is so entirely the talker and actor in all companies, that her good husband passes quite unnoticed; he is plain in appearance and called rather inferior in understanding." Jefferson was more damning: "Mr. Merry is . . . personally as desirable a character as could have been sent us," the president wrote, "but he is unluckily associated with one of an opposite character in every point. She has already disturbed our harmony extremely." As these dining room dramas played out in the partisan newspapers, Jefferson's animus toward Elizabeth Merry waxed stronger. He described her to James Monroe as "a virago"—a pejorative term that joined the mannish nature of an Amazon to the offensive personality of a termagant or scold. "In the short course of a few weeks," Jefferson declared, the minister's wife had "established a degree of dislike among all classes which one would have thought impossible in so short a time."[65]

From his male perspective, the president was distressed by Anthony Merry's subsequent refusals of dinner invitations from his cabinet officers—but not for his wife's sake. Jefferson, in fact, attributed all the minister's problems to the undue influence of an overbearing woman. "With respect to Merry," Jefferson declared, "I should be sorry to lose him as long as there remains a possibility of reclaiming him to the exercise of *his own* dispositions. If his wife perseveres, she must eat her soup at home, and we shall endeavor to draw him into society as if she did not exist."[66] In Jefferson's view of a healthy political order, whether in prerevolutionary France or at home in America, Elizabeth Merry and her kind had no legitimate place except as helpmates to their husbands.

CHAPTER EIGHT

All Men Are Created Equal

I laugh till my eyes are bedim'd with my tears,
When women neglect their domestic affairs,
And puzzle their heads with political cares;
When with zeal patriotic they puddings despise,
And chatter of taxes, of loans, and supplies.

—*Virginia Gazette,* October 7, 1773

Nature may by mental or physical disqualifications have marked
infants and the weaker sex for the protection rather than the direc-
tion of government, yet . . . the exclusion of a majority of our
freemen from the right of representation is merely arbitrary.

—Thomas Jefferson to John Hampden Pleasants, April 19, 1824

O N TUESDAY, June 11, 1776, two months after Abigail Adams had asked her husband to "Remember the Ladies, and be more generous and favourable to them than your ancestors," the Continental Congress designated John Adams, Benjamin Franklin, Thomas Jefferson, Roger Sherman of Connecticut, and Robert R. Livingston of New York a five-man committee responsible for drafting a statement to explain and justify the nation's decision to claim its independence from Great Britain.[1] In language that was largely Jefferson's, their Declaration of Independence expressed the basic and self-evident truths for which the War of Independence was fought and upon which the nation was built. Natural and inalienable rights. Life. Liberty. The pursuit of happiness— a splendid Jeffersonian amplification of John Locke's right to property. Government based upon the consent of the governed. America's list of self-evident truths began with Jefferson's statement "that all men are created equal." Abigail Adams was not the only female American hoping for more in 1776, but Thomas Jefferson meant every word that he had written, and he meant *men*.

WOMEN'S VOICES were heard throughout the thirteen colonies early in the 1770s as Americans grew increasingly dissatisfied with British rule, although Jefferson paid them little attention. *Virginia Gazette* editor Clementina Rind, who had inherited her newspaper from her late husband, published in September 1774 an appeal from the women of Virginia to their "countrywomen" in Pennsylvania, urging support of the intercolonial boycott of British tea and its duties. "Much, very much, depends upon the public virtue the ladies will exert at this critical juncture," the Virginians believed. "History may be hereafter filled with their praises, and teach posterity to venerate their virtues." By discouraging the use of tea and other imported luxuries, "A Planter's Wife" from South Carolina declared in another essay in Rind's *Gazette*, "we shall disappoint our enemies (who no doubt build much on our weakness in this respect) and greatly assist our husbands, brethren, and countrymen, in this *their* arduous struggle."[2]

As the quarrel with Britain accelerated from boycotts toward war, however, American women increasingly claimed the Revolution as their own as well as their husbands' and brothers' struggle. "The Complexion of the Times," a woman from Charleston proclaimed, "calls aloud to every Inhabitant of America, whether Male or Female, to exert themselves in Defence of those Rights which God and Nature has bestowed on us." Throughout the war, hundreds of American women traveled with the army as nurses, cooks, and laundresses. Others braved capture as couriers or spies. A few women dressed themselves as men and enlisted in the army. Anna Maria Lane fought in Washington's army at the Battle of Germantown in October of 1777 and later received a generous pension from the commonwealth of Virginia for her service "in the revolutionary war, in the garb, and with the courage of a soldier." Dozens of Virginia women manufactured munitions at the Westham forge and foundry near Richmond and the gunnery in Fredericksburg. Thousands of American women managed the family farm or business when their husbands enlisted in the army or spent months away from home as government officials.[3] Only a small percentage of the population, male or female, promoted the cause of American liberty by writing for the press.

Anne Dabney Terrel of Bedford County, where Jefferson had just acquired Poplar Forest from his father-in-law's estate, was one Virginia woman who wrote publicly about the Revolution and its implications. The mother of six children (and eventually of ten), Terrel was in her mid thirties in September 1776 when she rallied Virginia women to the cause of independence in a signed essay in Dixon and Hunter's *Virginia Gazette.* Her husband, Captain Harry Terrel, commanded a battalion of Virginia Continental troops for two years and then served in the commissary department for the rest of the war. "I am now absent from the tenderest of husbands," Terrel began, "because he is a soldier in the continental army, nobly supporting the glorious cause of liberty." Reflecting on the dangers of frontier life and the threats of British misrule, Terrel declared herself "not only willing to bear the absence of my dear husband for a short time, but . . . ready to start up with sword in hand to fight by his side in so glorious a cause." Responsible for the care of her family and farm, however, she summoned other Virginia women to "support ourselves under the absence of our husbands as well as we can, and as we are not well able to help them fight, let us pay attention to another branch of American politics." Terrel called upon her peers to demonstrate by "manufacturing our own wearing [apparel] . . . instead of the fine gew-gaws of Great Britain" that "American ladies have both ingenuity and industry, . . . and that we are free women."[4]

In 1776 Anne Terrel focused her attention on women's domestic contributions to the Revolution—on the "branch of American politics, which comes more immediately under our province." Terrel understood, as did Jefferson and his colleagues in Congress, that American independence could not be won only on the battlefield. Women's productive labor would be essential for a successful outcome. Terrel also recognized the vague boundaries between military and civilian life in revolutionary America. Civilians were vulnerable to attack as armies traveling with huge groups of noncombatants brought the war to hearths and homes throughout the colonies. Terrel knew implicitly that soldiers and statesmen were not the only political voices of the Revolution. Her own words—as in her assessment of "the wickedness of a cruel and abandoned [British] Ministry, who are forging chains, to bind not only us in the present age, but to bring out posterity into a lasting state of slavery"—reflected the political rhetoric of American patriots since the Stamp Act crisis. Nevertheless, Terrel explicitly raised the issue of gender differences as she linked the patriotic work of "free women" with their support for "our dear husbands [who] are nobly struggling in the army for that freedom."[5]

The American Revolution involved not only the transatlantic dispute about home rule within the British Empire but also, in most of the newly independent states, local contests over who should rule at home. As historian J. Franklin Jameson wrote eighty years ago, "The stream of revolution, once started, could not be confined within narrow banks, but spread abroad upon the land." While Anne Dabney Terrel focused her attention on the immediate measures necessary for victory against Great Britain, the values of the revolutionary era also inspired more insistent female voices in Jefferson's Virginia.

Hannah Lee Corbin was one Virginian who insisted upon her rights in a letter to her brother Richard Henry Lee, the Lee family's foremost statesman during the American Revolution. Widowed in her early thirties, Corbin was a fervent patriot and a force to be reckoned with. She was eager, as Abigail Adams had been, to see the Revolution sweep away the gender-based inequities of British property law. Enlisting her sister Alice to help persuade their brother, head of Virginia's congressional delegation, to "do something for the poor desolate widows," Hannah Lee Corbin wrote her brother indignantly in 1778, demanding to know why single women and widows remained subject to taxation when they had no hand in forming the laws or choosing those who did. For his part, Lee took his sisters' complaint seriously. Privately, Lee agreed that representation

ought to be extended as far as wisdom and policy can allow; nor do I see that either of these forbid widows having property from voting, notwithstanding [that] it has never been the practice either here or in England. Perhaps 'twas thought rather out of character for women to press into those tumultuous assemblages of men where the business of choosing representatives is conducted. And it might also have been considered as not so necessary, seeing that the representatives themselves, as their immediate constituents, must suffer the tax imposed in exact proportion as does all other property taxed.

None of the Lees said so in public, and Hannah Lee Corbin's death in 1782 ended their private discussion.[6]

As wartime governor in 1781, Jefferson faced the poignant complaints of the Philadelphia-born proprietress of Westover plantation, on the James River between Williamsburg and Richmond, who stood accused of treason. Mary Willing Byrd's dissolute husband, a third-generation member of the Governor's Council, had killed himself in 1777, and Jefferson had offered her legal advice about the management of the estate. Suspicions about her family's Tory sympathies were magnified by the fact that Benedict Arnold was married to her first cousin. Now Mary Willing Byrd was accused of unlawful communications with the British for attempting to reclaim property and slaves Arnold's troops had confiscated. Addressing herself to Jefferson "not only as Governor, but as an aquaintance, whom I have experienced kindness and some friendship from," Byrd asked, "What am I but an American? All my friends and connexions are in America; my whole property is here—could I wish ill to everything I have an interest in?"[7]

Mary Willing Byrd's interests went beyond property. Patriot troops had entered Westover with swords drawn while she and her daughters were asleep. Denouncing "the *savage* treatment I have met with," Byrd declared bitterly, "This cannot be called *Liberty*. I have sent a Soldier," presumably one of her four older stepsons, "who had lost his life in the Service of my Country. I have paid taxes and have not been Personally, or Virtually represented. My property is taken from me and I have no redress."[8] As the war ended, neither Mary Willing Byrd nor the patriot officers who had affronted her were ever brought to trial.

Six years later, faced with the same inequities of political representation, Anne Makemie Holden of Accomack County bought herself virtual representation at the cost of one hundred acres of land. Holden executed four deeds in 1787 that conveyed twenty-five acres to each of four male relatives with the explicit requirement that they "vote at the Annual Elections for the most Wise and Discreet men who have proved themselves real friends to the American Independence."[9] Thomas Jefferson was perhaps unaware of the women of Virginia who hoped that the American Revolution might improve their legal and political status. He was certainly indifferent, if not hostile, to their aspirations. But they were present in greater numbers than he imagined.

IN HIS authorship of the Declaration of Independence, Thomas Jefferson had John Locke's concepts of the origin of government in mind when he wrote (in a shortened version of the Lockean formulation of the Virginia Declaration of Rights) that "all men are created equal."[10] Contrary to some modern sensibilities, Jefferson's use of the word *men* did not necessarily invoke gender. The definition of *man* as a human being irrespective of sex or age went back to the Teutonic roots of the English language. In the Lockean context of the Declaration of Independence, Jefferson employed the gender-neutral terminology both of the Enlightenment (as exemplified in a 1752 essay by David Hume that described the universal traits found "in all men, male and female") and of the church (as in the biblical commentary from 1618 describing how "the Lord had [placed] but one paire of men in Paradise)."[11]

When dealing with a writer of extraordinary skill engaged in the drafting of a text as important as the Declaration of Independence, it is fair to recognize that talented authors often exploit the ambiguities and nuances of language. Thomas Jefferson's Declaration of Independence did not unthinkingly embrace the ancient gender-neutral terminology of the word *men*. With an intensity fueled by personal as well as theoretical considerations, Jefferson did *not* mean to say (as the women of the Seneca Falls Convention in 1848 did) "that all men and women are created equal."[12]

In his *Notes on the State of Virginia* and elsewhere, Jefferson's choice of a synonym for *women* was "the weaker sex." Not *the fair sex,* or *the distaff side,* but "the weaker sex." A cliché perhaps, but Jefferson—who was recurrently both attracted to strong women and uncomfortable about their strength—yearned to convince himself that human females were indeed the weaker sex. Because Jefferson believed that nature had "marked infants and the weaker sex for the protection rather than the direction of government," he contended that Virginia's constitution of

1776 was justified in "refusing to all but [male] freeholders any participation in the natural right of self-government."[13]

The convergence of Jefferson's personal and political sentiments about women is clear in the wholesale revision of Virginia's legal code that occupied Jefferson's attention from 1776 through 1779. Assisted in part by George Wythe and Edmund Pendleton, Jefferson's committee drafted legislation for elections, the state judiciary, and the elimination of primogeniture and entail. Their reform package—in all some 126 bills touching on everything from religious liberty and education to the prevention of smallpox and the regulation of ferries, roads, and taverns—fills 336 pages of Julian Boyd's edition of *The Papers of Thomas Jefferson*. Bill 27 protected the traditional dower rights of widows, and bill 21 guaranteed every sound-minded adult who was "not a married woman" the right to execute a last will and testament.[14] Except when mentioned as wives or widows, however, women were utterly invisible in Jefferson's reform of Virginia's laws and institutions. Some women may have benefited indirectly from the abolition of primogeniture, but if so, that boon was merely incidental to Jefferson's goal of removing a feudal provision of property and inheritance law designed to create and sustain aristocratic estates and family dynasties. Bill 79 of Jefferson's revisal outlined a statewide system of education for boys that eventually led to the creation of the University of Virginia, which remained an all-male undergraduate school until 1970. "A plan of female education," Jefferson later wrote, was "never a subject of my systematic contemplation." The education of females, he said, "occupied my attention only as the education of my own daughters occasionally required."[15]

JEFFERSON'S INDIFFERENCE to female education set him apart from more progressive Enlightenment contemporaries. His friend Dr. Benjamin Rush endorsed the betterment of women in an influential pamphlet entitled *Thoughts upon Female Education, Accommodated to the Present State of Society, Manners, and Government in the United States of America*, published in Philadelphia in 1787. "The equal share that every citizen has in the liberty," Rush wrote, "makes it necessary that our ladies should be qualified to a certain degree, by a peculiar and suitable education,

3 Juillet 1790.

N°. V.

JOURNAL

DE LA SOCIÉTÉ

DE 1789.

ART SOCIAL.

Sur l'admission des femmes au droit de cité.

L'HABITUDE peut familiariser les hommes avec la violation de leurs droits naturels, au point que parmi ceux qui les ont perdus personne ne songe à les réclamer, ne croie avoir éprouvé une injustice.

Il est même quelques-unes de ces violations qui ont échappé aux philosophes et aux législateurs, lorsqu'ils s'occupoient avec le plus de zèle d'établir les droits communs des individus de l'espèce humaine, et d'en faire le fondement unique des institutions politiques.

Par exemple, tous n'ont-ils pas violé le principe de l'égalité des droits, en privant tran-

A

Months after Jefferson had returned to the United States, the marquis de Condorcet published "On the Admission of Women to the Rights of Citizenship" in Journal of the Society of 1789, *which he edited. Condorcet, renowned as a mathematician and philosophe, and his wife, Sophie de Grouchy, used their apartments on the Left Bank as a salon for the discussion of political reform. An acquaintance of Jefferson and ally of the marquis de Lafayette and other liberal reformers who comprised the Society of 1789, Condorcet represented Paris in the Legislative Assembly of 1791. Parting company with these liberals over the fate of the monarchy, Condorcet sought to replace the monarchy with a republican constitution. An advocate of education for both sexes, Condorcet wrote the Legislative Assembly's report on public education, which was adopted in 1795 after his death. As a member of the National Convention that tried and executed Louis XVI, Condorcet voted to depose the king but against his execution. When the more radical Jacobins took power, Condorcet was forced into hiding, where he made his case for the perfectibility of mankind in his most famous work,* Outlines of an Historical View of the Progress of the Human Mind, *published in Paris and London in 1795. Discovered by the Jacobins during the Reign of Terror, Condorcet died in prison two days after his arrest in March 1794. A life-size statue of Condorcet stands in front of the old National Mint, now the Musée de la Monnaie, on the Seine at Quai Conti opposite the Louvre.*

Collection of the author.

to concur in instructing their sons in the principles of liberty and government."

In France, Jefferson's friend the marquis de Condorcet argued that their shared political faith required more than educational reform—it demanded the expansion of women's political and legal rights. "Can we think of a stronger proof of the power of custom over even enlightened men," Condorcet asked, "than the spectacle of a group of male legislators who invoke the principle of equality of rights to their own advantage, while, with absurd prejudice, they simultaneously ignore the rights of all women?"

Condorcet's essay "On the Admission of Women to the Rights of Citizenship," published in July 1790, directly challenged two of the justifications that Jefferson cited for excluding women from politics. "One cannot deny women civil rights because of their dependence on their husbands," Condorcet argued, "because this type of tyranny would be removed if they had civil rights and because one type of injustice cannot be used as justification for another." He also answered the claim "that one must fear women's influence on men"—an apprehension that Jefferson had expressed so vigorously to Washington. "To this," Condorcet wrote, "I should answer that we have far more reason to fear such influence in hidden discussions than in open ones."[16]

Condorcet was not alone among the philosophes. The great Immanuel Kant's "Answer to the Question: What Is Enlightenment?" spoke explicitly on behalf of men *and* women. "Enlightenment," Kant's essay began, "is man's exit from his self-incurred minority"—"the capacity to use one's intelligence without the guidance of another." Unlike Jefferson in the Declaration of Independence, however, Kant addressed both sexes when he castigated the enemies of the Age of Reason, who "see to it that the largest part of mankind, *including the entire 'fair sex,'* should consider the step into maturity, not only as difficult but as very dangerous."[17]

Eight years later, in 1792, Kant's friend Theodor Gottlieb von Hippel expanded the implications of his comment in the treatise *On Improving the Status of Women*, published in Berlin. "Do not the obstacles to a moral reform of the human race," Hippel asked, "arise chiefly from the fact that we . . . erect this temple of reform from our own sex alone, while the fair sex has been left to lie in ruins?" Mary Wollstonecraft posed a similar question to a far wider audience in her famous *Vindication of the Rights of*

A
VINDICATION
OF THE
RIGHTS OF WOMAN:
WITH
STRICTURES
ON
POLITICAL AND MORAL SUBJECTS.

BY MARY WOLLSTONECRAFT.

PRINTED AT BOSTON,
BY PETER EDES FOR THOMAS AND ANDREWS,
FAUST's Statue, No. 45, Newbury-Street.
MDCCXCII.

Completed on January 3, 1792, Mary Wollstonecraft's feminist manifesto, A Vindication of the Rights of Woman, *was published in England, France, and the United States before the year ended. Wollstonecraft argued for improved education for women and expanded opportunities to participate equally with men in economic and political affairs. "To be a good mother," she wrote, "a woman must have sense and that independence of mind which few women possess who are taught to depend entirely upon their husbands." With improved education, Wollstonecraft declared, many women "might have practiced as physicians, regulated a farm, managed a shop, and stood erect, supported by their own industry. . . . How much more respectable is the woman who earns her own bread by fulfilling her duty than the most accomplished beauty!"*

Collection of the author.

Woman, published that same year in Paris, London, Dublin, and Boston "It is time," she declared, "to effect a revolution in female manners time to restore them their lost dignity—and . . . to reform the world."[18]

Jefferson utterly rejected the view, advocated by contemporaries with whom he otherwise agreed, that the Enlightenment principle of equality of rights should extend to women. He embraced public education for young men as essential to the future of the republic. He was equally resolute in his conviction that young women needed training in the arts of domesticity and virtues of motherhood. During the American Revolution Jefferson was largely indifferent to reforms that might improve women's situation in American society. Then, from his experience in France in the 1780s, he drew the lesson that female meddling in public affairs was dangerous to liberty and republicanism. In Jefferson's rejection of women's aspirations and his attempts to supplant their influence in American politics, his private temperament and experience were closely aligned with his political theory.

JEFFERSON PENNED his most candid statement about women in public life in a brief and somewhat cryptic note written late in his presidency to Treasury Secretary Albert Gallatin: "The appointment of a woman to office is an innovation for which the public is not prepared, nor am I."[19] Although the president and his Treasury secretary regularly exchanged short notes in the course of their daily business (the equivalent of interoffice e-mail messages today), nothing in their correspondence in the six weeks prior to this January 13, 1807, note offers any context for Jefferson's blunt statement. Perhaps he was responding to a conversation with Gallatin (possibly about the difficulty of finding suitable appointees for the Louisiana Territory), perhaps to something in the newspapers, or perhaps even to a comment from the secretary's well-connected and politically astute wife, Hannah Nicholson Gallatin.[20]

Jefferson's definition of America as a white male polity had a relentless logic and an intensity rooted in his personal discomfort with women. He dismissed "the weaker sex" from any roles in public life except as republican wives and mothers. "By mental or physical disqualifications," Jefferson believed, nature had "marked infants and the weaker sex for the protection rather than the direction of government."

He applied the same logic to African Americans, who were "as incapable as children of taking care of themselves." Jefferson lumped infants, women, and slaves together and excluded them from any participation in government because they had no "rights of will and of property"[21]—impediments that Jefferson's revision of the Virginia legal code had done nothing whatsoever to change. While others like the marquis de Condorcet dreamt of ways to educate and empower women, Jefferson was entirely content with a world in which all white men were created equal. In fact, he was more than content with that patriarchal world. Its social assumptions were philosophically critical to his conception of legitimate republican government.

Once again, it is important to recognize that Jefferson used language with extraordinary skill and intelligence, even in a cryptic note describing "the appointment of a woman to office" as "an *innovation*."[22] Except in the context of science, Jefferson's vocabulary associated *innovation* with risk. In discussing various political topics, for example, he wrote of "dangerous innovations" in 1777 and 1801, of "perilous innovation" in his Second Inaugural Address, and of "rash and ruinous innovations" in 1816.[23] In the context of his attitudes toward women in person and in politics, Jefferson's use of the word *innovation* points toward something larger than patronage appointments or the novelty of female office-holding. In practice and in theory, Jefferson regarded women in political life as a threat to nothing less than the Lockean foundation of the nation's republican institutions.[24]

Jefferson and his contemporaries saw themselves as engaged in the great modern project of supplanting absolute monarchy with forms of government based on consent—a historical development they traced back to the English civil wars and the Glorious Revolution of the seventeenth century. The legitimacy of their republic (and of the modern liberal democratic state in general) rested on the fundamental premise, as Jefferson wrote in the Declaration of Independence, that "Governments are instituted among Men, deriving their just powers from the consent of the governed." If the authority of government no longer came from above, through the divine right of kings, then legitimacy demanded that "individuals must themselves consent, contract, agree, choose, or promise to enter" into relationships that created "political obligation and political authority."[25]

At some theoretical moment prior to the formation of human society and government, men *and women* had existed in a state of nature—a condition that Thomas Hobbes characterized as an "equality of ability" that fostered "a warre . . . of every man, against every man," and that John Locke described as "a State of perfect Freedom" and "a State also of Equality."[26] Regardless of whether that mythic state of nature had been benign or vicious, for Hobbes and Locke, and for Jefferson and the founders of the American republic, the critical event in history was the moment when government was created by civil compact: the moment when "our Fathers or Progenitors passed away their natural Liberty, and thereby bound up themselves and their Posterity to a perpetual subjection to the Government, which they themselves submitted to."[27]

Families were regarded as the fundamental units of social order in a state of nature. At the critical moment when civil government was created by compact, the state of nature ended and women simply disappeared from consent-based political theory. They disappeared as completely in Lockean theory as they did from English common law under the doctrine of coverture, and for basically the same reason: "by marriage, the husband and wife are one person in law; [and] . . . the very being or legal existence of the woman is suspended."[28] The result was that although Enlightenment philosophers expressly included women within their universal definitions of humanity in its original state of nature, they silently consigned women to domestic subordination as they imagined the progress of humanity from that state of nature, through the organization of patriarchal families, to the creation of civil society and government by social compact. By the middle of the eighteenth century, the French political philosopher and notorious misogynist Jean-Jacques Rousseau could entirely exclude women ("the sex that ought to obey") from his account of the creation of civil society. "Rousseau's ideal republic of free and equal heads of patriarchal families," Susan Moller Okin has written in words that seem equally applicable to Jefferson, "is necessarily built on the political exclusion, total confinement and repression of women."[29]

PRACTICE FOLLOWED theory as the eighteenth century drew to a close. At the beginnings of their respective revolutions, American and French women pressed for recognition as participants in political life. By the

mid-1790s, in both countries, revolutionary misogyny cloaked its rejection of female aspirations beneath the conciliatory icons of republican
motherhood and separate spheres. In America, the concepts of the
republican mother and the republican wife constricted the space in
which women could exercise their moral and intellectual capacities to
the home and family, and draped that narrow sphere even more tightly
in red, white, and blue.[30] The individual female voices of Abigail Adams,
Hannah Lee Corbin, Mary Willing Byrd, and Anne Holden were
drowned out by the program advocated by the likes of Dr. Benjamin
Rush and Judith Sargent Murray. Their reforms in women's education
were ultimately intended to benefit the sons and husbands of the republic. According to the anonymous "Lady" who published the essay "On
the Supposed Superiority of the Masculine Understanding" in the
Columbian Magazine, God had assigned to women "the care of making
the first impressions on the infant minds of the whole human race, a
trust of more importance than the government of provinces, and the
marshalling of armies."[31] Women were too important in the domestic
sphere to squander their energies in the public one. In New Jersey, where
the state constitution of 1776 had extended the suffrage to adult inhabitants worth fifty pounds, the propertied single women who had benefited from that provision were denied the vote after 1807.[32]

In France, ordinary women were prominent in street protests and
riots over the scarcity of bread, sugar, and other commodities. Women
participated in the taking of the Bastille in July 1789. They regularly
attended legislative sessions of the National Assembly and the Convention, and they demanded radical changes in discriminatory property and
divorce laws. Months before the publication of Wollstonecraft's *Vindication of the Rights of Woman,* a female orator and friend of the marquis
de Condorcet attacked the "gothic laws that abandon the . . . most
worthy half of humanity to a humiliating existence" in a speech to the
legislature in 1791. "Justice," declared Etta Palm d'Aelders, "calls all individuals to the equality of rights, without discrimination of sex; the laws
of a free people must be equal for all beings. . . . The powers of husband
and wife must be equal and separate."[33]

That same year a butcher's daughter, Olympe de Gouges, published a
Declaration of the Rights of Woman and the Female Citizen in twenty-
seven propositions. The "foolproof way to elevate the soul of women," de

Gouges argued, "is to join them in all the activities of men." Article 1 of her list of women's rights declared that "woman is born free and lives equal to man in her rights. Social distinctions can be based only on the common utility." Several pages later, article 27 concluded that "property belongs to both sexes whether united or separate; for each it is an inviolable and sacred right." De Gouges closed her pamphlet with a "Form for a Social Contract Between Man and Woman," which proposed to replace traditional marriage with conjugal unions "for the duration of our mutual inclination" in which both parties agreed "to make our wealth communal."[34]

Feminist agitation in France continued through 1792 and reached its peak in 1793 with the creation of the Society of Revolutionary Republican Women, which sided with Maximilien de Robespierre and his radical Jacobin faction against the moderate republicans known as Girondins. Once Robespierre had purged his rivals from the National Convention, however—sending twenty-two Girondin leaders to the guillotine in October of 1793—his Jacobins turned on their female allies with a vengeance. Acting on a complaint from a delegation of working-class women on October 28, 1793, the Jacobins responded two days later by outlawing all "women's societies and popular clubs." The Convention justified its action with two questions: "(1) Can women exercise political rights and take an active part in affairs of government? (2) Can they deliberate together in political associations or popular societies?" To both questions, the Jacobins who controlled the Convention answered no. As in America, male revolutionaries used the concepts of republican motherhood and separate spheres as their rationale to deflect feminist reforms. "Can women devote themselves to these useful and difficult functions?" asked the Committee on General Security.

> No, because they would be obliged to sacrifice the more important cares to which nature calls them. The private functions for which women are destined by their very nature are related to the general order of society. . . . Each sex is called to the kind of occupation which is fitting for it; its action is circumscribed within this circle. . . . We believe, therefore, that a woman should not leave her family to meddle in affairs of government . . . [and] that it is not possible for women to exercise political rights.[35]

Enforced by the fearsome Committee of Safety, the suppression of women's organized political activity was readily accomplished during the Reign of Terror. On November 3, 1793, six days after the Convention voted to ban all women's organizations, the author of the *Declaration of the Rights of Woman and the Female Citizen,* Olympe de Gouges, was beheaded. A few weeks later the de facto mayor of Paris invoked her name as a warning to all when he expelled all women from meetings of the commune, or city council. "Remember the impudent Olympe de Gouges," he proclaimed, "who was first to set up women's societies, who abandoned the cares of her household to get mixed up in the republic, and whose head fell beneath the avenging knife of its laws."[36]

Ultimately, the Jacobins were unable to sustain their version of Jean-Jacques Rousseau's ideal republic, but they did reestablish Rousseau's concept of women as "the sex that ought to obey" against the feminist aspirations of many revolutionary women.[37]

THOMAS JEFFERSON did not employ the avenging blade of a guillotine against the influence of women in the political affairs of his republic. Rather, after his election to the presidency in the "Revolution of 1800," he transformed the dining room of the White House into a political device. For a dozen years the social life of the executive branch (and the inevitable lobbying that went with it) had revolved around weekly social events established by Presidents Washington and Adams and their wives. Men had attended the presidents' formal receptions on Tuesdays and state dinners on Thursdays. On Fridays, women had flocked to Martha Washington's and Abigail Adams's levees.

President Jefferson changed all that. He opened the new White House only twice a year for public receptions, one on New Year's Day and the other on the Fourth of July. Jefferson replaced "levees, birthdays, royal parades, and the arrogation of precedence in society" with the *pêle-mêle* protocol of his occasional state banquets and the disarming informality of his numerous private dinners. Five nights a week he gathered as many as a dozen men around an oval table. He kept careful records of his guest lists to make sure that he reached virtually every member of Congress. The invitees for any given evening "were generally selected in reference to their tastes, habits, and suitability in all respects, which . . .

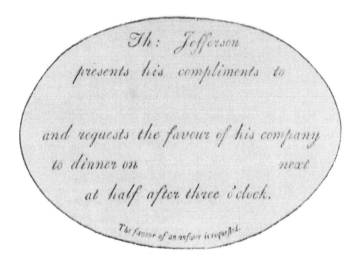

President Jefferson made effective political use of dinner parties, but his printed dinner invitations were meant to convey the impression that guests were invited in their private rather than public capacities.

Courtesy of the Library of Congress, Manuscript Division.

had a wonderful effect in making his parties more agreeable than dinner parties usually are." Acting as his own hostess, Jefferson personally inscribed his dinner invitations using a preprinted form that requested the pleasure of "his" company. With a dumbwaiter nearby and his French chef downstairs, the president served dinners himself. "At Mr. Jefferson's table," a frequent guest wrote, the president directed "the stream of conversation . . . with a *tact* so true and discriminating that he . . . dr[e]w forth the talents and information of each and all of his guests."[38]

By replacing levees and receptions with his intimate dinner parties, Jefferson not only deflected the social influence of women at the seat of government. At dinner after dinner Jefferson appropriated to his own purposes the role of hostess as practiced by the *salonnières* of Paris and their female counterparts in New York and Philadelphia. "His genius is of the *old French school*," Abigail's son John Quincy Adams perceptively remarked.[39]

Jefferson arranged the physical setting for his weekday dinners so that he was entirely in control of the room and its occupants. "A set of circular shelves were so contrived in the wall, that on touching a spring they turned into the room loaded with the dishes placed on them by servants," who remained out of sight. "You need not speak so low," Jefferson was able to assure his guests. "You see we are alone, and *our walls have no ears.*" Jefferson believed that eavesdropping servants fostered "domestic and even public discord . . . by the mutilated and misconstructed repetition of free conversation." Revolving shelves and dumbwaiters plugged those leaks.

His table was not rectangular but circular, or oval, a shape that symbolized equality for Jefferson and his guests as it had for King Arthur and his knights. More significant, however, the shape of Jefferson's table augmented his control of his guests and their conversation. "Instead of being arrayed in straight parallel lines, where they could not see the countenances of those who sat on the same side," Jefferson's dinner guests "all could see each other's faces, and feel the animating influence of looks as well as words." Everyone sat in plain view, participating in one "general conversation" that Jefferson could control as he wished, without the whispered asides that readily occur at the opposite ends and corners of a large banquet table.

Jefferson's careful arrangements for his dinners "prevented the company [from] forming little knots and carrying on in undertones separate conversations, a custom so common and almost unavoidable in a large party." In many respects, Jefferson fashioned these all-male weekday dinners to reflect his vision of the political nation: civility reigned. Women and servants were utterly excluded. Factional conversation was suppressed. Confrontation was avoided. Confidentiality was guaranteed and unruly passions tamed. Jefferson used his dinner parties as an essential element of his governance. At his table in the White House, a beneficent *salonnière* "with a *tact* so true and discriminating that he seldom missed his aim"[40] guided the gentlemen of the republic toward the common good.

"YESTERDAY I dined with the President," a Federalist from New Hampshire wrote on Christmas Day 1802. "His rule is to have about ten members of Congress at a time. We sat down to the table at four, rose at six. . . . The wine was the best I ever drank, particularly the champagne, which was indeed delicious. I wish his French politics were as good as his French wines."[41]

"Under the new order of things," a veteran Federalist congressman wrote a few days later,

> there are no Levees, but the members are invited to dine with the President in rotation, and what is strange (if anything done here can be strange), only Federalists or only Democrats are invited at the same time. The number in a day is generally eight, and when the Federalists are invited there is one of the heads of departments, which makes nine.[42]

Although in his second term he often invited a dozen guests at a time, Jefferson continued the practice of segregating his weekday dinner parties by political affiliation until the last year of his presidency. He believed that men of "good humor and politeness never introduce into mixed society a question on which they foresee there will be a difference of opinion." An unusual perspective for a lawyer and politician, perhaps, but it was all the more revealing as a maxim that other men applied only to social rather than political conduct. Jefferson's weekday dinners created a social forum that cloaked his political agenda: bringing congressmen and the president together to "know one another and have opportunities of little explanations of circumstances, which, [if] not understood might produce jealousies and suspicions injurious to the public interest."[43]

Women were never present at Jefferson's *weekday* White House dinners—and he never engaged his daughter Martha or the wives of colleagues, such as Dolley Madison, as hostesses for them. During the congressional session of 1804–05, for example, Dolley Madison was present at three of only seven dinners served to a mixed company. Jefferson's remaining fifty-six dinners that season were all-male events. The myth of Dolley Madison's role as the surrogate hostess for Jefferson's White House rests on the misreading of a letter in which Jefferson explained to James Monroe that he had "been in the habit, *when I invited female company* (having no lady in my family) to ask one of the ladies of the four [cabinet] secretaries to come and take care of my company." When Jefferson courted the support of the men with whom he shared responsibility for governing the United States—whether at his weekday dinner table or in the meetings of his cabinet, which he called "his family"— Jefferson himself, not Dolley Madison, played the role of hostess and *salonnière*.[44]

Margaret Bayard Smith—wife of a Jeffersonian newspaperman, close friend of Dolley Madison, and frequent guest at the White House when Jefferson did invite mixed parties to dinner—recorded her first impressions of the president in the opening pages of her published account of *Forty Years in Washington Society.* "Is this," Smith asked herself,

> the violent democrat, the vulgar demagogue, the bold atheist and profligate man I have so often heard denounced by the federalists? Can this man so meek and mild, yet dignified in his manners, with a voice so soft and low, with a countenance so benignant and intelligent, can he be that daring leader of a faction, that disturber of the peace, that enemy of all rank and order?

Although Alexander Hamilton accused Jefferson of "a womanish attachment to France and a womanish resentment against Great Britain," Margaret Bayard Smith was the first perceptive observer, but certainly not the last, to describe Jefferson's mature conduct and temperament as "almost femininely soft and gentle." Later in the nineteenth century, the great American historian Henry Adams concluded that Jefferson's disdain for "whatever was rough or coarse, and his yearning for sympathy was almost feminine"—a perception echoed by some recent biographers.[45]

By describing Jefferson as feminine, Smith and Adams drew a sharp contrast between his temperament and the military swagger of his rival Alexander Hamilton or the robust masculinities of John Marshall and George Washington. More clearly than other observers, Margaret Bayard Smith recognized that Jefferson's effectiveness as president depended upon the very same "feminine" aptitude for genteel political maneuvering under the cloak of sociability that he had denounced as "female intrigue" on the part of dangerous and unruly women. Jefferson excluded women from his weekly political dinners as thoroughly as he expunged them from the consent-based Lockean theory of American representative institutions and from the seemingly universal promise that all men were created equal.

. . .

THOMAS JEFFERSON was nearly sixty years old when he was elected president of the United States. Throughout the course of his earlier life, he had mastered his personal fear of women by contriving ways to protect his autonomy against their influence. During and after the American Revolution, he carefully guarded America's transition from a patriarchal monarchy to a democratic nation based on civic republicanism and the consent of the governed from the perceived dangers of female discord. He consistently opposed any expansion of women's participation in public life, any departure from an exclusively domestic role as republican wives and mothers, any relaxation of their subordination in law, culture, and education. Jefferson's personal aversion to and fear of women in public life shaped American laws and traditions in ways that echo into the twenty-first century.

APPENDIX A

THE JEFFERSON - WALKER AFFAIR

Although Thomas Jefferson's attempts to seduce Elizabeth Moore Walker began in the summer of 1768, the surviving evidence about his misconduct was not committed to paper until some thirty years later. Pertinent documents are printed below in chronological sequence, with annotation identifying a few other documents that are not known to have survived. The editorial policy for these transcriptions is stated on page xiii. The fourth paragraph of Henry Lee's letter of September 18, 1806 (printed below), suggests that John Walker alone possessed (and probably destroyed in 1809) other documents in which Jefferson addressed his misconduct toward Elizabeth Walker.[1]

A close reading of the extant documents suggests that all parties were acutely aware that Jefferson's misconduct could have led to a duel.[2] Mrs. Walker waited to reveal the details of Jefferson's misconduct to her husband until after Jefferson had left for Paris in the 1780s, "from her fear of its consequence which might have been fatal." In that context, the situation in 1802–06 demanded both exoneration of Elizabeth Walker and, although jarring to modern sensibilities, satisfaction for John Walker's injured honor.

In 1802 the Walker affair first received public attention in newspaper accounts that both Jefferson and John Walker tried to suppress, apparently with some success. Three years later, however, the allegations surfaced again in debates on the floor of the Massachusetts legislature when a Federalist legislator, Mr. Hulbert, of Sheffield, described Jefferson's attempted seduction of Mrs. Walker, his liaison with Sally Hemings, and his response to Banastre Tarleton's raid of 1781 in his attack on the president's character, religion, and policies.[3] This second round of criticism was widely reprinted in American newspapers, and it led to a second round of public commentary in prose and verse. In both instances, General Henry "Light-Horse Harry" Lee, a Virginia Federalist hostile to Jefferson and related to the Walkers by marriage, served as an intermediary on John Walker's behalf. In 1806, when the second round of public attention prompted John

Walker to demand formal attestations to the authenticity of Jefferson's earlier correspondence, Episcopal bishop James Madison (a cousin of Jefferson's secretary of state) and Chief Justice John Marshall were enlisted for that purpose.

Thomas Jefferson to John Walker, April 13, 1803,
Virginia Historical Society (Mss2 J3595 a 29)[4]

Washington. Ap[ri]l 13 1803
Sir.

Your letter of the fourth did not come to hand 'till last night. it covered a copy of that of May 15th 1788[5]—which I had only hastily read in the hands of Gen[era]l Lee.

I think its miscarriage unfortunate, as had I received it I should without hesitation have made it my first object to have called on you on my return to this country,[6] & to have come to an understanding as to the course we were to pursue, as was the object of the letters. time, silence, & the circumstances growing out of them have unfavorably affected the case. With respect to the newspapers, 'tho the silencing them would be very desirable yet it would be as difficult if not desperate.

However if Callender & Coleman & Caldwell can be silenced, the others are but copyers or answerers of them. Wayne, Relf, Russell, have not pretended to originate information.[7] but these people slander for their bread, & as long as customers can be found who will read & relish & pay for their lies, they will fabricate them for the market. As for the antagonist presses, I have with conscientious exactness approved the smallest interference with them further than to have public documents published in them. The present occasion however will justify my using the intermediation of friends to direct the discretion of those of them of the principal circulation. With respect to the Bee[8] which you particularly mention, I know not the editor & scarcely ever see his paper. but through a friend who knows him I can have a total silence recommended to him probably with effect. through the same channel the Aurora & American Citizen may probably be induced to silence. these are the only papers of considerable circulation on that side: & if their antagonists can be brought to be silent, they can have no reason not to be so. however my best endeavors shall be used by these & all other means to consign this unfortunate matter to all the oblivion of which it is susceptible. I certainly could have no objection to your shewing my letter to Mr. Nicholas[9] to the Ladies of your family. My greatest anxieties are for their tranquility. I salute them & yourself with respect

TH. JEFFERSON
John Walker esqr

{Two attestations dated 1806 appear at the bottom of this document.}

I certify this to be a true Copy from the Original—{*signed*} J MADI-
SON B[isho]p of the Pr[otestant] Ep[iscopal] Church in Virginia
April 20th 1806

A true copy from the original shown me by Mr. Walker which I
believe to be in the hand writing of Mr. Jefferson
{*signed*} J MARSHALL C[hief] J[ustice] of the US
May 13th 1806

Statement by John Walker in the handwriting
of Henry Lee, 1805, TJP[10]

I was married at Chelsea the seat of my wifes father on 6th of June [17]64. I
was educated at W[illia]m & Mary where was also educated Mr. J[efferson].

We had previously grown up together at a private school & our boys
acquaintance was strengthened at college. We loved (at least I did sincerely)
each other.

My father was one his fathers ex[ecuto]r & his own guardian & advanced
money for his education[11] for which my father gave me an order on him
returned from france & is the act to which he refers in our correspondence.

I took Mr. J[efferson] with me the friend of my heart to my wedding. He
was one of my bridemen.

This as I said ~~before~~ above ~~happened?~~ took place in [17]64.

In [17]68 I was called to Fort Stanwix being secretary or clerk to the Virginia
Commission at the treaty with the Indians there held by Sir W[illiam] Johnson
which was composed of Gen'l A[ndrew] Lewis & my father.

I left my wife & infant daughter at home, relying on Mr. Jefferson as my
~~near~~ neighbor & fast friend having in my will made before my departure, named
him first among my executors.

I returned in Nov[embe]r having been absent more than 4 months.

During my absence Mr. J[efferson's] conduct to Mrs W[alker] was improper
so much so as to have ~~subtly~~ laid the foundation of her constant objection to my
leaving Mr. J[efferson] my ex[e]c[u]t[or] telling me that she wondered why I
could place such confidence in him.

At Shadwell his own house in [17]69 or [17]70 on a visit common to us being
neighbors & as I felt true fr[ien]ds. he renewed his caresses ~~&~~ placed in Mrs
W[alker]'s gown ~~cuff~~ sleeve cuff a paper tending to convince her of the innocence ~~of~~ of promiscuous love.

This Mrs W[alker] on first glance tore to pieces.

After this we went on a visit to Col. Coles a mutual acquaintance & distant
neighbor. Mr. Jefferson was there. On the ladys retiring to bed he pretended to
be sick, complained of a headache & left the gentlemen among whom I was.

Instead of going to bed as his sickness authorized a belief he stole into my
room where my wife was undressing or in bed.

He was repulsed with indignation & menaces of alarm & ran off.

In [17]71 Mr. J[efferson] was married[12] and yet continued his efforts to destroy my peace until the latter end[13] of the year [17]79.

One particular instance I remember.

My old house[14] had a passage upstairs with ~~bed~~ private rooms on each side & opposite doors.

Mr. J[efferson] and wife slept in one. I & my wife in the other.

At one end of the passage was a small room used by my wife as her private apartment.

She visited it early & late. On this morning Mr. J[efferson]'s knowing her custom was found in his shirt ready to seize her on her way from her Chamber—indecent in manner.

In [17]83 Mr. J[efferson] went to France his wife died previously.[15]

From [17]79 Mr. J[efferson] desisted in his attempts on ~~her~~ my peace.

All this time I believed him to be my best frd & so felt & acted toward him.

All this time I held him first named in my will, as Excr. ignorant of every thing which had passed.

Soon after his sailing for France was known Mrs W[alker] then recurred to my will & being as before asked her objections, she ~~told me~~ related to me these base transactions apologizing for her past ~~the~~ silence ~~by her~~ from her fear of its consequence which might have been fatal to me.

I constantly wrote to him. You have our correspondence & you go now to Mr. J[efferson]. My injury is before you. Let my redress be commensurate. It cannot be complete & therefore ought to be as full as possible.

John Walker to Henry Lee, March 28, 1805, TJP

Shirley March 28th 1805

My dear Sir—

Yours of the 11th Inst[ant] reached me yesterday. It was unfortunate that Mr J—— had left Washington previous to your arrival. The debate of the Massachusetts Assembly has been sent me by a friend. How Mr. Hubbert had acquired his knowledge of my affair, & the part you took in it, I know not. You are well assured, that my communication with Mr. Kinloch was never meant for the Public eye. That this Debate may be resorted to by Mr. J—— as an excuse for not acceding to my demand is very possible & even probable; but how this can be done with *justice,* I can not comprehend. For you must remember, that by an express article of that negotiation, some mode was to be devised whereby it might be made known to the world, that satisfaction had been given to me. This was required as *indispensable.* How has it been complied with? And untill it is, the only possible mode of self defence that occurs to me, is the showing our correspondence to friends who may by that means possess the [tools] of correcting such misrepresentations as they frequently hear.

This I have done & this I must continue to do untill that stipulation is fulfilled. From what I hear of the malignity with which this subject is handled by some of his friends & abettors, I fear a publication will soon be unavoidable, unless he takes some decisive measure to prevent it. He may still continue to say 'it will not be my cross' but I can say with truth, that he & his friends have rendered it unavoidable. For this, & other reasons I long to see you, as I shall take no such step without consulting you particularly, altho' by some I have already been urged to it.

It grieves me to find that Mrs. Lee's health is still so precarious. Should her destination be to the Springs, we shall of course have the pleasure of seeing you both. If to sea, God grant her pleasant gales & a happy Issue.

I am so unacquainted with the money'd Gentry of James river, that I know not how to answer your question on that subject. I wish however the attempt may be made, & with success: the more so as it may afford one the pleasure of seeing both you & your brother, & in good humour, tho' that is nothing rare.

I am sorry poor little {*manuscript torn*}ith has lost his nurse but hope he will not miss her long.

The children here, have I believe, the whooping cough, & even the grown have dreadful colds. Poor little Kinloch is just recovering from a most obstinate fever, which lasted near twenty days without intermission.

That all manner of happiness may attend you & yours is the fervent wish of

> My dear Sir
> Your ever affectionate
> Jno Walker

Thomas Turner, "Letter," printed in *The Balance and Columbian Repository* (Hudson, N.Y.), June 18, 1805, American Philosophical Society

Sir,

After my note of last week, I shall, without circumlocution, enter upon the several subjects embraced by your letter of the 14th ultimo, and answer the interrogatories therein proposed, with all the perspicuity in my power, and all the light, afforded by *my own* knowledge of facts, and by *respectable information* recently obtained in Richmond. . . .

The third subject alluded to, in your letter, is "the affair of Mr. Walker"—an affair whose monstrous atrocity, whose diabolical turpitude, whose extensive, continued, and deliberate villainy, defy the powers of the strongest pen, and can only be conceived by those, who have seen, and attentively perused, the documents unfolding the whole of this unparalleled transaction—*This I have done*. I will as briefly as I can, give you the substance of, and dispatch the hateful subject.

The father of Col. John Walker was the guardian of Mr. Jefferson, and advanced a part of those funds, which were applied to the education of the latter—an education affording those talents, which have been strangely perverted, which have been insidiously employed, in the conception of schemes, foul, ungrateful, horrible. At a very early period of their lives, Colonel Walker, and Mr. Jefferson contracted an attachment which grew up with their years, and ripened into the closest intimacy—Their professions were mutual; their confidence unbounded—whilst things were in this situation Mr. Jefferson was meditating the unnatural purpose, of seducing the wife of his best friend, and to this end, (taking advantage of the confidence of Mr. Walker, and availing himself of the timidity of the lady, whose affection for her husband forbade the disclosure of a transaction, which might lead to an exposure of his life) devoted himself for ten years, repeatedly and assiduously making attempts, which were as repeatedly, and with horror repelled. For ten years was this purpose pursued, and at last abandoned, (*as he himself acknowledges*) from the inflexible virtue of the lady, and followed (as he also acknowledges) by the deepest and most heart wounding remorse—All this, I HAVE SEEN; NOT in Newspapers, not in extracts, not in copies of letters—I HAVE SEEN IT, in the ORIGINAL CORRESPONDENCE BETWEEN Messrs. WALKER and JEFFERSON, every letter of which, bears the signature of the writer, or has been since acknowledged by him, under his own hand. In this correspondence Mr. Jefferson repeatedly, and fervently confesses, that the guilt is all his own—the innocence all Mrs. Walker's; and that he shall never cease to revere, and attest the purity of her character, and to deprecate his unpardonable, and unsuccessful attempt to destroy her. His contrition, his misery is asserted in the warmest terms, and his acquittal of Mrs. Walker, pronounced in the strongest language of his pen—Amongst other concessions, he owns, that in order to cover the real cause of the separation between Col. Walker and himself, he did FABRI-CATE A NOTE respecting an unsettled account which he said, had produced the schism, and which he expressly acknowledges had no foundation in truth.—Let it not be forgotten, that the attempts against the honor of Mrs. Walker were carried on during the life of Mrs. Jefferson, than whom a better woman, and better wife never existed.

Thomas Jefferson to Robert Smith, July 1, 1805,
Henry E. Huntington Library and Art Gallery[16]

Dear Sir   Washington July 1, 1805
The inclosed copy of a letter to Mr. Lincoln will so fully explain it's own object, that I need say nothing in that way. I communicate it to par-

ticular friends because I wish to stand with them on the ground of truth, neither better nor worse than that makes me. You will perceive that I plead guilty to one of their charges, that when young & single I offered love to a handsome lady. I acknolege it's incorrectness; it is the only one, founded in truth, among all their allegations against me. Before I had sent the original to Mr. Lincoln I was advised to detach from it what related to transactions during the invasion of Virginia, a person in that state having undertaken to have that matter fully established, & communicated thro' one of the presses there. I will thank you for these papers when perused, & to consider their contents as communicated with the same latitude, as well as restriction, as to Mr. Lincoln, and that you will ascribe the trouble I give you in reading them to my counting you among those whose esteem I value too much to risk it by silence.

I shall leave this [city] on the 15th but Mr. Gallatin proposes a temporary absence about the 10th. Before that time, say the 7th, I must pray you to visit us, in order to consult as to consult on two important questions. 1. What conduct shall we pursue as to naval spoliations & insults on our coast? and what as to the territorial contest with Spain? Accept affection salutations & assurances of constant esteem & respect.

Th. Jefferson

Henry Lee to Thomas Jefferson, February 24, 1806, TJP

Occaquan 24th February 18[06]
Sir,

In addition to my letter of this day, I beg leave to ask your attention to some matters which I have long desired to call the appropriation of a few moments of your time.

Shortly after I had the honor of an interview with you in Albermarle I learnt from several Porterfields. . . . [17]

You will oblige me also by stating to me, what occurrence you allude to in your letter to Mr W[alker], during the conference I had the honor to hold with you, on his affair, which you considered violating that decorum I had before observed. I never could have expected such animadversions, being unconscious of such deviations, & sure that I never intended any departure from the strict line of propriety & respect.

I have the honor to be sir, with due respect & consideration your most obedient servant

Henry Lee

Thomas Jefferson to Henry Lee, Washington, March 29, 1806, TJP[18]

I mentioned in a letter to Mr. Walker that "a single incident only on your part at our meeting, I had considered as *not right*" this is the only expression meant for the incident. it becomes quite unimportant, because not noticed at the time, and should require too many recollections & too long a recapitulation for the bound of a letter. unimportant as it is however, I shall state it to you with frankness if you shall desire it whenever we may happen to meet. I return you mr Strode's and Mr Washington's letters, & salute you with respect & consideration.

TH JEFFERSON

Henry Lee to Thomas Jefferson, September 18, 1806, TJP

{A contemporary notation written sideways in the margin of the second page of this document reads: "Letter from Genl. Lee to Mr. Jefferson (rough copy)."}

Belvoir 8th Sept 18[06]
Sir

The claims on my time ~~ever since January~~ [*February?*] ~~been so pressing the failure of there~~ *(illegible)* ~~indebted for~~ ever since I was introduced by Mr Walker in this intercourse which I have had the honor to hold with you that I cannot without noting enter further, delay commending to you the result of the conversation with Mr W[alker] since my return from Monticello. I stated to him fully & distinctly what had passed at our last interview. I repeated my conviction of your sincere desire to do every thing which truth & honor would warrant to give peace to his mind & service to the cause of his disquietude. At the same time I told him that solicitous as you was s[ai]d to be you never could assent to any terms in the least derogatory to your own sense of what was due to your station & character. That you considered the planting of any sort of contemp[t], no matter how designated, for the purpose of news paper publication degrading & of course inadvisable. He has after much pressure suggested a course, which is free at present from the objection stated by you ~~& may~~ always ~~a preference.~~

He wishes a written paper from you going only to his, & his Ladys entire exculpation, without the tincture of any inculpation of yourself.[19]

This paper the signature he desires should be acknowledged before any two of your friends known in the world to prevent at any future day the insinuation of its being a forgery.

This document he engages to hold upon the express condition of using it, instead of the correspondence in his possession, whenever self defence shall require it & upon the condition that after your retirement from public life he may publish the same should a resurrection of the charges ag[ain]st him & his lady demand it in his judgement.

If sir this proposition meets your approbation I will do myself the pleasure to wait upon you when ever you shall desire it for the purpose of concluding (I trust for ever) a correspondence unpleasant altho intended to produce a desircable end.

The servant will reach Monticello late in the evening & has orders to wait till the morning that you may have the requisite leisure ~~which~~ to make up your decision.

{~~illegible~~} I must add that in my report to Mr W[alker] I dwelt on your declaration of the ~~the~~ happy moment you enjoyed after our conference in march ~~first~~ not only from your expectation that a controversy most painful to you was closed, but also from a consequential hope, that social intercourse would be resumed between two friends from earliest youth I was truely gratified in finding kindred feelings in his breast.

{Not signed}

{The following fragment, written upside down at bottom of the final page of Lee's letter, may have been intended as an insertion at note 19 above.}

stigmatizing by your marked ~~animm~~ reprobation the malignant calamnys levelled ag[ain]st the honor of his name heretofore so {*illegible*} profusely averred & which may be repeated whether proceedings from indiscreet friends or venomous foes.

William Armistead Burwell, "Narrative," ca. 1808, TJP[20]

You no doubt recollect the celebrated letter of Tom Turner, written to some man in Boston & publish'd in the Repertory. It was received with great interest by the fed[era]l Editors & became the text for the most vile, slanders, they triumphed with indecent joy at the exposure of Mr. Jefferson by a man who had affixed his name, & pledged himself for the truth of the allegations; the friends of Mr J[efferson] naturally felt hurt at the use made of that letter. . . . Mr Turner's letter surprised me very much[.] I had long known him, had passed much time in his company without discovering those traits of party malignity in his temper evinced in his letter, & am convinced he was deceived, & stimulated by his connections with the Walker family (John Walker) to asperse a man who never injur[e]d him; & of whose moral conduct he could not impartially judge. The affair of Mr. J[efferson] & Mrs Walker, formed a part of T[urne]rs letter, & I have good reason to believe was grossly misrepresented. Mr. J[efferson] declared to me, it was without premeditation & produced by an accidental event.

It however gave him great pain, & it was only by his knowledge that Mrs. W[alker] herself countenanced the publication in the N[ew-England] P[alladium][21] his sensibility ceases—he told me the affair had long been known & that Hamilton about the time he was attacked for his connection with Mrs Reynolds had threatened him with a public disclosure. The noise this transaction has made, the purpose for which it was unfolded, & the uneasiness it gave Mr. W[alker] and J[efferson] were attributable to the pretended friends of Mr W[alker] & the irreconciliable enemies of Mr J[efferson]. . . . It was said that in addition to the wickedness of violating the confidence reposed in him by his friend Mr. W[alker] & the obligations he ow'd to Mr W[alker's] father (his guardian) he had fabricated a falsehood to explain the cause of their rupture, & charged Mr. W[alker] with an attempt to defraud him in some money transactions. Mr W[illia]m Skipwith a relative of the family . . . explained that matter to me. When Mr. J[efferson] returned from France, he was asked by his Daughters why he ceased to visit at Dr. J[ohn] Walkers, knowing [how] intimate they were before he went to F[rance]—to quiet them *{i.e., Jefferson's daughters}* he said some difference had arisen about money matters; they were afterwards interrogated by Mr. D[avid] M[eade] R[andolph] & incautiously assign[e]d that as the reason, thus an explanation intended to preserve the happiness & tranquility of his daughters, & *never* given elsewhere was made the basis of that charge against him & handled and attributed to the iniquity of his heart. I have since received a confirmation of this statement from Skipwith which convinces me of its truth.

APPENDIX B

CHILDREN BORN TO MARTHA WAYLES SKELTON JEFFERSON AND TO SALLY HEMINGS

Martha Wayles was born in October 1748 and married Bathurst Skelton on November 20, 1766, at the age of eighteen.

1. Their son, John Skelton, was born on November 7, 1767.
Bathurst Skelton died September 30, 1768.
John Skelton died on June 10, 1771.

Martha Wayles Skelton married Thomas Jefferson at the Forest on January 1, 1772, at the age of twenty-three.

1. Martha Jefferson was born on September 27, 1772, and died at age sixty-four in 1836.

Computed date of conception:	January 5, 1772
Birth to next conception:	9.6 months

2. Jane Randolph Jefferson was born on April 3, 1774, and died seventeen months later in September 1775.
Thomas and Martha Wayles Jefferson were at the Forest from June 11 to July 10, 1773.

Computed date of conception:	July 11, 1773
Interval since previous birth:	9.6 months
Birth to next conception:	29.5 months

3. An unnamed son was born on May 28, 1777, and survived only two weeks.
Jefferson was in Philadelphia from May 14 to September 3, 1776; Martha Wayles Jefferson joined him early in August.

Computed date of conception:	September 4, 1776
Interval since previous birth:	29.5 months
Birth to next conception:	5.5 months

4. Mary Jefferson was born on August 1, 1778, and died at age twenty-six on April 17, 1804; her children both died without issue.
Thomas and Martha Wayles Jefferson were in Williamsburg for the General Assembly session from October 20, 1777, to January 25, 1778.

Computed date of conception: November 8, 1777

Interval since previous birth: 5.5 months

Birth to next conception: 19.5 months

5. The first Lucy Elizabeth Jefferson was born on November 30, 1780, and died five months later on April 15, 1781.

Thomas and Martha Wayles Jefferson were at Monticello from late February 1780 to March 14, 1780.

Computed date of conception: March 9, 1780

Interval since previous birth: 19.5 months

Birth to next conception: 8.6 months

6. The second Lucy Elizabeth Jefferson was born on May 8, 1782, and died of whooping cough at age two and a half around October 13, 1784.

Thomas and Martha Wayles Jefferson left Monticello on June 4, 1781, and were together at Poplar Forest until August 15, 1781.

Computed date of conception: August 14, 1781

Interval since previous birth: 8.6 months

Martha Wayles Skelton Jefferson died on September 6, 1782, 122 days after her last birth. The mean interval between these six births and five subsequent conceptions is 13.9 months.

Sally Hemings was born in 1773 and turned twenty-one in 1794.

1. Harriet Hemings was born on October 5, 1795; she died in December 1797.

Jefferson was at Monticello from January 16, 1794, to February 20, 1797.

Computed date of conception: January 11, 1795

Birth to next conception: 20.4 months

2. Beverley Hemings was born on April 1, 1798.

Jefferson was at Monticello from July 11 to December 4, 1797.

Computed date of conception: July 8, 1797

Interval since previous birth: 20.4 months

Birth to next conception: 11.3 months

3. A daughter was born to Sally Hemings early in December 1799; the child died in infancy.

Jefferson was at Monticello from March 8 to December 21, 1799.

Computed date of conception: early March 1799

Interval since previous birth: 11.3 months

Birth to next conception: 8.5 months

4. The second Harriet Hemings was born in May 1801.

Jefferson was at Monticello from May 29 through November 24, 1800.

Computed date of conception: August 1800

Interval since previous birth: 8.5 months

Birth to next conception: 44.3 months

5. Madison Hemings was born on January 19, 1805.

Jefferson was at Monticello from April 5 to May 11, 1804.

Computed date of conception: April 27, 1804

Interval since previous birth: 44.3 months

Birth to next conception: 31.7 months

6. Eston Hemings was born on May 21, 1808.

Jefferson was at Monticello from August 5 to October 1, 1807.

Computed date of conception:	August 28, 1807
Interval since previous birth:	31.7 months

Thomas Jefferson died in 1826. Sally Hemings died in 1835. The mean interval between these six births and five subsequent conceptions is 17.7 months.

Sources: Malone, *Jefferson the Virginian,* 434; *Memorandum Books,* xlvi–liii, 422, 513, 912, 966, 999, 1020; Lucia Stanton, *Free Some Day: The African-American Families of Monticello* (Charlottesville, 2000); Fraser D. Neiman, "Coincidence or Causal Connection? The Relationship Between Thomas Jefferson's Visits to Monticello and Sally Hemings's Conceptions," *WMQ,* 3d ser., 57 (2000): 205.

Computed dates of conception are based on an average human gestation period of 266 days. Conception dates for Martha Wayles Skelton Jefferson were calculated by the same formula—"subtracting 267 days from each of the . . . birthdays"—that Fraser D. Neiman used in his examination of Sally Hemings's reproductive history. Reliable statistics for premature births are not available for the early republic, but in the United States in 2002, 10.4 percent of infants, 58.2 percent of twins, and 92.4 percent of triplets were born less than thirty-seven weeks (259 days) after conception (National Center for Health Statistics, *National Vital Statistics Reports* 52 [17 December 2003]).

APPENDIX C

DIALOGUE BETWEEN
MY HEAD AND MY HEART,
THOMAS JEFFERSON TO MARIA COSWAY,
OCTOBER 12, 1786

Thirty years ago, when I first examined Jefferson's encounter with Maria Cosway for a magazine article, their flirtation in Paris seemed to be intensely romantic.[1] The primary sources then available (as well as the scholarship I relied upon) suggested that their many weeks together initiated an emotional love affair, if not a physical one, that continued by correspondence for the rest of their lives. The assessment now presented in chapter 5 is quite different, however, because key details about chronology forced me to reconsider everything I thought I knew about the romantic myth told by many of Jefferson's biographers during the past half century.

My friend John P. Kaminski recently summarized three prevalent interpretations of the Jefferson-Cosway relationship in the introduction to his splendid edition of Jefferson and Cosway's correspondence from 1786 to 1790. "Jefferson's relationship with Cosway was unique in his life," Kaminski wrote, "and historians have long disagreed about it. Some have attacked Cosway as a spoiled, pampered coquette who added Jefferson to her salon of admirers. Others have said it was a romantic friendship filled with flirtation but no physical consummation."[2] Kaminski continued, "And yet others have sensed a passion between the two that never appeared between Jefferson and any other woman"—except presumably his late wife. "Given this passion," Kaminski concluded,

> along with Maria's unhappy marriage and Jefferson's loneliness as a widower, it would not seem unlikely that they consummated their love. The sexual mores of late-eighteenth-century France would have been less critical of their relationship than would those of later generations. Whatever the case, these letters are evidence of a deep and passionate love between Thomas and Maria.[3]

Well put. But ultimately this third alternative depends on the key phrase "given this passion"—and the argument for "a deep and passionate love" assumes that they spent more time together in Paris than in fact they did.[4] Jefferson and Mrs. Cosway did not spend seven, or six, or even four weeks in each other's company in 1786. As described in chapter 5, their excursions occurred on only ten or twelve days during a period of exactly two weeks, with two more outings on October 4 and 6. The fundamental premise of the romantic myth—"given the passion"—rests on errors of chronology made by two influential scholars who published modern editions of the Head and Heart dialogue in 1945 and 1954, soon after the University of Virginia acquired Jefferson's letterpress copy along with two dozen related letters.

The Head and Heart dialogue had been reprinted several times since its first publication in 1828,[5] but the honor of publishing an authoritative text from the newly acquired letterpress manuscript fell to Helen Duprey Bullock, of the Library of Congress and the University of Virginia, who had participated in the detective work that led to its discovery and acquisition. Working from then-available sources (chiefly the newly acquired manuscripts, John Trumbull's memoirs, and Jefferson's then unpublished account books), Bullock presented the dialogue as the centerpiece of her charming book entitled *My Head and My Heart*. She also stated, first, that Jefferson met Maria Cosway in mid-August 1786 and, second, that he injured his wrist on September 4. Neither date proved correct, but Bullock's scholarship was long regarded as definitive. Anyone who consulted her book "knew" that Jefferson and Maria Cosway spent at least six weeks together before she left for London with her husband early in October (a date firmly established by the dialogue itself). Biographer Marie Kimball also relied upon Bullock's chronology for her treatment of the Jefferson-Cosway relationship, published in 1950.[6]

In 1954, nine years after Helen Bullock published *My Head and My Heart*, editor Julian P. Boyd published the dialogue in volume 10 of the comprehensive modern edition of *The Papers of Thomas Jefferson* that he had founded. Although influenced by Bullock's scholarship as well as Kimball's biography, Boyd's annotation suggested that Jefferson had met the Cosways even earlier, in August 1786, because "a large packet of letters from America" had arrived on August 1. Boyd and his team of editors corrected Bullock's account of the dislocation of Jefferson's wrist by determining the exact date of the injury, September 18 (which had the effect of adding two weeks to Bullock's chronology). The editorial team's inference about the day on which Jefferson first met the Cosways, however, ignored Jefferson's own frank admission, in the text of the dialogue itself, that the excuse of urgent dispatches was a falsehood. Insofar as Boyd's documentary edition supplanted Bullock's book as the preferred text for scholars interested in the Head and Heart dialogue, Boyd's notes were also responsible for spreading the mistaken impression that Jefferson and Maria Cosway had met at the very beginning of August and spent seven weeks together until he injured his wrist in mid-September 1786.[7]

With the publication in 1995 of Jefferson's detailed account books, however, it became possible to determine with certainty that Jefferson first met the

Cosways at the Halle au Blé on Sunday, September 3, 1786. Jefferson's recollection of the events of the day ("after dinner to St. Cloud [and] from St. Cloud to Ruggieri's") precisely match his account-book entry for September 3: "P[ai]d. seeing gallery St. Cloud 6 f[rancs]."[8] Jefferson dislocated his wrist two weeks after he had met the Cosways. During the first two weeks of their acquaintance, as we have seen, Jefferson saw the Cosways on ten or twelve days. And he saw them again only on October 4 and 6 as they were departing for London. In all, between September 3 and October 6, 1786, Jefferson and Mrs. Cosway spent "half days, and whole days together," as he later complained, during a sustained period of only two weeks. These outings had generally been in the company of John Trumbull, William Short, Maria's husband, or the author and antiquarian Pierre-François Hugues d'Hancarville, yet another of Maria's admirers.[9]

Maria Cosway's copy of the Head and Heart dialogue, which John Trumbull delivered to her, is not extant. We know that she showed it to her acquaintances in London, one of whom described it in a letter to Jefferson as "your Excellencies Verses."[10] Jefferson's retained letterpress copy, from which this and all other transcriptions of the Head and Heart dialogue have been made, is in the Jefferson Papers at the Library of Congress. The first page, of twelve, is reproduced on page 205. The editorial policy for this transcription is stated on page xiii.

My Dear Madam,   Paris Octob.12.1786.
Having performed the last sad office of handing you into your carriage at the Pavillon de St. Denis, and seen the wheels get actually into motion, I turned on my heel & walked, more dead than alive, to the opposite door, where my own was awaiting me. Mr. Danquerville was missing. he was sought for, found, & dragged down stairs. We were crammed into the carriage, like recruits for the Bastille, & not having soul enough to give orders to the coachman, he presumed Paris our destination, & drove off. after a considerable interval, silence was broke with a "je suis vraiment affligh du depart de ces bons gens." this was the signal for a mutual confession of distress. we began immediately to talk of mr. and mrs. Cosway, of their goodness, their talents, their amiability; & tho we spoke of nothing else, we seemed hardly to have entered into matter when the coachman announced the rue St. Denis, & that we were opposite mr. Danquerville's. he insisted on descending there & traversing a short passage to his lodgings. I was carried home.[11] Seated by my fire side, solitary & sad, the following dialogue took place between my Head & my Heart.

HEAD. Well, friend, you seem to be in a pretty trim.
HEART. I am indeed the most wretched of all earthly beings. overwhelmed with grief, every fibre of my frame distended beyond it's

Jefferson retained a letterpress copy of his twelve-page October 12, 1786, Head and Heart letter to Maria Cosway.

Courtesy of the Library of Congress, Manuscript Division.

natural powers to bear, I would willingly meet whatever catastrophe should leave me no more to feel or to fear.

HEAD. These are the eternal consequences of your warmth & precipitation. this is one of the scrapes into which you are ever leading us. you confess your follies indeed: but still you hug & cherish them. & no reformation can be hoped, where there is no repentance.

{Page two}

HEART. Oh, my friend! this is no moment to upbraid my foibles. I am rent into fragments by the force of my grief! if you have any balm, pour it into my wounds. if none, do not harrow them by new torments. spare me in this awful moment! at any other I will attend with patience to your admonitions.

HEAD. On the contrary I never found that the moment of triumph with you was the moment of attention to my admonitions. while suffering under your follies you may perhaps be made sensible of them, but, the paroxysm over, you fancy it can never return. harsh therefore as the medicine may be, it is my office to administer it. You will be pleased to remember that when our friend Trumbull used to be telling us of the merits & talents of these good people, I never ceased whispering to you that we had no occasion for new acquaintance: that the greater their merits & talents, the more dangerous their friendship to our tranquillity, because the regret at parting would be greater.

HEART. Accordingly, Sir, this acquaintance was not the consequence of my doings. it was one of your projects which threw us in the way of it. It was you, remember, & not I, who desired the meeting at Legrand & Molinos. I never trouble myself with domes[12] nor arches. The Halle aux bleds might have rotted down before I should have gone to see it. but you, forsooth, who are eternally getting us to sleep with your diagrams & crotchets, must go & examine this wonderful piece of architecture. and when you had seen it, oh! it was the most superb thing on earth! what you had seen there was worth all you had yet seen in Paris! I thought so too. but I meant it of the lady & gentleman to whom we had been presented, & not of a parcel of sticks & chips put together in pens. you then, Sir, & not I, have been the cause of the present distress.

{Page three}

HEAD. It would have been happy for you if my diagrams & crotchets had gotten you to sleep on that day, as you are pleased to say they eternally do. my visit to Legrand & Molinos had public utility for it's object. a market is to be built in Richmond. what a commodious plan is that of Legrand & Molinos: especially if we put on it the noble dome of the Halle aux bleds. if such a bridge as they shewed us can be thrown across the Schuylkill at Philadelphia, the floating bridges taken up & the navigation of that river opened, what a copious resource will be added, of wood & provisions, to warm & feed the poor of that city while I was occupied with these objects, you were dilating with your new acquaintances, & contriving how to prevent a separation from them. every soul of you had an engagement for the day. yet all these were to be sacrificed, that you might dine together. lying messengers were to be despatched into every quarter of the city with apologies for your breach of engagement. you particularly had the effrontery to send word to the Dutchess Danville that, in the moment we were setting out to dine with her, dispatches came to hand which required immediate attention. you wanted me to invent a more ingenious excuse; but I knew you were getting into a scrape, & I would have nothing to do with it. well, after dinner to St. Cloud, from St. Cloud to Ruggieri's, from Ruggieri to Krumfoltz, & if the day had been as long as a Lapland summer day, you would still have contrived means, among you, to have filled it.

HEART. Oh! my dear friend, how you have revived me by recalling to my mind the transactions of that day! how well I remember them all, & that when I came home at night & looked back to the morning, it seemed to have been a month agone. go on then, like a kind comforter[13] & paint to me the day we went to St. Germains. how beautiful was every object! The Port de Reuilly, the hills along the Seine, the rainbows of the machine of Marly, the terrace of St. Germains, the chateaux, the

{Page four}

gardens, the statues of Marly, the pavillon of Lucienne. recollect too Madrid, Bagatelle, the King's garden, the Dessert. how grand the idea excited by the remains of such a column! the spiral staircase too was beautiful. every moment was filled with something agreeable. the wheels of time moved on with a rapidity of which those of our carriage gave but a faint idea. and yet in the evening when one took a retrospect of the day, what a mass of happiness had we travelled over! retrace all those scenes to me, my good companion, & I will forgive the unkindness with which you were chiding me. the day we went to St. Germains was a little[14] too warm, I think, was it not?

HEAD. Thou art the most incorrigible of all the beings that ever sinned! I reminded you of the follies of the first day, intending to deduce from thence some useful lessons for you. but instead of listening to these, you kindle at the recollection, you retrace the whole series with a fondness which shews you want nothing but the opportunity to act it over again. I often told you during it's course that you were imprudently engaging your affections under circumstances that must cost you a great deal of pain: that the persons indeed were of the greatest merit, possessing good sense, good humour, honest hearts, honest manners, & eminence in a lovely art: that the lady had moreover qualities & accomplishments, belonging to her sex, which might form a chapter apart for her: such as music, modesty, beauty, & that softness of disposition which is the ornament of her sex & charm of ours. but that all these considerations would increase the pang of separation: that their stay here was to be short: that you rack our whole system when you are parted from those you love, complaining that such a separation is worse than death, inasmuch as this ends our sufferings, whereas that only begins them: & that the separation would in this instance be the more severe as you would probably never see them again.

HEART. But they told me they would come back again the next year.

HEAD. But in the meantime see what you suffer: & their return too depends on so many circumstances that if you had a grain of prudence you would not count upon it. upon the whole it is improbable & therefore

{Page five}

you should abandon the idea of ever seeing them again.

HEART. May heaven abandon me if I do!

HEAD. Very well. suppose then they come back—they are to stay two months, & when these are expired, what is to follow? perhaps you flatter yourself they may come to America?

HEART. God only knows what is to happen. I see nothing impossible in that supposition. and I see things wonderfully contrived sometimes to make us happy. where could they find such objects as in America for the exercise of their enchanting art? especially the lady, who paints landscapes so inimitably. she wants only subjects worthy of immortality to render her pencil immortal. the Falling spring, the Cascade of Niagara, the Passage of the Potowmac thro the Blue mountains, the Natural bridge. it is worth a voiage across the Atlantic to see these objects: much more to paint, and make them, & thereby ourselves, known to all ages. and our own dear Monticello, where has Nature spread so rich a mantle under the eye? mountains, forests, rocks, rivers. with what majesty do we there ride above the storms! how sublime to look down into the workhouse of nature, to see her clouds, hail, snow, rain, thunder, all fabricated at our feet! and the glorious Sun, when rising as if out of a distant water, just gilding the tops of the mountains, & giving life to all nature!—I hope in god no circumstance ~~may~~ may ever make either seek an asylum from grief! with what sincere sympathy I would open every cell of my composition to receive the effusion of their woes! I would pour my tears into their wounds: & if a drop of balm could be found on the top of the Cordilleras, or at the remotest sources of the Missouri, I would go thither myself to seek & to bring it. deeply practised in the school of affliction, the human heart knows no joy which I have not lost, no sorrow of which I have not drank! Fortune can present no grief of unknown form to me! who then can so softly bind up the wound of another as he who has felt the same wound himself? but Heaven forbid they should ever know a sorrow!—let us turn over another leaf, for this has distracted me.

{Page six}

HEAD. Well. let us put this possibility to trial then on another point. when you consider the character which is given of our country by the lying newspapers of London, & their credulous copyers in other countries; when you reflect that all Europe is made to believe we are a lawless banditti, in a state of absolute anarchy, cutting one another's throats, & plundering without distinction, how can you expect that any reasonable creature would venture among us?

HEART. But you & I know that all this is false: that there is not a country on earth where there is greater tranquillity, where the laws are milder, or better obeyed: where every one is more attentive to his own business, or meddles less with that of others: where strangers are better received, more hospitably treated, & with a more sacred respect.

HEAD. True. you & I know this, but your friends do not know it.

HEART. But they are sensible people who think for themselves. they will ask of impartial foreigners who have been among us, whether they saw or heard on the spot any instances of anarchy. they will judge too that a people occupied as we are in opening rivers, digging navigable canals, making roads, building public schools, establishing academies, erecting busts & statues to our great men, protecting religious freedom, abolishing sanguinary punishments, reforming & improving our laws in general, they will judge I say for themselves whether these are not the occupations of a people at their ease, whether this is not better evidence of our true state than a London newspaper, hired to lie, & from which no truth can ever be extracted but by reversing everything it says.

HEAD. I did not begin this lecture my friend with a view to learn from you what America is doing. let us return then to our point. I wished to make you sensible how imprudent it is to place your affections, without reserve, on objects you must so soon lose, & whose loss when it

{Page seven}

comes must cost you such severe pangs. remember the last night. you knew your friends were to leave Paris to-day. this was enough to throw you into agonies. all night you tossed us from one side of the bed to the other. no sleep, no rest. the poor crippled wrist too, never left one moment in the same position, now up, now down, now here, now there; was it to be wondered at if it's pains returned? the Surgeon then was to be called, & to be rated as an ignoramus because he could not divine the cause of this extraordinary change.—In fine, my friend, you must mend your manners. this is not a world to live at random in as you do. to avoid those eternal distresses, to which you are forever exposing us, you must learn to look forward before you take a step which may interest our peace. everything in this world is matter of calculation. advance then with caution, the balance in your hand. put into one scale the pleasures which any object may offer; but put fairly into the other the pains which are to follow, & see which preponderates. the making an acquaintance is not a matter of indifference. when a new one is proposed to you, view it all round. consider what advantages it presents, & to what inconveniences it may expose you. do not bite at the bait of pleasure till you know there is no hook beneath it. the art of life is the art of avoiding pain: & he is the best pilot who steers clearest of the rocks & shoals with which it is beset. pleasure is always before us; but misfortune is at our side: while running after that, this arrests us. the most effectual means of being secure against pain is to retire within ourselves, & to suffice for our own happiness. those, which depend on ourselves, are the only pleasures a wise man will count on: for nothing is ours which another may deprive us of. hence the inestimable value of intellectual pleasures. ever in our power, always leading us to something new, never cloying, we ride ~~placid,~~ serene & sublime, above the concerns of this mortal world, contemplating truth & nature, matter & motion, the laws which bind up their existence, & that eternal

{Page eight}

being who made & bound them up by these laws. let this be our employ. leave the bustle & tumult of society to those who have not talents to occupy themselves without them. friendship is but another name for an alliance with the follies & the misfortunes of others. our own share of miseries is sufficient: why enter then as volunteers into those of another? is there so little gall poured into our own cup that we must needs help to drink that of our neighbor? a friend dies or leaves us: we feel as if a limb was cut off. he is sick: we must watch over him, & participate of his pains. his fortune is shipwrecked; ours must be laid under contribution. he loses a child, a parent or a partner: we must mourn the loss as if it was our own.

HEART. And what more sublime delight than to mingle tears with one whom the hand of heaven hath smitten! to watch over the bed of sickness, & to beguile it's tedious & it's painful moments! to share our bread with one to whom misfortune has left none! this world abounds indeed with misery: to lighten it's burthen we must divide it with one another. but let us now try the virtues of your mathematical balance, & as you have put into one scale the burthens of friendship, let me put it's comforts into the other. when languishing then under disease, how grateful is the solace of our friends! how are we penetrated with their assiduities & attentions! how much are we supported by their encouragements & kind offices! when Heaven has taken from us some object of our love, how sweet is it to have a bosom whereon to recline our heads, & into which we may pour the torrent of our tears! grief, with such a comfort, is almost a luxury! in a life where we are perpetually exposed to want & accident, yours is a wonderful proposition, to insulate ourselves, to retire from all aid, & to wrap ourselves in the mantle of self-sufficiency! for assuredly nobody will care for him who care for nobody. but friendship is precious, not only in the shade but in

{Page nine}

the sunshine of life: & thanks to a benevolent arrangement of things, the greater part of life is sunshine. I will recur for proof to the days we have lately passed. on these indeed the sun shone brightly! how gay did the face of nature appear! hills, vallies, chateaux, gardens, rivers, every object wore it's liveliest hue! whence did they borrow it? from the presence of our charming companion. They were pleasing, because she seemed pleased. alone, the scene would have been dull & insipid: the participation of it with her gave it relish. let the gloomy Monk, sequestered from the world, seek unsocial pleasures in the bottom of his cell! Let the sublimated philosopher grasp visionary happiness while pursuing phantoms dressed in the garb of truth! their supreme wisdom is supreme folly: & they mistake for happiness the mere absence of pain. had they ever felt the solid pleasure of one generous spasm of the heart, they would exchange for it all the frigid speculations of their lives, which you have been vaunting in such elevated terms. believe me then, my friend, that that is a miserable arithmetic which would estimate friendship at nothing, or at less than nothing. respect for you has induced me to enter into this discussion, & to hear principles uttered which I detest & abjure. respect for myself now obliges me to recall you into the proper limits of your office. when nature assigned us the same habitation, she gave us over it a divided empire. to you she allotted the field of science, to me that of morals. when the circle is to be squared, or the orbit of a comet to be traced; when the arch of greatest strength, or the solid of least resistance is to be investigated, take you the problem: it is yours: nature has given me no cognisance of it. in like manner in denying to you the feelings of sympathy, of benevolence, of gratitude, of justice, of love, of friendship, she has excluded you from their controul. to these she has adapted the mechanism of the heart. morals were too essential to the happiness of man to be risked on the incertain combinations of the head. she laid their foundation therefore in sentiment, not in science. that she gave to all, as necessary to all: this to a few only, as sufficing with a few.

{*Page ten*}

I know indeed that you pretend authority to the sovereign controul of our conduct in all it's parts: & a respect for your grave saws & maxims, a desire to do what is right, has sometimes induced me to conform to your counsels. a few facts however which I can readily recall to your memory, will suffice to prove to you that nature has not organized you for our moral direction. when the poor wearied souldier, whom we overtook at Chickahominy with his pack on his back, begged us to let him get up behind our chariot, you began to calculate that the road was full of souldiers, & that if all should be taken up our horses would fail in their journey. we drove on therefore. but soon becoming sensible you had made me do wrong, that tho we cannot relieve all the distressed we should relieve as many as we can, I turned about to take up the souldier; but he had entered a bye path, & was no more to be found: & from that moment to this I could never find him out to ask his forgiveness. Again, when the poor woman came to ask a charity in Philadelphia, you whispered that she looked like a drunkard, & that half a dollar was enough to give her for the ale-house. those who want the dispositions to give, easily find reasons why they ought not to give. when I sought her out afterwards, & did what I should have done at first, you know that she employed the money immediately towards placing her child at school. If our country, when pressed with wrongs at the point of the bayonet, had been governed by it's heads instead of it's hearts, where should we have been now? hanging on a gallows as high as Haman's. you began to calculate & to compare wealth and numbers: we threw up a few pulsations of our warmest blood: we supplied enthusiasm against wealth and numbers; we put our existence to the hazard, when the hazard seemed against us, and we saved our country: justifying at the same time the ways of Providence, whose precept is to do always what is right, and leave the issue to him. in short, my friend, as far as my recollection serves me, I do not know that I ever did a good thing on your suggestion, or a dirty one without it. I do for ever then disclaim your interference in my province. fill paper as you please with triangles & squares: try how many ways you can hang & combine them together. I shall never envy nor controul your sublime delights.

{*Page eleven*}

but leave me to decide when & where friendships are to be contracted. You say I contract them at random. so you said the woman at Philadelphia was a drunkard. I receive no one into my esteem till I know they are worthy of it. wealth, title, office, are no recommendations to my friendship. on the contrary great good qualities are requisite to make amends for their having wealth, title, & office. you confess that in the present case I could not have made a worthier choice. you only object that I was so soon to lose them. we are not immortal ourselves, my friend; how can we expect our enjoiments to be so? we have no rose without its thorn; no pleasure without alloy. it is the law of our existence; & we must acquiesce. it is the condition annexed to all our pleasures, not by us who receive, but by him who gives them. true, this condition is pressing cruelly on me at this moment. I feel more fit for death than life. but when I look back on the pleasures of which it is the consequence, I am conscious they were worth the price I am paying. notwithstanding your endeavours too to damp my hopes, I comfort myself with expectations of their promised return. hope is sweeter than despair and they were too good to mean to deceive me. in the summer, said the gentleman; but in the spring, said the lady: & I should love her forever, were it only for that! know then, my friend, that I have taken these good people into my bosom: that I have lodged them in the warmest cell I could find: that I love them, & will continue to love them through life: that if fortune should dispose them on one side the globe, & me on the other, my affections shall pervade it's whole mass to reach them. knowing then my determination, attempt not to disturb it. if you can at any time furnish matter for their amusement, it will be the office of a good neighbor to do it. I will in like manner seize any occasion which may offer to do the like good turn for you with Condorcet, Rittenhouse, Madison, La Cretelle, or any other of those worthy sons of science whom you so justly prize.

I thought this a favorable proposition whereon to rest the issue of the dialogue. so I put an end to it by calling for my night-cap. Methinks I hear you wish to heaven I had called a little sooner, & so spared you the ennui of such a tedious sermon. I did not interrupt them sooner because I was in a mood for hearing sermons. you too were the subject; & on such a thesis I never think the theme long; not even if I am to write it,

[*Page twelve*]

and that slowly & awkwardly, as now, with the left hand. but that you may not be discouraged from a correspondence which begins so formidably, I will promise you on my honour that my future letters shall be of a reasonable length. I will even agree to express but half my esteem for you, for fear of cloying you with too full a dose. but, on your part, no curtailing. if your letters are as long as the bible, they will appear short to me. only let them be brim full of affection. I shall read them with the dispositions with which Arlequin in les deux billets spelt the words "je t'aime" and wished that the whole alphabet had entered into their composition.[15] We have had incessant rains since your departure. these make me fear for your health, as well as that you have had an uncomfortable journey. the same cause has prevented me from being able to give you any account of your friends here. this voiage to Fontainbleau will probably send the Count de Moustier & the Marquise de Brehan to America. Danquerville promised to visit me, but has not done it as yet. De la Tude comes sometimes to take family soup with me, & entertains me with anecdotes of his five & thirty years imprisonment. ~~you know that this was imposed~~ how fertile is the mind of man which can make the Bastille & Dungeon of Vincennes yeild interesting anecdotes. you know this was for making four verses on Mme de Pompadour. but I think you told me you did not know the verses. they were these. Sans esprit, sans sentiment, Sans etre belle, ni neuve, En France on peut avoir la premier ament: Pompadour en es l'epreuve.[16] I have read the memoir of his three escapes. As to myself my health is good, except my wrist which mends slowly, & my mind which mends not at all, but broods constantly over your departure. the lateness of the season obliges me to decline my journey into the South of France. present me in the most friendly terms to mr. Cosway, & receive me into your own recollection with a partiality & a warmth, proportioned, not to my own poor merit, but to the sentiments of sincere affection & esteem with which I have the honour to be, my dear Madam, your most obedient humble servant.

Th. Jefferson

A NOTE ON SOURCES

During the course of my research, in addition to traditional research through books and manuscripts at many archives and libraries, I frequently compared published texts of Jefferson's letters and other documents with the original manuscripts accessible online. Rather than citing cumbersome (and mutable) URLs, my footnotes provide the basic information (author, title, publication date, repository) with which readers using the major search engines can access primary sources online through the finding aids at the following websites:

American Memory (Library of Congress)
    George Washington Papers
    Thomas Jefferson Papers
Family Letters Project (Papers of Thomas Jefferson: Retirement Series, Monticello)
John D. Rockefeller Jr. Library (Colonial Williamsburg Foundation)
    Virginia Gazette and index for 1736–80
Thomas Jefferson Digital Archive (University of Virginia Library Electronic Text Center)
Thomas Jefferson: A Comprehensive, Annotated Bibliography of Writings About Him, 1826–1997, ed. Frank Shuffelton (University of Virginia Library Electronic Text Center)
Virginia Heritage: Guides to Manuscript and Archival Collections in Virginia

In addition, for access to a variety of printed sources I relied on several subscription-based resources at major research libraries:

America's Historical Newspapers, 1690–1922
American Periodicals Series Online, 1740–1900

Eighteenth Century Collections Online
JSTOR
Project MUSE

Finally, I gratefully acknowledge my frequent use of the online catalogues of the Library of Virginia, the University of Virginia Library, the Virginia Historical Society, and the Library of Congress.

The following abbreviations are used in the notes:

ANB	*American National Biography.*
Bear, *Monticello*	James A. Bear, Jr. *Jefferson at Monticello.* Charlottesville, 1967.
Cappon, *Letters*	Lester J. Cappon, ed. *The Adams-Jefferson Letters.* Chapel Hill, 1959.
CW	John D. Rockefeller Jr. Library, Colonial Williamsburg Foundation.
Domestic Life	Sarah N. Randolph. *The Domestic Life of Thomas Jefferson, Compiled from Family Letters and Reminiscences by His Great-Granddaughter.* 1871. Reprint, Charlottesville, 1985.
DVB	*Dictionary of Virginia Biography.* Richmond, 1988–. 3 vols. to date.
Family Letters	Edwin M. Betts and James A. Bear, Jr., eds. *Family Letters of Thomas Jefferson.* Charlottesville, 1966.
Farm Book	Edwin Morris Betts, ed. *Thomas Jefferson's Farm Book.* 1953. Reprint, Charlottesville, 1976.
Ford, *Writings*	Paul Leicester Ford, ed. *The Writings of Thomas Jefferson.* New York, 1904–05.
Garden Book	Edwin M. Betts, ed. *Thomas Jefferson's Garden Book, 1766–1824.* Philadelphia, 1985.
ICJS	Robert H. Smith International Center for Jefferson Studies. Thomas Jefferson Memorial Foundation. Charlottesville.
Jefferson Papers	Julian P. Boyd et al., eds. *Papers of Thomas Jefferson.* Princeton, 1950–. 34 vols. to date.

Jefferson Papers: Retirement Series	J. Jefferson Looney et al., eds. *Papers of Thomas Jefferson: Retirement Series.* Charlottesville, 2004–. 3 vols. to date.
Kaminski, *Jefferson in Love*	John P. Kaminski, ed. *Jefferson in Love: The Love Letters Between Thomas Jefferson and Maria Cosway.* Madison, Wis., 1999.
LVA	Library of Virginia, Richmond.
Malone, *Jefferson the Virginian*	Dumas Malone. *Jefferson the Virginian.* Vol. 1 of *Jefferson and His Time.* Boston, 1948.
Malone, *Rights of Man*	Dumas Malone. *Jefferson and the Rights of Man.* Vol. 2 of *Jefferson and His Time.* Boston, 1951.
Malone, *Ordeal of Liberty*	Dumas Malone. *Jefferson and the Ordeal of Liberty.* Vol. 3 of *Jefferson and His Time.* Boston, 1962.
Malone, *First Term*	Dumas Malone. *Jefferson the President: First Term, 1801–1805.* Vol. 4 of *Jefferson and His Time.* Boston, 1970.
Malone, *Second Term*	Dumas Malone. *Jefferson the President: Second Term, 1805–1809.* Vol. 5 of *Jefferson and His Time.* Boston, 1974.
Malone, *Sage of Monticello*	Dumas Malone. *The Sage of Monticello.* Vol. 6 of *Jefferson and His Time.* Boston, 1981.
Memorandum Books	James A. Bear, Jr., and Lucia C. Stanton, eds. *Jefferson's Memorandum Books: Accounts, with Legal Records and Miscellany, 1767–1826.* Princeton, 1997.
Notes	Thomas Jefferson. *Notes on the State of Virginia.* Ed. William Peden. Chapel Hill, 1955.
Peterson, *Writings*	Thomas Jefferson. *Thomas Jefferson: Writings.* Ed. Merrill D. Peterson. New York , 1984.
Randall, *Life of Thomas Jefferson*	Henry S. Randall. *The Life of Thomas Jefferson.* 3 vols. New York, 1858.
TJP	Thomas Jefferson Papers. Series 1, General Correspondence, 1651–1827. Library of Congress, Washington, D.C.
UVA	University of Virginia Library, Charlottesville.

Virginia Guide	*Virginia: A Guide to the Old Dominion Compiled by Workers of the Writers' Program of the Works Projects Administration in the State of Virginia.* New York, 1940. 2d ed., Richmond, 1992.
VMHB	*Virginia Magazine of History and Biography.*
Wilson, *Commonplace Book*	Thomas Jefferson. *Jefferson's Literary Commonplace Book.* Ed. Douglas L. Wilson. *Papers of Thomas Jefferson:* Second Series. Princeton, 1989.
WMQ	*William and Mary Quarterly.*

NOTES

CHAPTER ONE: MR. PETERMAN'S SHIRT

1. J. Peterman Company, *Owner's Manual* (n.p., 1988–); quoted by permission.

2. David Brion Davis, Annette Gordon-Reed, James Horton, and Peter Onuf were the panelists in a session entitled "Thomas Jefferson, Sally Hemings, and the DNA Evidence" at the 1999 annual meeting of the Southern Historical Association in Fort Worth, Texas. The DNA test results were announced in "Jefferson Fathered Slave's Last Child," *Nature* 396 (5 Nov. 1998): 27–28, and Eric S. Lander and Joseph J. Ellis, "Founding Father," *Nature* 396 (5 Nov. 1998): 13–14. Callender's charges first appeared in the *Richmond Recorder* (1 Sept. 1802). See Fawn M. Brodie, *Thomas Jefferson: An Intimate History* (New York, 1974); and Annette Gordon-Reed, *Thomas Jefferson and Sally Hemings: An American Controversy* (Charlottesville, 1997).

3. Winthrop D. Jordan, "Hemings and Jefferson: Redux," in *Sally Hemings and Thomas Jefferson: History, Memory, and Civic Culture,* ed. Jan Ellen Lewis and Peter S. Onuf (Charlottesville, 1999), 51 n. 12.

4. Winthrop D. Jordan, *White over Black: American Attitudes Toward the Negro, 1550–1812* (Chapel Hill, 1968), 462. Kenneth A. Lockridge misquoted Jordan by silently deleting three sentences from Jordan's text, including the words "that female passion must and can only be controlled by marriage." See *On the Sources of Patriarchal Rage: The Commonplace Books of William Byrd and Thomas Jefferson and the Gendering of Power in the Eighteenth Century* (New York, 1992), 71.

5. Jack P. Green, *Landon Carter: An Inquiry into the Personal Values and Social Imperatives of the Eighteenth-Century Virginia Gentry* (Charlottesville, 1967), 20; Gordon S. Wood, *The Creation of the American Republic, 1776–1787* (Chapel Hill, 1969), 69; Philip Greven, *The Protestant Temperament: Patterns of Child-Rearing, Religious Experience, and the Self in Early America* (New

York, 1977), 247–56; Joyce Appleby, "Thomas Jefferson and the Psychology of Democracy," in *The Revolution of 1800: Democracy, Race, and the New Republic,* ed. James Horn, Jan Ellen Lewis, and Peter S. Onuf (Charlottesville, 2002), 155–72; Andrew Burstein, *Jefferson's Secrets: Death and Desire at Monticello* (New York, 2005), 89–91.

6. Malone, *Jefferson the Virginian,* 81; Jefferson to William Fleming, 20 Mar. 1764, Jefferson to John Page, 9 Apr. 1764, *Jefferson Papers* 1:16, 17.

7. Jefferson to John Harvie, 14 Jan. 1760, *Jefferson Papers* 1:3.

8. Ibid. Years later Jefferson described his arrival at the college somewhat differently in his correspondence with Patrick Henry's biographer William Wirt. "In the winter of 1759–1760," Jefferson wrote, "on my way to the college I passed the Christmas holydays at Col. [Nathaniel West] Dandridge's in Hanover, to whom Mr. [Patrick] Henry was a near neighbor. During the festivity of the season, I met him in society every day, and we became well acquainted, altho' I was much his junior, being then but in my seventeenth year, and he a married man." "Mr. Henry," Jefferson continued in a second letter to Wirt, "had a little before broken up his store, or rather it had broken him up, but his misfortunes were not to be traced either in his countenance or conduct." The evidence suggests that Jefferson (who came to William and Mary in March 1760) actually met Henry in the winter of 1760–61, when he was seventeen and after Henry had closed his store in the autumn of 1760. Perhaps they met around Christmas 1760 in Hanover County when Jefferson was en route *back* to the college. Jefferson to Wirt, 12 Apr. 1812 and 5 Aug. 1815, TJP; William Wirt Henry, *Patrick Henry: Life, Correspondence and Speeches* (New York, 1891), 1:18–19; and Robert Douthat Meade, *Patrick Henry: Patriot in the Making* (Philadelphia and New York, 1957), 90–91, 368n.

9. Jefferson to Thomas Jefferson Randolph, 24 Nov. 1808, TJP.

10. The Mattaponi and Pamunkey Rivers flow below the fall line before they merge at West Point to form the York, Virginia's fourth great tidal river.

11. Malone, *Jefferson the Virginian,* 426–27.

12. Jefferson Randolph Anderson, "Tuckahoe and the Tuckahoe Randolphs," *VMHB* 45 (1937): 55–86.

13. Married first to Anne Cary and after her death to Gabriella Harvey, Thomas Mann Randolph of Tuckahoe (1741–93) was the father of fifteen children and gave his name to a son by each wife: Thomas Mann Randolph of Edgehill (1768–1828), who married Jefferson's eldest daughter, Martha, and Thomas Mann Randolph of Tuckahoe (1791–1851). See ibid.

14. Jon Kukla, *Speakers and Clerks of the Virginia House of Burgesses, 1643–1776* (Richmond, 1981), 129–33, 150, 152; Patricia M. Samford et al., *Archaeological Excavations on the Tazewell Hall Property* (Williamsburg, 1986; reissued 2001), 1–7; Jonathan Daniels, *The Randolphs of Virginia* (Garden City, N.Y., 1972), x–xxi; and Anderson, "Tuckahoe Randolphs," 55–86. The Peyton Randolph House is maintained by Colonial Williamsburg. Tazewell Hall stood between the side entrance of the Williamsburg Lodge and the front court-

yard of the Abby Aldrich Rockefeller Folk Art Center. Altered and moved about 1908 when South England Street was extended, the house was sold and dismantled in 1954 and rebuilt in Newport News by the late Lewis A. McMurran, Jr.

15. Jefferson to Thomas Jefferson Randolph, 24 Nov. 1808, TJP.
16. Jefferson to Dabney Carr, 19 Jan. 1816, TJP.
17. Malone, *Jefferson the Virginian*, 42, 85, 160–61, 170–71, 430.
18. Keith Ryan Nyland, "Doctor Thomas Walker (1715–1794): Explorer, Physician, Statesman, Surveyor and Planter of Virginia and Kentucky" (Ph.D. diss., Ohio State University, 1971), 2–32.
19. Lyon G. Tyler, "Education in Colonial Virginia, Part II: Private Schools and Tutors," *WMQ*, 1st ser., 6 (1897): 4.
20. "Berkeley Manuscripts: Copy of Records in an Old Prayer Book," in *WMQ*, 1st ser., 6 (1898): 146; John E. Selby, *ANB*, s.v. "Page, John"; and John Frederick Dorman, ed., *Adventurers of Purse and Person: Virginia 1607–1624/5*, 3d ed. (Richmond, 1987), 409–12.
21. Jane Carson, *James Innes and His Brothers of the F. H. C.* (Williamsburg, 1965) and "The Fat Major of the F. H. C.," in *The Old Dominion: Essays for Thomas Perkins Abernethy*, ed. Darrett B. Rutman (Charlottesville, 1964), 79–95.
22. *Virginia Gazette*, 23 Sept. 1775; and Maud Potter, *The Willises of Virginia*, rev. ed. (Mars Hill, N.C., 1968), 83. Darrett B. Rutman and Anita H. Rutman's classic examinations of parental death and remarriage in colonial Virginia are "'Now Wives and Sons-in-Law': Parental Death in a Seventeenth-Century Virginia County," in *The Chesapeake in the Seventeenth Century: Essays on Anglo-American Society*, ed. Thad W. Tate and David Ammerman (Chapel Hill, 1979), 153–82, and *A Place in Time: Middlesex County, Virginia, 1650–1750: Explicatus* (New York, 1984), 79–81.
23. These and other comments in the Jefferson-Page-Fleming correspondence from 25 Dec. 1762 to 9 Apr. 1764, *Jefferson Papers*, 1:5–18, are discussed in chap. 1.

CHAPTER TWO: REBECCA BURWELL

1. B. Noland Carter, *A Goodly Heritage: A History of the Carter Family in Virginia* (Richmond, 2003), 240; and Andrew Levy, *The First Emancipator: The Forgotten Story of Robert Carter, the Founding Father Who Freed His Slaves* (New York, 2005), 11, 20–21.
2. Jefferson to Page, 20 Jan. 1763, *Jefferson Papers*, 1:8.
3. Ibid., 1:7.
4. Jefferson to Page, 25 Dec. 1762 and 20 Jan. 1763, ibid., 1:5, 7.
5. Using facial hair "as a marker for biological maturation, since it is triggered by testosterone," Herbert Moller suggests that "the onset of beard growth in the past can be used as proxy for unavailable data on sexual maturation and, specifically, on testosterone circulation in the blood." Today "about half of

American boys reach this stage at 16 years of age; the great majority have a shavable beard at 17." Citing examples from antiquity through the eighteenth century that point to twenty-three years as the average age for full beard development, Moller concludes that "in the late eighteenth century beard growth still occurred in general about two to three years later in life than it does today." Herbert Moller, "The Accelerated Development of Youth: Beard Growth as a Biological Marker," *Comparative Studies in Society and History* 29 (1987): 748–62. Jefferson's awkwardness may bring to mind that of younger men today, but I know talented marine lieutenants in their mid-twenties who can emphathize with his experience.

6. Elizabeth Jaquelin Ambler Brent Carrington to Ann Ambler Fisher, 1 Jan. 1807, Ambler Family Papers, CW. For Rebecca Lewis Burwell Ambler's daughters, see Catherine Kerrison, "Elizabeth Jaquelin Ambler Brent Carrington (1765–1842)," *DVB*, and "By the Book: Elizabeth Ambler Brent Carrington and Conduct Literature in Late Eighteenth-Century Virginia," *VMHB* 105 (1997): 27–52.

7. Jefferson to Page, 25 Dec. 1762. The Bollings later moved to Chesterfield County; Julian Boyd's mislocation of Fairfields ignored Dumas Malone's scholarship in *Jefferson the Virginian,* 38–39.

8. Ibid., 4–5. For ease of comprehension, I substituted *rip* where Jefferson wrote *rent* as a noun based on the verb *rend.*

9. Jefferson to John Page, 25 Dec. 1762, 20 Jan. 1763, and 15 July 1763, ibid., 1:5, 7, 11.

10. Jefferson to William Fleming, Oct. 1763, *Jefferson Papers,* 1:12.

11. The earliest known reference to the Apollo Room is "in the 1751 diary of John Blair—just prior to the first indications of a 'Great Room' at Wetherburn's tavern in 1752. It may be that the wing was built shortly after Alexander Finnie's purchase of the property in 1749. Together with construction of the Governor's ballroom wing early in the 1750s, the addition of these public rooms to the town's two largest taverns, marked a mid-century 'building boom' which coincided with the decision to rebuild the burned-out Capitol after its destruction by fire in 1747." See Mark R. Wenger, "The Construction of Raleigh Tavern: A Brief Report on Its Eighteenth-Century Development," Department of Architectural Research, 31 Dec. 1989, CW.

12. Jefferson to John Page, 7 Oct. 1763, *Jefferson Papers,* 1:11–12.

13. Ibid. Jefferson first visited Great Britain in 1784 en route to his diplomatic assignment in Paris, and then he spent two months in England during 1786; George Green Shackelford, *Thomas Jefferson's Travels in Europe, 1784–1789* (Baltimore, 1995), 8, 43–63.

14. Jefferson to John Page, 25 Dec. 1762, 20 Jan. 1763, 15 July 1763, and Jefferson to William Fleming, Oct. 1763, *Jefferson Papers,* 1:6, 7, 10, 11, 13.

15. Jefferson to John Page, 19 Jan. 1764 and 23 Jan. 1764, ibid., 1:13–15.

16. Jefferson to John Page, 15 July 1763, ibid., 1:11.

17. Jefferson to John Page, 19 Jan. 1764, ibid., 1:13–14. Julian Boyd noted that in

addition to disguising Rebecca's nickname in Greek throughout this letter, Jefferson also "attempted, somewhat ineffectually, to reinforce the disguise by using masculine pronouns" in his references to Rebecca Burwell. See ibid., 14n.

18. Jefferson to Page, 23 Jan. 1764.

19. Ibid. (emphases added).

20. In May 1763 Page had urged Jefferson to "go immediately and lay siege in form," a phrase that Jefferson quoted in his reply on 15 July 1763. Page's phrase "siege in form" alluded to a passage (bk. 9, chap. 3) in Henry Fielding's 1751 novel *Amelia*, about a husband who foiled the attempted seduction of his wife.

21. Jefferson to William Fleming, 20 Mar. 1764, *Jefferson Papers*, 1:16.

22. Jefferson to John Page, 9 Apr. 1764, ibid., 1:17.

23. Jefferson acknowledged Page's May 1763 warning in his reply on 15 July and offered both his absence and his impending trip as excuses for Rebecca's attraction to someone else: "The rival you mentioned I know not whether to think formidable or not as there has been so great an opening from him during my absence." Then, evading his own responsibility for the derailed courtship, Jefferson added, "I say 'has been' because I expect there is one no longer since you [i.e., Page] have undertaken to act as my attorney."

24. Elizabeth Jaquelin Ambler to Ann Ambler, Feb. 1785, Ambler Family Papers, CW.

25. Jefferson to Fleming, 20 Mar. 1764.

26. Elizabeth Carrington to Frances Caines, Mar. 1795, Ambler Family Papers, CW. Frances Caines was the niece of wealthy widow Susannah Riddell, who owned the residence now known as the Brush-Everard House on the Palace Green in Williamsburg. Frances Caines lived in Bristol, England. See Kerrison, "By the Book," 37, 39n.

27. "Mr. Jacqlin Ambler is our Treasurer in the room of Colonel Brooke— empty as the strong Box is I am told there was a warm contest for this Office," Edmund Pendleton informed James Madison on 22 Apr. 1782. "Mr. Ambler is well esteemed." See David J. Mays, ed., *Letters and Papers of Edmund Pendleton, 1721–1803* (Charlottesville, 1967), 392.

28. Charles F. Hobson, "Jaquelin Ambler (1742–1798)," *DVB*; and "Inventory of the Estate of Richard Ambler, February 15, 1768," *York County Wills and Inventories* 21, *1760–1771* (original at LVA; transcription at CW), 392–96. "Consumption" was "the hereditary weakness" of the Ambler family. See Elizabeth Carrington to Ann Ambler Fisher, 10 Oct. 1796 and 1 Jan. 1807, Ambler Family Papers, CW. See also n. 49 below.

29. Elizabeth Carrington to Ann Ambler Fisher, undated [1807–9], Ambler Family Papers, CW.

30. Ibid.

31. Stuart E. Brown, Jr., *Burwell: Kith and Kin of the Immigrant Lewis Burwell (1621–1653) and Burwell Virginia Tidewater Plantation Mansions* (Berryville,

Va., 1994), 4–7, 23–28; John L. Blair, "The Rise of the Burwells," *VMHB* 72 (1964): 304–29; William Hamilton Bryson, ed., "A Letter of Lewis Burwell to James Burrough, July 8, 1774," *VMHB* 81 (1973): 405–14; Daphne Gentry, "Carter Burwell (1716–1756)," *DVB;* John L. Blair, "Lewis Burwell (1622–1652)," *DVB;* Christopher F. Lee, "Lewis Burwell (1651–1710)," *DVB;* Alan Simpson, "Lewis Burwell (d. 1743)," *DVB;* Randall Shrock, "Lewis Burwell (1711–1756)," *DVB;* Brent Tarter, "Lewis Burwell (d. 1779)" and "Robert Burwell (1720–1777)," *DVB;* and Richard L. Morton, *Colonial Virginia* (Chapel Hill, 1960), 580, 598.

32. Brown, *Burwell: Kith and Kin,* 23–28; Shrock, "Lewis Burwell."
33. Elizabeth Carrington to Ann Ambler Fisher, 1 Jan. 1807, Ambler Family Papers, CW.
34. Elizabeth Carrington to Ann Ambler Fisher, 1809, Ambler Family Papers, CW.
35. "After asking ourselves who we are, and what we are," Rebecca's eldest daughter wrote, "it naturally arises *from whom* we are." Elizabeth Carrington to Ann Ambler Fisher, 10 Oct. 1796, Ambler Family Papers, CW.
36. Kevin R. Hardwick, "Narratives of Villainy and Virtue: Governor Francis Nicholson and the Character of the Good Ruler in Early Virginia," *Journal of Southern History* 72 (2006): 39–74; Kathleen M. Brown, *Good Wives, Nasty Wenches, and Anxious Patriarchs: Gender, Race, and Power in Colonial Virginia* (Chapel Hill, 1996), 254–58.
37. Byrd quoted in Parke Rouse, Jr., *James Blair of Virginia* (Chapel Hill, 1971), 135.
38. Kathleen M. Brown, "Lucy Burwell (1683–1716)," *DVB;* Fairfax Downey, "The Governor Goes A-Wooing: The Swashbuckling Courtship of Nicholson of Virginia, 1688–1705," *VMHB* 55 (1947): 6–9. The manuscripts documenting Nicholson's pursuit of Lucy Burwell are in the Francis Nicholson Papers, ms. 43.4, CW. Lucy was the fifth child among Lewis Burwell (d. 1710) and Abigail Smith Burwell's six daughters and four sons; Lewis Burwell and his second wife, Martha Lear Cole Burwell, had three more daughters, a son named Nathaniel (d. 1744), and possibly another son who died in infancy. See Brown, *Burwell: Kith and Kin,* 19.
39. Lewis Burwell to Francis Nicholson, 6 Jan. 1703; Polly Cary Legg, "The Governor's 'Extacy of Trouble,'" *WMQ,* 2d ser., 22 (1942): 393–94.
40. Francis Nicholson to Lucy Burwell, 7 Jan. 1703; ibid., 394; and Downey, "Governor Goes A-Wooing," 15.
41. Council of Virginia to the Queen, 20 May 1703, quoted in Rouse, *James Blair,* 136.
42. Samuel Claude McCulloch, "The Fight to Depose Governor Francis Nicholson—James Blair's Affidavit of June 7, 1704," *Journal of Southern History* 12 (1946): 403–22; and Legg, "Governor's 'Extacy,'" 397–98.
43. John Custis to William Byrd II, 30 Mar. 1717, in *Correspondence of the Three William Byrds of Westover, Virginia, 1684–1776,* ed. Marion Tinling (Char-

lottesville, 1977), 297–99. Custis named four gentry women "dead of the measles" along "with many others." Lucy Burwell Berkeley's gravestone at Barn Elms testified to the measure of happiness that her independent choice afforded women in the Burwell family:

> Here lyeth the Body of
> LUCY BERKELEY, who departed this
> Life the 16th day of December, 1716, in the 33rd
> Year of her Age, after she had been
> Married 12 years and 15 Days. She left behind
> her 5 children viz. 2 Boys and 3 Girls.
> I shall not pretend to give her full
> Character; it would take too much room
> for a Grave stone; shall only say that
> She never neglected her duty to her
> Creator in Publick or Private. She was
> Charitable to the poor; a kind mistress
> and indulgent mother and obedient wife.
> She never in all the time she lived
> with her Husband gave him so much
> as once cause to be displeased with Her.

"Tombstones in Middlesex County," *WMQ*, 1st ser., 12 (1904): 244.

44. The 1687 wedding of Sarah Harrison to the Rev. James Blair remained a well-known story from Lucy Burwell's youth. In response to the Prayer Book's standard questions for the bride, Sarah Harrison repeated her famous reply "No obey" three times—a clear signal to the formidable Commissary Blair that he had met his match. See Suzanne Lebsock, *Virginia Women, 1600–1945: "A Share of Honour"* (Richmond, 1987), 21.

45. Elizabeth Smith Shaw spoke for many eighteenth-century women when she observed that the choice of a husband was "*the* important Crisis, upon which our Fate depends"; Shaw to Abigail Smith Adams, 27 Nov. 1786, quoted in Mary Beth Norton, *Liberty's Daughters: The Revolutionary Experience of American Women, 1750–1800* (Boston, 1980), 42.

46. Elizabeth Carrington to Ann Ambler Fisher, 1 Jan. 1807, Ambler Family Papers, CW.

47. Elizabeth Carrington to Ann Ambler Fisher, 1809, Ambler Family Papers, CW.

48. Elizabeth Carrington to Ann Ambler Fisher, 1 Jan. 1807. In this letter Carrington attributed some information about the early Ambler residents of Jamestown Island to "my highly respected Aunt Martha who I well remember told me she was born in the year 1701 . . . and after living near a whole century retained her powers of amusing and instructing to the last years of her life."

49. Ann Ambler Fisher to Elizabeth Carrington, 1802, and passim, Ambler

Family Papers, CW. R. Kent Newmyer described "an acute form of chronic depression" that plagued Rebecca's daughter Mary Willis Ambler Marshall in his *John Marshall and the Heroic Age of the Supreme Court* (Baton Rouge, 2001), 34. "Consumption" was "the hereditary weakness" of the Ambler family. See n. 28 above.

50. Elizabeth Carrington to Ann Ambler Fisher, 1 Jan. 1807 and Mar. 1809, Ambler Family Papers, CW. "War in itself, however distant, is indeed terrible, but when brought to our very doors . . . is indeed overwhelming. . . . Should it be confirmed that the British are really coming up James River, my poor Mother will not continue a moment—poor dear soul what sufferings are hers." See also Betsey J. Ambler (later Elizabeth Carrington) to Mildred Smith, [May–June] 1781, Ambler Family Papers, CW. Thirty years later she remained convinced "that another revolutionary war can never happen to affect and ruin a family so completely as ours have been"; Elizabeth Carrington to Ann Ambler Fisher, 1810, Ambler Family Papers, CW. Jaquelin Ambler entered a claim against the British for the loss of real and personal property valued at £418 during the siege of 1781. See Martha Woodruff Hiden, "Losses of York County Citizens in British Invasion, 1781," *WMQ*, 2d ser., 7 (1927): 132.

51. Carrington to Fisher, Mar. 1809.

52. Carrington to Fisher, 1809, Ambler Family Papers, CW.

53. Ambler to Smith, [May–June] 1781. Malone, *Jefferson the Virginian*, 359, quotes this letter from *Atlantic Monthly* 84 (1899): 538.

54. Ambler to Smith, [May–June] 1781.

55. Malone, *Jefferson the Virginian*, 352–59.

56. Ambler to Smith, [May–June] 1781.

57. Except for the 1781 anecdote about their escapes from Tarleton, the Ambler family letters mentioned Jefferson only twice, and both references date from after Rebecca's death. Like many Americans after the French Revolution, the Amblers were highly critical of deism. Toward the end of Jefferson's second term as president, Rebecca's daughter disparaged Thomas Paine's *Age of Reason* (1794) and William Godwin's radical *Enquiry Concerning Political Justice, and Its Influence on General Virtue and Happiness* (1793) and referred to Jefferson as "a more insinuating distinguished personage [who] gave his lessons at home." See Elizabeth Carrington to Ann Ambler Fisher, undated [1807–9], Ambler Family Papers, CW. Three years later, in a lengthy passage about the virtues of her brother-in-law John Marshall, she accused Jefferson of slanders that "insidiously" exaggerated Marshall's "most trifling failings into crimes of blackest dye." See Carrington to Fisher, 1810.

58. Jefferson to William Fleming, Oct. 1763, *Jefferson Papers*, 1:13.

59. Jefferson to Fleming, 20 Mar. 1764; James Bear, comp., "Medical Chronology: Thomas Jefferson," Monticello Research Files, ICJS; John D. Battle, Jr., "The 'Periodical Head-achs' of Thomas Jefferson," *Cleveland Clinic Quarterly* 51 (1984): 531–39; and A. K. Thould, "The Health of Thomas Jef-

ferson (1743–1826)," *Journal of the Royal College of Physicians of London* 23 (1989): 50–52. There is no evidence about when this first severe headache ceased. My inference that it lasted at least three days is based on the letter to Fleming (written at "11. o'clock at night"), which opens with a "violent head ach, with which I have been afflicted these two days," and closes with "My head achs, my candle is just going out, and my boy [i.e., slave] asleep, so must bid you adieu."

It is noteworthy that 1764 was also the year in which Jefferson commenced his lifelong practice of bathing his feet in cold water every morning, a habit to which he later attributed his resistance to the common cold. In a volume that Jefferson owned and read, the English physician Edward Baynard recommended cold-water baths as both a preventive measure for head colds and a cure for headaches. See Baynard, *ψυχρολουσια [Psychrolousia]*; *or, The History of Cold Bathing . . .* , 3d ed. (London, 1709), 138, 365–66. Jefferson owned Baynard's 2d ed. (London, 1706); E. Millicent Sowerby, comp., *Catalogue of the Library of Thomas Jefferson*, 5 vols. (Washington, D.C., 1952–59), 1:417. "I have for 50 years bathed my feet in cold water every morning," Jefferson wrote to James Maury on 16 June 1815, "and have been remarkably exempted from colds." Sowerby, *Catalogue*, 1:417n; Battle, " 'Periodical Head-achs,' " 536; and Bear, "Medical Chronology."

60. Battle, " 'Periodical Head-achs,' " 531, 533, 538. Summarizing his diagnosis of Jefferson's ailment as tension, or muscular-contraction, headaches rather than migraines, Battle noted: (1) their long duration (from several days to several weeks); (2) their association with frustration or stress; (3) their greater severity during the day than at night; (4) the absence of "symptoms so common in migraines such as premonitory visual aura, . . . nausea or vomiting"; and (5) their apparent remission after his retirement from the presidency. In addition, Battle noted that Jefferson's symptoms excluded cluster headaches, formerly called histaminic cephalgia or Horton's headache (short recurrent attacks generally at night accompanied by tearing of the eyes, runny nose, or nasal obstruction); malaria (which is accompanied by fever); or a combination of migraines and muscular-contraction (tension) headaches.

Battle's article remains the most reliable account of Jefferson's headaches. A brief note by J. M. S. Pearce ("The Headaches of Thomas Jefferson," *Cephalagia* 23 [2003]: 472–73) is flawed by the mistaken belief that Jefferson's "headaches are first mentioned in 1803." Gary L. Cohen and Loren A. Rolak amplified the reasons that Battle rejected cluster headaches as a diagnosis ("Thomas Jefferson's Headaches: Were They Migraines?" *Headache: The Journal of Head and Face Pain* 46 [2006]: 492–97), but less persuasive is their suggestion that "those with migraine can proudly claim him as a likely fellow victim." Cohen and Rolak failed to notice Jefferson's headache in Feb. and Mar. 1784 (*Memorandum Books*, xlix) and were wrong about an alleged headache in Sept. 1789; see chap. 4, n. 67.

61. *Headache Disorders and Public Health: Education and Management Implications,* World Health Organization report msd/mbd/00.9 (Geneva, 2000), 1–4; David H. Brendel, "A Pragmatic Consideration of the Relation Between Depression and Melancholia," *Philosophy, Psychiatry, and Psychology* 10, no. 1 (Mar. 2003): 53–55; Jennifer Radden, "The Pragmatics of Psychiatry and the Psychiatry of Cross-Cultural Suffering," *Philosophy, Psychiatry, and Psychology* 10, no. 1 (Mar. 2003), 63–66; David H. Leibowitz, "The Glial Spike Theory: I. On an Active Role of Neuroglia in Spreading Depression and Migraine," *Proceedings: Biological Sciences* 250, no. 1329 (22 Dec. 1992): 287–95; and Edward Bever, "Witchcraft Fears and Psychosocial Factors in Disease," *Journal of Interdisciplinary History* 30 (2000): 577–81.

62. Battle, " 'Periodical Head-achs,' " 532, 535; *Notes,* 24–25; Jefferson to Martha Jefferson Randolph, 16 Mar. 1807, *Family Letters,* 302; Jefferson to Albert Gallatin, 20 Mar. 1807, TJP; and Donald R. Hickey, "The Monroe-Pinckney Treaty of 1806: A Reappraisal," *WMQ,* 3d ser., 44 (1987): 65–88. In scholarship keenly attentive both to Jefferson's health and to his extensive reading and library, Andrew Burstein observed that "these tension headaches ceased after he retired to Monticello in 1809." See *The Inner Jefferson: Portrait of a Grieving Optimist* (Charlottesville, 1995), 245. Accordingly, headaches are scarcely mentioned in Burstein's detailed examination of Jefferson's health-related preoccupations in retirement. See *Jefferson's Secrets: Death and Desire at Monticello* (New York, 2005), passim.

63. Jefferson to Fleming, 20 Mar. 1764.

64. Ibid. In the year that Victoria came to the throne and lent her name to reticence about such matters, the first publication of this letter in the *Southern Literary Messenger* (3 [1837]: 305) omitted the sentences referring to 1 Cor. 7:9. The King James translation reads, "But if they [unmarried and widows] cannot contain, let them marry: for it is better to marry than to burn." Jefferson clearly recognized that in Saint Paul's advice about ethical problems in the congregation at Corinth, *burn* referred to sexual desire (not the fires of hell). The passage is more effectively translated in the New English Bible: "To the unmarried and to widows I say this: it is a good thing if they stay as I am myself; but if they cannot control themselves, they should marry. Better be married than burn with vain desire." See Margaret E. Thrall, *The First and Second Letters of Paul to the Corinthians* (Cambridge, 1965), 50–52; Morton Smith, "Paul's Arguments as Evidence of the Christianity from Which He Diverged," *Harvard Theological Review* 79 (1986): 256; and John Morris, "Early Christian Orthodoxy," *Past and Present* 3 (1953): 5.

65. A. Roger Ekirch, *At Day's Close: Night in Times Past* (New York, 2005), 197–202; Ellen K. Rothman, *Hands and Hearts: A History of Courtship in America* (New York, 1984), 45–50; "A Justification of the Custom of Bundling," *Columbian Magazine* (Oct. 1788): 559; "A Dissertation upon Bundling," *Time-Piece, and Literary Companion* (4 Sept. 1797): 1; Herbert Moller, "Sex Composition and Correlated Culture Patterns of Colonial

America, *WMQ*, 3d ser., 2 (1945): 144–45; Edward Shorter, "Illegitimacy, Sexual Revolution, and Social Change in Modern Europe," *Journal of Interdisciplinary History* 2 (1971): 243–44; Philip Benedict, "The Huguenot Population of France, 1600–1685: The Demographic Fare and Customs of a Religious Minority," *Transactions of the American Philosophical Society*, n.s., 81 (1991): 80n; Daniel Scott Smith and Michael S. Hindus, *Journal of Interdisciplinary History* 5 (1975): 548, 556; Edwin G. Burrows, " 'Notes on Settling America': Albert Gallatin, New England, and the American Revolution," *New England Quarterly* 58 (1985): 452; Samuel Middlebrook, "Samuel Peters: A Yankee Munchausen," *New England Quarterly* 20 (1947): 75, 80–81; H. B. Parkes, "New England in the Seventeen-Thirties," *New England Quarterly* 3 (1930): 408–9; and W. J. Hoffman, "Folk-Lore of the Pennsylvania Germans," *Journal of American Folklore* 1 (1888): 131–32.

66. The nineteenth-century abhorrence of masturbation began a century earlier with the anonymous *Onania; or, The Heinous Sin of Self-Pollution, and All Its Frightful Consequences . . .* (London, ca. 1712) and was fueled by Samuel Auguste David Tissot's *Onanism; or, A Treatise upon the Disorders Produced by Masturbation . . .* (London, 1761) and scores of competing texts published in dozens of editions; Thomas W. Laqueur, *Solitary Sex: A Cultural History of Masturbation* (New York, 2003); and Helen Lefkowitz Horowitz, *Rereading Sex: Battles over Sexual Knowledge and Suppression in Nineteenth-Century America* (New York, 2002), 86–122. Less familiar is the survival of an earlier perspective based on the humoral theories of the Greek physician Galen (A.D. 129–199) and by Jefferson's day also associated with the third-century philosopher Diogenes Lartius. In this Galenic tradition, semen was regarded as an important bodily fluid, a humor similar to blood, to be kept in balance for good health. The elimination of excess or pent-up semen was a therapeutic measure analogous to bloodletting. Some writers contended, as did the theologian John Duns Scotus, that retained semen eventually became poisonous. Jefferson surely knew that Galen wrote in the century after the apostle Paul. It may also be significant that Denis Diderot and other Enlightenment philosophes held similar views; *Encyclopédie ou Dictionnaire Raisonné des Sciences, des Arts et des Métiers*, 28 vols. (Paris, 1751–72), s.v. "Manstupration," "Semence"; "D'Alembert's Dream," in *Diderot's Selected Writings*, ed. Lester G. Crocker (New York, 1966), 216–19; Théodore Tarczylo, "Moral Values in 'La Suite de l'Entretien,' " in *'Tis Nature's Fault: Unauthorized Sexuality During the Enlightenment*, ed. Robert Purks Maccubbin (Cambridge, 1987), 43–60; Burstein, *Jefferson's Secrets*, 34–37, 156–58; Laqueur, *Solitary Sex*, 90–95; and Michael Stolberg, "Self-Pollution, Moral Reform, and the Venereal Trade: Notes on the Sources and Historical Context of *Onania* (1716)," *Journal of the History of Sexuality* 9 (2000): 37–61. See also my discussion of Tissot in chap. 6 and 255 nn. 55–59.

67. Burstein, *Jefferson's Secrets*, 158. In an observation equally applicable to British North America in the 1760s, U. R. Q. Henriques observed that "early

nineteenth-century Britain was a morally predatory society. 'Respectable' families kept their daughters well guarded, while young men could not think of marriage until they had inherited or earned enough to maintain a wife and family according to their proper station. It was not surprising that they seduced pretty milkmaids"; Henriques, "Bastardy and the New Poor Law," *Past and Present* 37 (1967): 128. Equally descriptive is Bertram Wyatt-Brown's observation about the antebellum South: "Attitudes toward male fornication were permissive. Male lust was simply a recognized fact of life. . . . Outright libertinism also suggested unmanly self-indulgence and inner weaknesses. But a healthy sex life without regard to marriage was quite in order." See Wyatt-Brown, *Southern Honor: Ethics and Behavior in the Old South* (New York, 1982), 295.

68. Despite a paucity of documentary evidence, historians agree that Williamsburg had its share of prostitutes. Nevertheless, a recent publication purporting to be a reprint of *Armitage's Impartial List of the Ladies of Pleasure of Williamsburg, with a Preface by a Celebrated Wit* (Williamsburg, 1775)— quoted in Andrew Levy, *The First Emancipator: The Forgotten Story of Robert Carter, the Founding Father Who Freed His Slaves* (New York, 2005), 17, 225— is actually a parody sold to tourists.

69. Joshua D. Rothman, *Notorious in the Neighborhood: Sex and Families Across the Color Line in Virginia, 1787–1861* (Chapel Hill, 2003); Joshua Rothman, "James Callender and Social Knowledge of Interracial Sex in Antebellum Virginia," in *Sally Hemings and Thomas Jefferson: History, Memory, and Civic Culture*, ed. Jan Ellen Lewis and Peter S. Onuf (Charlottesville, 1999), 87–113; Philip D. Morgan, *Slave Counterpoint: Black Culture in the Eighteenth-Century Chesapeake and Lowcountry* (Chapel Hill, 1998), 398–413; and Philip D. Morgan, "Interracial Sex in the Chesapeake and the British Atlantic World, c. 1700–1820," in Lewis and Onuf, *Sally Hemings and Thomas Jefferson*, 52–84.

70. Burstein, *Jefferson's Secrets*, 28–30; *Memorandum Books*, 207–10, 349. Jefferson's editors translated his shorthand entries for payments of six shillings on 4 Aug. and five shillings on 5 Sept. 1770 to "Molly Dudley," who may have been George Dudley's wife, Mary, a midwife. The editors translated his shorthand entries for 14 and 28 Oct. 1770 as "Sukey at Smith." The editors describe these entries (for which no payment was listed) as likely references to a boardinghouse operated by William and Mary Smith and, much more speculatively, a slave girl named Sukey or Suck, whose future husband, Jupiter, boarded there. The editors regard her identity as a "remote possibility," but if correct, she and Jupiter were both owned by Jefferson's law client and future father-in-law, John Wayles.

71. Dr. Thomas Watkins to Jefferson, 14 May 1815, TJP, quoted (p. 29) and discussed in Burstein, *Jefferson's Secrets*, 28–30.

72. Watkins's successor, Dr. Robley Dunglison, "found that the prostatic portion [of Jefferson's urethra] was affected with stricture, accompanied and

apparently produced by enlargement of the prostate gland," for which Dunglison prescribed the use of a "bougie," or catheter. See Samuel X. Radbill, ed., "The Autobiographical Ana of Robley Dunglison, M.D.," *Transactions of the American Philosophical Society*, n.s., 53, no. 8 (1963): 26; and Burstein, *Jefferson's Secrets*, 29.

73. The two scholars who have closely examined the evidence for misogyny in Thomas Jefferson's notebooks reached radically different conclusions about the intensity, timing, and duration of Jefferson's hostility toward women. In the introduction to his edition of the *Literary Commonplace Book*, Douglas L. Wilson contended that Jefferson's "defiance and rebellion, as well as frank misogyny, were presumably things he had either outgrown or gained control of." Kenneth A. Lockridge, in contrast, saw in these notebook entries "the confessional turning point of a life characterized at first by problematic and later by carefully delimited and controlled relationships with women." See *On the Sources of Patriarchal Rage: The Commonplace Books of William Byrd and Thomas Jefferson and the Gendering of Power in the Eighteenth Century* (New York, 1992), 77. Wilson and Lockridge disagree about how many of Jefferson's 407 notebook entries expressed misogynistic attitudes. Wilson listed 17 entries under his index entry for "misogyny." Lockridge quoted all or part of 55 entries in his text. My independent assessment of the text added 4 entries to Wilson's list for a total of 21 misogynistic entries. In part, the differences are matters of definition, exemplified by Lockridge's interest in the "entwined subjects of power, rebellion, evil women, and death" (61). Wilson indexed 54 entries under "death" as well as 19 entries under "defiance" (8 of which are also indexed under "rebellion"). For clarity, Jefferson's own notebook entries in Wilson, *Commonplace Book*, are cited with the symbol § and Wilson's editorial comments are cited by page number.

74. Douglas L. Wilson, "Thomas Jefferson's Early Notebooks," *WMQ*, 3d scr., 42 (1985): 433–52; and *Memorandum Books*, "Descriptive Notes," xxxvii–xl.

75. *Memorandum Books*, 154.

76. Wilson, *Commonplace Book*, §284, copied ca. 1762–64 from James Thomson's *The Seasons* (1730). "That this corresponds to the period in which Jefferson was enamored of Rebecca Burwell," Wilson noted, "would seem to be no coincidence" (ibid., 185).

77. Ibid., §285, also copied ca. 1762–64 from Thomson's *The Seasons*.

78. Ibid., §301, from Thomas Otway's *The Orphan; or, The Unhappy Marriage*, which Jefferson probably read in *A Select Collection of English Plays*, 6 vols. (Edinburgh, 1755). Wilson (*Commonplace Book*, 227) cautiously dated this entry as "pre-1763." If that date is accurate, Jefferson may have echoed Otway's play in his letter to Fleming just as John Page echoed Fielding's *Amelia* when he advised Jefferson to "lay siege in form" (n. 20 above).

79. Wilson, *Commonplace Book*, §303, also from Otway's *The Orphan*. Describing the play's major characters as "tormented by conflicts between their natural appetites and their social/rational beings," Jessica Munns explained the

context of the passage that Jefferson quoted. The speaker, a male character reacting to his rejection by the woman he desires, declared, "in effect, that the only difference between man and beast is that man can talk about his desires as well as enact them." See "The Interested Heart and the Absent Mind: Samuel Johnson and Thomas Otway's *The Orphan*," *English Literary History* 60 (1993): 616.

CHAPTER THREE: ELIZABETH MOORE WALKER

1. Jefferson to John Page, 23 Jan. 1764, *Jefferson Papers*, 1:15.
2. Jefferson to Robert Smith, 1 July 1805; this and other critical documents in the Jefferson-Walker affair are printed in app. A.
3. Keith Ryan Nyland, "Doctor Thomas Walker (1715–1794): Explorer, Physician, Statesman, Surveyor and Planter of Virginia and Kentucky" (Ph.D. diss., Ohio State University, 1971), 2–32.
4. Ibid.
5. Ibid., 122.
6. Lyman C. Draper, "Life of Daniel Boone: Appendices," Draper Papers, Wisconsin Historical Society, Madison, 5B11–18.
7. Franklin Minor, "Memoranda of Inquiries About Dr. Thomas Walker My Great Grand Father," 10 Jan. 1853, Draper Papers, Wisconsin Historical Society, Madison, 13ZZ1–41.
8. Peyton Neale Clarke, *Old King William Homes and Families* (Louisville, Ky., 1897), 31. Clarke's identification of Spotswood's daughter as Anne Butler Spotswood is an error. I am grateful to Sandra Gioia Treadway for this and much other information about Elizabeth Walker and her family. Jefferson to Smith, 1 July 1805.
9. *Two Children of the Moore Family*, by Charles Bridges (oil on canvas, 40 in. × 50 in.), is reproduced and discussed in Graham Hood, *Charles Bridges and William Dering: Two Virginia Painters, 1735–1750* (Williamsburg and Charlottesville, 1978), 63, and as *Bernard Moore and a Sister* in *VMHB* 25 (1917), facing p. 336. The artist was active in Virginia from 1735 to 1743. The portrait is in a private collection; the photograph reproduced on p. 46 is preserved by the Virginia Historical Society, acc. no. IMG06710.
10. See Raleigh Travers Green, comp., *Genealogical and Historical Notes on Culpeper County, Virginia* (Baltimore, 1983).
11. *VMHB* 25 (1917): 435–37. The only known birth dates for Elizabeth and her siblings are for her younger siblings: Ann born in 1746, Lucy born in 1747, and Alexander Spotswood Moore born in 1763. Estimations of the dates of Bernard and Ann Spotswood Moore's marriage and their children's births are complicated by the fact that his father's will (dated 20 Jan. and proved 18 Aug. 1743) named only three grandchildren (the offspring of Bernard's two sisters) and no grandchildren by Bernard and Ann. Assuming that

Bernard Moore married Ann Spotswood in 1741 at the age of twenty-one, and that his father may have chosen only to name in his will his grandchildren by his daughters, the plausible dates of single births between their marriage in 1741 and the fifth child (Ann) in 1746 would place the birth of Elizabeth Moore (Walker) about 1745. Elizabeth's aunt Lucy Moore, who was born about 1720, the same year as her father, married Speaker John Robinson of King and Queen County (his second wife) about 1740 and died by 1759. Robinson married his third wife, Susanna Chiswell, on 21 Dec. 1759 and invested heavily in her father's lead mines.

12. "Gorsuch and Lovelace Families," *VMHB* 25 (1917): 431–37.

13. Ann Harrison Booker Darst, " 'Parson Skyring': The Reverend Henry Skyring, 1729–1795" (King William Co., 1995), 1; and *VMHB* 25 (1917): 435–37.

14. Clarke, *Old King William Homes*, 31.

15. Charles Campbell, *Genealogy of the Spotswood Family in Scotland and Virginia* (Albany, 1868), 31.

16. Governor Francis Fauquier to Horatio Sharpe, 12 Apr. 1760, George Reese, ed., *Official Papers of Francis Fauquier, Lieutenant Governor of Virginia, 1758–1768* (Charlottesville, 1980), 346.

17. *Virginia Gazette* (Rind), 14 Apr. 1768; *Virginia Gazette* (Purdie and Dixon), 1 Dec. 1768.

18. Jon Kukla, *Speakers and Clerks of the Virginia House of Burgesses, 1643–1776* (Richmond, 1981), 22–24, 123–28; Jack P. Greene, " '*Virtus et Libertas*': Political Culture, Social Change, and the Origins of the American Revolution in Virginia," in *The Southern Experience in the American Revolution*, ed. Jeffrey J. Crow and Larry E. Tise (Chapel Hill, 1978), 55–108; and Jack P. Greene, "The Attempt to Separate the Offices of Speaker and Treasurer in Virginia, 1758–1766," *VMHB* 71 (1963): 11–18. The first complete account of the Robinson scandal, and still the best, appears in the biography of Robinson's executor: David J. Mays, *Edmund Pendleton, 1721–1803: A Biography* (Cambridge, Mass., 1952), 174–208, 358–75. Moore's debt to the Robinson estate was about £8,500. See David J. Mays, ed., *Letters and Papers of Edmund Pendleton, 1721–1803* (Charlottesville, 1967), 71. The leading beneficiary of Robinson's illegal loans, to the tune of some £10,000, was John Chiswell, father of Robinson's third wife, Susanna Chiswell.

19. John M. Hemphill II, ed., "John Wayles Rates His Neighbors," *VMHB* 66 (1958): 306. Wayles, who would become Jefferson's father-in-law, was the Virginia agent for the Bristol tobacco-importing firm of Farrell & Jones.

20. *Virginia Gazette* (Purdie and Dixon), 31 Mar. and 1 Dec. 1768, 21 Dec. 1769, 8 Mar., 5 Apr., 19 Apr., 18 Oct., and 8 Nov. 1770, 27 June 1771, 12 Nov. 1772; *Virginia Gazette* (Rind), 14 Apr. 1768, 27 July, 19 Oct., and 28 Dec. 1769, 5 Apr., 11 Oct., and 8 Nov. 1770, 5 May 1771; *Virginia Gazette* (Pinckney), 12 Dec. 1774; *Virginia Gazette* (Dixon), 24 Oct. 1777; and *Virginia Gazette*

(Purdie), 24 Oct. 1777. Jefferson's involvement as a trustee of Bernard Moore's estate surfaced again after his retirement from the presidency. See Edmund Pendleton, Jr., to Jefferson, 15 May 1809, John Minor to Jefferson, 17 May 1809, Jefferson to John Minor, 10 July and 6 Oct. 1809, *Jefferson Papers: Retirement Series*, 1:200, 204, 338–39, 585. Kate Moore's dower rights are mentioned in auction notices in the *Virginia Gazette* (Rind), 10 Jan. and 21 Feb. 1771, and *Virginia Gazette* (Purdie and Dixon), 10 Jan. 1771.

21. In a formal notice dated 3 Nov. 1770, Bernard Moore "deliver[ed] up, upon oath, [his] whole estate, of every kind whatever, to Messrs. *Carter Braxton, George Webb, Thomas Walker, Thomas Jefferson,* and *Jack Power,* as trustees, to dispose of it for the benefit of [his] creditors, in such order as the law directs." See *Virginia Gazette* (Purdie and Dixon), 8 Nov. 1770; and *Virginia Gazette* (Rind), 8 Nov. 1770. Three sales of Bernard Moore's property are also documented in *Jefferson Papers*, 1:59–60, 64–65. Despite his desperate financial situation, in 1771 George Washington and other close friends lent Moore money to buy slaves for his own and his family's use. See W. W. Abbot et al., eds., *Papers of George Washington: Colonial Series*, 10 vols. (Charlottesville, 1983–), 9:44–45. Kate Moore was related through the Dandridge family to Martha Washington.

22. Minor, "Dr. Thomas Walker."

23. The Walker family's assets were also complicated by the fact that Jack's mother had been a widow of twenty-one when she married Dr. Walker and that there were temporary title restrictions on some of their land in Albemarle County that had belonged to her first husband, Nicholas Meriwether. Walker had bought Castle Hill in 1760, but clear title had to await confirmation until John Syme, Jr. (his wife's grandchild), reached maturity in 1780. See William Buckner McGroaty, "Wives of Doctor Thomas Walker," *VMHB* 42 (1934): 244–46; and Nyland, "Doctor Thomas Walker," 117–19, 157–59.

24. Green, *Culpeper County,* 73; there is an obvious transcription error in the signature.

25. Ibid.

26. Dr. Thomas Walker and his wife, Mildred Thorton Meriwether Walker, built Castle Hill early in the 1760s. See Nyland, "Doctor Thomas Walker," 119. John Walker built Belvoir in 1764, presumably after his graduation that spring and his marriage that June. See Nancy S. Pate, "Belvoir," Works Progress Administration of Virginia Historical Inventory, 6 Sept. 1937, LVA.

27. Benjamin J. Hillman, ed., *Executive Journals of the Council of Colonial Virginia, June 20, 1754–May 3, 1775* (Richmond, 1966), 291–93.

28. Ibid.; Woody Holton, "The Ohio Indians and the Coming of the American Revolution in Virginia," *Journal of Southern History* 60 (1994): 457–61; Peter Onuf, "Toward Federalism: Virginia, Congress, and the Western Lands," *WMQ,* 3d ser., 34 (1977): 363; Daniel J. Hulsebosch, "Imperia in Imperio: The Multiple Constitutions of Empire in New York, 1750–1777," *Law and*

History Review 16 (1998): 363–64; Clarence E. Carter, "British Policy Towards the American Indians in the South, 1763–8," *English Historical Review* 33 (1918): 37–56; Max Farrand, "The Indian Boundary Line," *American Historical Review* 10 (1905): 782–91; John R. Alden, *John Stuart and the Southern Colonial Frontier, 1754–1775* (Ann Arbor, 1944); and Jack M. Sosin, *Whitehall and the Wilderness: The Middle West in British Colonial Policy* (Lincoln, Neb., 1961).

29. Hillman, *Executive Journals*, 293.
30. John Walker's statement, 1805, in the handwriting of Henry "Light-Horse Harry" Lee, 1805 (TJP, 161:28252–53), is printed in app. A. Malone's transcription in *Jefferson the Virginian*, 449–50, is basically sound, though it omits one passage. Malone objected that "these documents are not a constituent part of the Jefferson Papers as he left them," and that "they were acquired later by the Library of Congress and incorporated in them, with doubtful propriety." See ibid., 450n.
31. *Virginia Gazette* (Purdie and Dixon), 1 Dec. 1768.
32. Jefferson saw John Walker on 26 Nov. See *Memorandum Books*, 84.
33. *Virginia Gazette* (Purdie and Dixon), 1 Dec. 1768.
34. Gene Waddell, "The First Monticello," *Journal of the Society of Architectural Historians* 46 (1987): 6–14, 27; and *Memorandum Books*, 76.
35. *Memorandum Books*, 43–84.
36. Jefferson's letter to William Preston, 18 Aug. 1768, *Jefferson Papers*, 1:23, was written on behalf of an aspirant to the post of chaplain to the House of Burgesses.
37. Jefferson to Smith, 1 July 1805.
38. John Walker's statement.
39. Jefferson had been in Williamsburg from 24 May through 21 June, when he left by way of Yorktown to spend the night with friends in Gloucester. On 23 June he caught the ferry at West Point and spent the night in King William County (where his account book indicates that he frequently visited Susanna Chiswell Robinson, widow of the late Speaker, perhaps in connection with the Bernard Moore estate). After breakfast on 24 June in King William, Jefferson could readily have made it back to Albemarle County by 26 June. He was certainly back at Shadwell by 30 June, when he paid one of his slaves for 13½ quarts of grass seed. See *Memorandum Books*, 77–84. Of course, Walker could have named Jefferson executor without consulting him in person. Prior to his departure for New York, Walker's last documented meeting with Jefferson occurred on 9 May 1768. See ibid., 76.
40. Jefferson "gave J. Walker's Michael 2/6" on 8 July; he engaged to handle a lawsuit for Elizabeth's father on 12 Sept.; and again he "gave J. Walker's Michael 2/6" on 13 Sept. See *Memorandum Books*, 62, 80, 81.
41. Jefferson to William Fleming, Oct. 1763, *Jefferson Papers*, 1:13.
42. E. M. Halliday, *Understanding Thomas Jefferson* (New York, 2001), 26.
43. Ibid.

44. On the question of whether Jefferson and Mrs. Walker consummated a sexual affair in 1768, E. M. Halliday and Dumas Malone draw opposite conclusions from their fundamental agreement about Jefferson's personality and character. Both men concluded (plausibly) that "there is reason to think that [Jefferson] was still quite inexperienced in love" (*Understanding Thomas Jefferson*, 26). Malone says that Jefferson "was not bold toward women and . . . was much more in character as a devoted husband and kind father than as an aggressive lover, and it is hard to believe that he would have persisted in the face of rebuffs at any age" (*Jefferson the Virginian*, 155). Halliday echoed Malone's viewpoint by alluding to "the certainty, from all that is known about him, that aggressive sexual advances upon a woman who had given no signal of invitation were contrary to his nature and his code of conduct" (*Understanding Thomas Jefferson*, 26). In short, if the aggressor's conduct was out of character, then the victim must have been responsible! See also Mia Bay, "In Search of Sally Hemings in the Post–DNA Era," *Reviews in American History* 34 (2006): 414.

45. Jefferson to Smith, 1 July 1805.

46. John Walker's statement.

47. Ibid. The second incident happened at Enniscorthy, the home of their mutual friend John Coles (1745–1808) and Rebecca Tucker Coles, sixteen miles south of Charlottesville; *Virginia Guide*, 622. See "Letters of Edward Coles," *WMQ*, 2d ser., 7 (1927): 32n.

48. Jefferson to Smith, 1 July 1805; John Walker's statement.

49. Wilson, *Commonplace Book*, §303, from Thomas Otway's *The Orphan*.

50. John Walker's statement.

51. Ibid.

52. Ibid. One wonders whether the death in 1785 of their only daughter, Mildred Walker Kinloch, had any connection to this sequence of events.

53. Joanne B. Freeman, *Affairs of Honor: National Politics in the New Republic* (New Haven, 2001), 115, 269–70, 317 n. 19.

54. Walker stated in 1805 that "I constantly wrote to him." See John Walker's statement. In 1803, Henry Lee showed Jefferson a letter that Walker had written to him on 15 May 1788, which is not known to be extant; Jefferson to John Walker, 13 Apr. 1803, Virginia Historical Society (Mss2 J3595 a 29), printed in app. A. For Jefferson's problems with transatlantic mail, see p. 249, n. 3, and *Jefferson Papers*, 7 passim.

55. The will was entered in court on 7 Jan. 1811, Albemarle County Will Book, 1809–1814, LVA, 407. Again I am grateful to Sandra Gioia Treadway for this and other information about the Walker family.

56. William J. Van Schreeven, Robert L. Scribner, and Brent Tarter, eds., *Revolutionary Virginia: The Road to Independence, a Documentary Record*, 7 vols. (Charlottesville, 1973–83), 2:338, 3:419, 421n, 4:184–92, 7:245, 491.

57. H. R. McIlwaine et al., eds., *Journals of the Council of State of Virginia*,

1776–1791, 5 vols. (Richmond, 1931–82), 1:315–16; 5:172, 175; Washington to William Thornton, 7 Oct. 1799, W. W. Abbot et al., eds., *Papers of George Washington: Retirement Series,* vol. 4 (Charlottesville, 1998–99), 339.

58. McIlwaine et al., *Journals,* 2:150, 160; McGroaty, "Wives of Doctor Thomas Walker," 244; John Walker to Jefferson, 13 June 1780, *Jefferson Papers,* 3:441.

59. Minor, "Dr. Thomas Walker."

60. McIlwaine et al., *Journals,* 5:172, 175, 407. Walker's appointment *was* a high honor even though he was the second choice—the governor and council first offered the Senate seat to Virginia's aged and distinguished planter-statesman George Mason of Gunston Hall (who habitually declined appointments and elections to office except in times of crisis).

61. The first house the Walkers built at Belvoir in 1764 was moved to Milton and then to "the Creek." The Walkers built a larger house at Belvoir about 1790; it was destroyed by fire in 1836. See Pate, "Belvoir."

62. James Callender's initial revelations were published in the *Richmond Recorder,* 1, 22, and 29 Sept., 5 Nov., and 1 Dec. 1802. See Annette Gordon-Reed, *Thomas Jefferson and Sally Hemings: An American Controversy* (Charlottesville, 1997), 59–63, 264.

63. Robert M. S. McDonald, "Thomas Jefferson and the Sally Hemings Story," *Southern Cultures* 4 (1998): 46–63; Jacob Katz Cogan, "The Reynolds Affair and the Politics of Character," *Journal of the Early Republic* 16 (1996): 389–417; and Freeman, *Affairs of Honor,* 68–72, 308 n. 15.

64. Jefferson to Walker, 13 Apr. 1803.

65. "Jefferson's Works on Satin" (Hudson, N.Y.), *Balance and Columbian Repository,* 30 Apr. 1805, American Philosophical Society. (This item originated in the *Boston Repertory.*) Thomas Turner, "Letter," *Balance and Columbian Repository,* 18 June 1805 (emphasis added), printed in app. A.

66. John Walker's statement.

67. John Walker to Henry Lee, 28 Mar. 1805, TJP, printed in app. A.

68. Freeman, *Affairs of Honor,* 185.

69. *Balance and Columbian Repository,* 26 Feb. 1805. As late as June 1809, New England legislators were still investigating Jefferson's conduct in the Walker affair in an attempt to find grounds for impeachment by linking him to a series of Connecticut libel prosecutions aimed at his critics. See *Jefferson Papers: Retirement Series,* 1:278–79; and Leonard W. Levy, *Emergence of a Free Press* (New York, 1985), 343–47.

70. Jefferson to Smith, 1 July 1805.

71. Ron Chernow, *Alexander Hamilton* (New York, 2004), 364–70, 409–18, 529–45.

72. Gerard W. Gawalt, ed., " 'Strict Truth': The Narrative of William Armistead Burwell," *VMHB* 101 (1993): 118–20; excerpted in app. A.

73. Turner, "Letter."

74. Gawalt, " 'Strict Truth,' " 118–20.

75. William D. Meriwether to Charles Meriwether, 17 Sept. 1809, Meriwether Family Papers, Southern Historical Collection, University of North Carolina; and *Richmond Enquirer,* 2 Jan. 1810.

CHAPTER FOUR: MARTHA WAYLES SKELTON JEFFERSON

1. "Autobiography," Peterson, *Writings,* 5.
2. Jefferson paid the fiddler on Friday, 3 Jan. 1772. See *Memorandum Books,* 285.
3. Ibid.
4. William H. Gaines, Jr., *Thomas Mann Randolph: Jefferson's Son-in-Law* (Baton Rouge, 1966), 5–8.
5. Jack McLaughlin, *Jefferson and Monticello: The Biography of a Builder* (New York, 1988), 28–29, 153–60.
6. Martha Jefferson Randolph quoted in Randall, *Life of Thomas Jefferson,* 1:64. Randall created an invaluable record of the family's recollections of Martha Wayles Jefferson, but his genealogical details about the Wayles family are not reliable.
7. Ibid.
8. "Autobiography," Peterson, *Writings,* 46.
9. Thomas and Martha Jefferson's children are listed in app. B.
10. "Patsy [Martha] Jefferson was tall like her father," Isaac Jefferson continued. "Polly [Mary] low like her mother." See "Memoirs of a Monticello Slave as Dictated to Charles Campbell," in Bear, *Monticello,* 5.
11. Randall, *Life of Thomas Jefferson,* 1:62–64.
12. Ellen Randolph Coolidge Letter Book, ICJS, 4:66–67. I am indebted to Anna Berkes for sending a copy of this letter and for much other assistance.
13. Malone, *Jefferson the Virginian,* 432–34; Philip D. Morgan, "Interracial Sex in the Chesapeake and the British Atlantic World, c. 1700–1820," in *Sally Hemings and Thomas Jefferson: History, Memory, and Civic Culture,* ed. Jan Ellen Lewis and Peter S. Onuf (Charlottesville, 1999), 76–77; and Joshua D. Rothman, *Notorious in the Neighborhood: Sex and Families Across the Color Line in Virginia, 1787–1861* (Chapel Hill, 2003), 18–20. Betty Hemings and her youngest children initially moved to Elk Hill, one of several plantations the Jeffersons inherited from John Wayles.
14. Malone, *Jefferson the Virginian,* 155–58; and *Memorandum Books,* 64.
15. "Autobiography," Peterson, *Writings,* 5. Jefferson estimated the value of the Wayles estate at £30,000 prior to the settlement of his debts, which totaled between £10,000 and £16,000. The heirs' decision to split the estate prior to settling its debts, a course then complicated by the Revolution, contributed to Jefferson's insolvency at his death in 1826. See Herbert E. Sloan, *Principle and Interest: Thomas Jefferson and the Problem of Debt* (Charlottesville, 1995), 14–18.
16. Randall, *Life of Thomas Jefferson,* 1:64.

17 *Memorandum Books*, 36 and n.; Jefferson to Thomas Adams, 1 June 1771, *Jefferson Papers*, 1:71.

18. Winthrop D. Jordan, *White over Black: American Attitudes Toward the Negro, 1550–1812* (Chapel Hill, 1968), 462; Randall, *Life of Thomas Jefferson*, 1:63; Jefferson, Fragment on Marriage. Based only on the handwriting, Marie Kimball dated Jefferson's commentary to the 1760s, "some time after the termination of his tenuous affair with Rebecca Burwell." See *Jefferson: The Road to Glory, 1743–1776* (New York, 1943), 166, 323n. The Library of Congress subsequently (and plausibly) catalogued this two-page fragment as a letter intended for his eldest daughter, Martha, written about 23 Feb. 1790, the date of her marriage to Thomas Mann Randolph, Jr. The document was not published under that date in *Jefferson Papers*.

19. Mary Deverell, "On Marriage, Addressed to a Sister," in *The Ladies' Literary Companion; or, A Collection of Essays, Adapted for the Instruction and Amusement of the Female Sex* (Burlington, N.J., 1792), 82–83.

20. Jefferson, Fragment on Marriage.

21. Jordan, *White over Black*, 462; Randall, *Life of Thomas Jefferson*, 1:63; and Nancy F. Cott, "Passionlessness: An Interpretation of Victorian Sexual Ideology, 1790–1850," *Signs* 4 (1978): 219–22. In his examination of Jefferson's misogyny, Kenneth A. Lockridge quoted from this same page of Jordan's *White over Black* but silently deleted three entire sentences (including the observation that "female passion must and could only be controlled by marriage") and thereby subtly distorted Jordan's perceptive argument. See *On the Sources of Patriarchal Rage: The Commonplace Books of William Byrd and Thomas Jefferson and the Gendering of Power in the Eighteenth Century* (New York and London, 1992), 71.

22. Jefferson, Fragment on Marriage.

23. Other eighteenth-century examples abound: in one of Richard Steele's essays for *The Spectator* an idealized wife described herself as possessing "no other Concern but to please the Man I love: he's the End of every Care I have; if I dress 'tis for him, if I read a Poem or a Play 'tis to qualify my self for a Conversation agreeable to his Taste: He's almost the End of my Devotions, half my Prayers are for his Happiness"; quoted in Katherine M. Rogers, *The Troublesome Helpmate: A History of Misogyny in Literature* (Seattle, 1966), 179. Steele (1672–1729) and Joseph Addison (1672–1719) published 510 essays in *The Spectator* between 1 Mar. 1711 and 6 Dec. 1712. Jefferson owned editions of *The Spectator* and frequently recommended Steele and Addison's essays on his reading lists for young men and women.

24. Thomas E. Buckley, S.J., *The Great Catastrophe of My Life: Divorce in the Old Dominion* (Charlottesville, 2002), 188–207.

25. Of 47 cases of marital conflict in the records of three Virginia counties between 1675 and 1750, "3 focused on the husband's physical cruelty." See Kathleen M. Brown, *Good Wives, Nasty Wenches, and Anxious Patriarchs:*

Gender, Race, and Power in Colonial Virginia (Chapel Hill, 1996), 464–65 nn. 39, 44. Forty-two percent of women who petitioned for divorce in antebellum Virginia were battered wives. Although "women from across Virginia and from every class and rank in society sought divorces on the grounds of battery, . . . battering husbands tended to come from lower socioeconomic levels than their wives." See Buckley, *Great Catastrophe,* 168. Carol Shammas's observation about New England—where "doubts have been raised as to how frequently town officers actually prosecuted wife beating, because recorded cases are so rare"—is surely applicable to Virginia as well; "Anglo-American Household Government in Comparative Perspective, *WMQ,* 3d ser., 52 (1995): 117.

26. Jefferson, Fragment on Marriage.
27. Jefferson to Martha Jefferson Randolph, 4 Apr. 1790, *Family Letters,* 51.
28. Deverell, "On Marriage," 85.
29. Mary Jefferson Eppes to Jefferson, 8 Dec. 1797, and Jefferson to Mary Jefferson Eppes, 7 Jan. 1798, *Family Letters,* 150, 151–52. Mary had married John Wayles Eppes on 13 Oct. 1797.
30. Jefferson to Eppes, 7 Jan. 1798.
31. Ibid. (emphasis added).
32. Jefferson to François Barbé-Marbois, 5 Dec. 1783, *Jefferson Papers,* 6:374.
33. "Autobiography," Peterson, *Writings,* 46.
34. "Memoirs of a Monticello Slave," 5; Lucia Stanton, *Free Some Day: The African-American Families of Monticello* (Charlottesville, 2000), 33. Jefferson bought Ursula from the estate of John Fleming in Cumberland. See *Memorandum Books,* 334.
35. Stanton, *Free Some Day,* 102–3.
36. Martha Wayles Skelton Jefferson, Household Accounts, 1772–1782, TJP.
37. Ibid.
38. Ibid.
39. Ibid.
40. Ibid.
41. Jefferson, Fragment on Marriage.
42. Martha Wayles Skelton Jefferson to Eleanor Conway Madison, 8 Aug. 1780, *Jefferson Papers,* 3:532–33; *Virginia Gazette* (Dixon and Nicholson), 9 Aug. 1780; Suzanne Lebsock, *Virginia Women, 1600–1945: "A Share of Honour"* (Richmond, 1987), 51; Cokie Roberts, *Founding Mothers: The Women Who Raised Our Nation* (New York, 2004), 124–30. Treasurer Jaquelin Ambler to Speaker John Tyler, 31 May 1784; Treasurer Jaquelin Ambler to Speaker Thomas Mathews, 18 Nov. 1790, Virginia General Assembly, House of Delegates, Speaker, Executive Communications (acc. 36912), State Government Records Collection, LVA. I am grateful to Sandra Gioia Treadway for finding these documents. The original letter to Nelly Madison is in the collections of the North Carolina Office of Archives and History in Raleigh.
43. Patricia Brady, *Martha Washington: An American Life* (New York, 2005),

235–36, 256; Dolley Madison's similar destruction of private correspondence is described in Catherine Allgor, *A Perfect Union: Dolley Madison and the Creation of the American Nation* (New York, 2006), 411–12.

44. Daniel Blake Smith, *Inside the Great House: Planter Family Life in Eighteenth-Century Chesapeake Society* (Ithaca, 1980), 26–27; Jan Lewis and Kenneth A. Lockridge, " 'Sally Has Been Sick': Pregnancy and Family Limitation Among Virginia Gentry Women, 1780–1830," *Journal of Social History* 22 (1998): 5–19.

45. Randall, *Life of Thomas Jefferson*, 1:62–64 (emphasis added); McLaughlin, *Jefferson and Monticello*, 187–88. For Rebecca Ambler and her daughters, see chap. 2.

46. See app. B. Dumas Malone observed that Jefferson "had no advanced ideas about women" and that "something more than jocularity may be perceived in his later remark to his sister-in-law about her woman's 'trade.' His own wife engaged in it far beyond her strength." See *Jefferson the Virginian*, 397. When read in full context, Jefferson's actual comment seems less disparaging. Upon learning that his sister-in-law and her family were all in good health after the birth of her second child, he wrote, "You improve in your trade I see, and I heartily congratulate you." On the other hand, writing to his eldest daughter, Martha, he referred to her sister Mary's impending childbirth as a "knock of an elbow in February." Mary died two months after giving birth to her second child. Jefferson to Elizabeth Wayles Eppes, 12 July 1788, *Jefferson Papers*, 13:347; and Jefferson to Martha Jefferson Randolph, 23 Jan. 1804, *Family Letters*, 254.

47. "Memoirs of a Monticello Slave," 5.

48. Paul A. Treckel, "Breastfeeding and Maternal Sexuality in Colonial America," *Journal of Interdisciplinary History* 20 (1989): 25–52; Smith, *Inside the Great House*, 26–27; and Lewis and Lockridge, " 'Sally Has Been Sick,' " 5–19.

49. James Monroe to Jefferson, 6 May 1782, and Jefferson to the Speaker of the House of Delegates [John Tyler], 6 May 1782, *Jefferson Papers*, 6:179.

50. James Monroe to Jefferson, 11 May 1782, ibid., 183.

51. John Tyler to Jefferson, 16 May 1782, ibid., 183–84.

52. Ibid.

53. Jefferson to James Monroe, 20 May 1782, ibid., 186.

54. Martha Jefferson Randolph quoted in Randall, *Life of Thomas Jefferson*, 1:382.

55. Lines Copied from *Tristram Shandy* by Martha and Thomas Jefferson, 1782, *Jefferson Papers*, 6:196–97 and nn.

56. Jefferson to John Adams, 13 Nov. 1818, Cappon, *Letters*, 529. See also Jefferson to John Page, 25 June 1804, *The Founders on Religion: A Book of Quotations*, ed. James H. Hutson (Princeton, 2005), 9–10.

57. Edmund Bacon's recollections in Hamilton Wilcox Pearson, ed., *Jefferson at Monticello: The Private Life of Thomas Jefferson*, reprinted in Bear, *Monticello*, 99–100. Only three of Martha's children were then alive; Bacon's account of

this deathbed scene was based on narratives that the slaves who had been present recounted to his wife. Another of Monticello's former slaves, Israel Jefferson, affirmed "that it was a general statement among the other servants at Monticello, that Mr. Jefferson promised his wife, on her death bed, that he would not again marry." See "Life Among the Lowly, No. 3," *Pike County (Ohio) Republican,* 25 Dec. 1873, reprinted in Annette Gordon-Reed, *Thomas Jefferson and Sally Hemings: An American Controversy* (Charlottesville, 1997), 252. "It seems entirely possible," Andrew Burstein suggests, "that Jefferson was a man increasingly fixed in his habits who found self-sufficiency preferable to having a partner whom he would feel obliged to consult. In his world, such a choice did not have to result in celibacy." See Burstein, *Jefferson's Secrets: Death and Desire at Monticello* (New York, 2005), 187.

58. Martha Jefferson Randolph quoted in Randall, *Life of Thomas Jefferson,* 1:382.

59. Edmund Randolph to James Madison, 20 Sept. 1782; James Madison to Edmund Randolph, 30 Sept. 1782; quoted in *Jefferson Papers,* 6:199–200n.

60. "Reminiscences of Th.J. by MR," quoted ibid., 200n.

61. Ibid.

62. Jefferson to the marquis d'Chastellux, 26 Nov. 1782, *Jefferson Papers,* 6:203.

63. Ibid.

64. Robert R. Livingston to Jefferson, 13 Nov. 1782; Jefferson to Robert R. Livingston, 26 Nov. 1782; Jefferson to James Monroe, 26 Nov. 1782, ibid., 202, 206–7. Julian Boyd's editorial note (207n.) documents informal communications from several friends in mid-November before Jefferson received the official letter of appointment from Livingston.

CHAPTER FIVE: MARIA COSWAY

1. Steven Gwynn, *Memorials of an Eighteenth Century Painter, James Northcote* (London, 1898), 150.

2. Maria Cosway to Sir William Cosway, 24 May 1830, Gerald Barnett, *Richard and Maria Cosway: A Biography* (Cambridge, 1995), 260.

3. Barnett, *Richard and Maria Cosway,* 51–52; Gwynn, *James Northcote,* 150.

4. Barnett, *Richard and Maria Cosway,* 16–38; Stephen Lloyd, *Richard and Maria Cosway: Regency Artists of Taste and Fashion* (Edinburgh, 1995), 14–29. Lloyd observes that "very few of Cosway's erotic miniatures have survived, a notable exception being *An unknown lady* painted c. 1780," which Lloyd reproduced as color plate 16, p. 27.

5. John Thomas Smith quoted in George C. Williamson, *Richard Cosway R. A.* (London, 1905), 38–39.

6. "If the Italian women fuck as well in Italy as they do here, you must be happy indeed—I am such a zealot for them, that I'll be damned if I ever fuck an English woman again (if I can help it)": Cosway to unidentified, 24 Feb. 1772, Townley Manuscripts, British Museum, quoted in Lloyd, *Richard and*

Maria Cosway, 29–31; Horace Walpole to Lady Ossory, 27 Jan. 1786, *Horace Walpole's Correspondence with the Countess of Upper Ossory,* ed. W. S. Lewis and A. Dayle Wallace (London and New Haven, 1965), 2:510–11.

7. Williamson, *Richard Cosway,* 31–32, 38; Henry Angelo, *Reminiscences of Henry Angelo* (London, 1828), 357–59, quoted in Lloyd, *Richard and Maria Cosway,* 29–31; and John Thomas Smith, *Nollekens and His Times* (London, 1828), 2:393, quoted in Lloyd, *Richard and Maria Cosway,* 30.

8. Lloyd, *Richard and Maria Cosway,* 48; Roy Porter, "The Sexual Politics of James Graham," *British Journal for Eighteenth-Century Studies* 5 (1982): 199–206; Allan Cunningham, *Lives of the Most Eminent British Painters, Sculptors, and Architects,* vol. 2 (London, 1830), 350; and Barnett, *Richard and Maria Cosway,* 69.

9. Horace Walpole to Sir Horace Mann, 29 May 1786, *Horace Walpole's Correspondence with Sir Horace Mann and Sir Horace Mann the Younger,* ed. W. S. Lewis et al. (London and New Haven, 1971), 646; Williamson, *Richard Cosway,* 27.

10. Gouverneur Morris, *A Diary of the French Revolution,* ed. Beatrix Cary Davenport (New York, 1939), 1:488; and Lloyd, *Richard and Maria Cosway,* 49.

11. Lyman H. Butterfield and Howard C. Rice, Jr., "Jefferson's Earliest Note to Maria Cosway, with Some New Facts and Conjectures on His Broken Wrist," *WMQ,* 3d ser., 5 (1948): 27. Although most American writers follow Jefferson's spelling *Halle aux Bleds* (as I did in "Flirtation and *Feux d'Artifices:* Mr. Jefferson, Mrs. Cosway, and Fireworks," *Virginia Cavalcade* 26 [Autumn 1976]: 52–63), the correct form *Halle au Blé* literally means the corn (or grain) market, one of many commodity markets that stood in the area known as Les Halles. The former Halle au Blé was replaced by the Bourse du Commerce. The wood-framed dome that interested Jefferson was destroyed by fire in 1802 and replaced with a structural iron dome in 1809–11. See Howard C. Rice, Jr., *Thomas Jefferson's Paris* (Princeton, 1975), 18–21.

12. Arthur Young, *Travels in France and Italy During the Years 1787, 1788 and 1789,* ed. Miss Betham-Edwards (London, 1909), 93; Mark K. Deming, *La Halle au Blé de Paris, 1762–1813: "Cheval de Troie" de l'abondance dans la capitale des Lumières* (Brussels, 1984); and George Green Shackelford, *Thomas Jefferson's Travels in Europe, 1784–1789* (Baltimore, 1995), 21–23.

13. Howard C. Rice, Jr., *L'Hôtel de Langeac: Jefferson's Paris Residence, 1785–1789* (Paris and Monticello, 1947). The site of Jefferson's house is now marked with a plaque at the corner of the Champs-Elysées and rue de Berri a few blocks east of the Arc de Triomphe. Rue de Rivoli, now a larger thoroughfare than rue Saint-Honoré, was extended past the Louvre by Napoleon. The tireless guide and translator for my exploration of Jefferson's Paris in 2004 was Jennifer Anne Kukla, assisted by Alice Jouve, co-author with her husband, Daniel Jouve, of *Paris: Birthplace of the U.S.A.: A Walking Guide for the American Patriot* (Paris, 1994).

14. Jefferson to Maria Cosway, 12 Oct. 1786, app. C; and Deming, *La Halle au Blé*, 101–10.

15. Julian Boyd suggested (*Jefferson Papers*, 10:454n) that Jefferson met the Cosways early in August because "a large packet of letters from America" arrived on 1 Aug. This ignored Jefferson's admission that the excuse of urgent dispatches was false (ibid., 445, and app. C). Recalling in that letter the day they met, Jefferson described their trip "after dinner to St. Cloud [and] from St. Cloud to Ruggieri's" in terms that precisely matched his account-book entry for 3 Sept.: "Pd. seeing gallery St. Cloud 6f" (*Memorandum Books*, 637). Unfortunately, John Trumbull's otherwise detailed autobiography sheds no light on the relationship because the pages of his diary from 19 Aug. through 10 Sept. were lost before he prepared the text for publication. See *Autobiography of Colonel John Trumbull: Patriot-Artist, 1756–1843*, ed. Theodore Sizer (New Haven, 1953), 120.

16. Malone, *Rights of Man*, 70.

17. It is uncertain whether they visited the library on Monday or Tuesday— probably because Jefferson recorded these memorandum-book entries weeks later, *after* he injured his right wrist on 18 Sept. All his entries from 4 Sept. through 9 Nov. were written with his left hand. See *Memorandum Books*, 638–39 and nn. 54, 65.

18. Ibid.; Rice, *Jefferson's Paris*, 26, 30, 103–4; Jefferson to the marquis de Chastellux, Oct. 1786, *Jefferson Papers*, 10:498; and Shackelford, *Jefferson's Travels*, 65–66.

19. *Memorandum Books*, 638; Rice, *Jefferson's Paris*, 45–49; Jefferson to Cosway, 12 Oct. 1786 (italics and capitalization added). The stock characters of an English harlequinade played in mime, those of an eighteenth-century Parisian *arlequinade* usually spoke in verse; *Oxford English Dictionary*, s.v. "harlequinade."

20. Jefferson's account-book entry for 14 Sept. (*Memorandum Books*, 639) was "Pd. seeing machine 3f." Except for the verb *seeing*, the entry might also refer to a concert at Salle des Machines in the north wing of the Tuileries. See Rice, *Jefferson's Paris*, 30. The waterworks at Marly are described in Shackelford, *Jefferson's Travels*, 65–66.

21. *Memorandum Books*, 639; Diana Ketcham, *Le Désert de Retz: A Late Eighteenth-Century French Folly Garden: The Artful Landscape of Monsieur de Monville* (Cambridge, Mass., 1994); and Jefferson to Cosway, 12 Oct. 1786.

22. *Memorandum Books*, 639, 784; and Shackelford, *Jefferson's Travels*, 70. Fixing the exact date of Jefferson's accident, even in otherwise reliable secondary accounts, has been problematic. Henry Stevens Randall, in *The Life of Thomas Jefferson* (New York, 1858), 1:456, dated the injury to 4 Sept., and Helen Duprey Bullock's pioneering *My Head and My Heart: A Little History of Thomas Jefferson and Maria Cosway* (New York, 1945) followed his lead. Lyman H. Butterfield and Howard C. Rice, Jr., narrowed the range of dates to 13–22 Sept. in "Earliest Note to Maria Cosway," 26–33. Butterfield subse-

quently discovered in Benjamin Franklin's papers a letter dated 20 Sept. mentioning that the "day before yesterday Mr. Jefferson dislocated his right wrist when attempting to jump over a fence in the Petit Cours. The wrist is in place all right but he has suffered a great deal and I do not see how he can write for another month" (*Jefferson Papers*, 10:432n). The 18th is further confirmed by Jefferson's daily log of morning and afternoon temperatures (*Memorandum Books*, 784), which is complete from 1 May 1786 to 27 Feb. 1787, except for the three days immediately after Jefferson "P[ai]d two Surgeons 12f" on 18 Sept. (639).

23. Jefferson to William Stephens Smith, 22 Oct. 1786, *Jefferson Papers*, 10:478; and Randall, *Life of Thomas Jefferson*, 1:456. See also Fawn M. Brodie, *Thomas Jefferson: An Intimate History* (New York, 1974), 208.

24. Jefferson to the prévôt des Marchands et Echevins de Paris, 27 Sept. 1786, "in Short's hand, including signature," *Jefferson Papers*, 10:407–9.

25. Jefferson to Maria Cosway, 5 Oct. 1786, *Jefferson Papers*, 10:431–32.

26. Maria Cosway to Jefferson, 5 Oct. 1786, ibid., 433 (emphasis added).

27. Jefferson to Lewis Littlepage, 10 Oct. 1786, *Jefferson Papers*, 10:442 ed. n., 453–54.

28. Jefferson to Cosway, 12 Oct. 1786.

29. Andrew Burstein, *Letters from the Head and Heart: Writings of Thomas Jefferson* (Charlottesville, 2002), 30; Malone, *Rights of Man*, 75–76.

30. Jefferson to Maria Cosway, 24 Apr. 1788, *Jefferson Papers*, 13:104; Kaminski, *Jefferson in Love*, 103; and Sizer, *Colonel John Trumbull*, 120. The loss might have been worse. "I kept a journal of each day's occupation," Trumbull wrote in 1841, "which has narrowly escaped perishing by dampness" (93).

31. Malone, *Rights of Man*, 72.

32. Jefferson to Cosway, 24 Apr. 1788, 104; and Kaminski, *Jefferson in Love*, 103.

33. Malone, *Rights of Man*, 72.

34. Jefferson to Maria Cosway, 19 Nov. 1786, *Jefferson Papers*, 10:543; and Kaminski, *Jefferson in Love*, 72.

35. Kaminski, *Jefferson in Love*, 138–39; Lucy Ludwell Paradise to Jefferson, 5 May 1789, *Jefferson Papers*, 15:95. Jefferson was vigilant about the security of *all* his correspondence. See Jefferson to André Limozin, 29 July and 6 Aug. 1787, *Jefferson Papers*, 11:642, 700.

36. Jefferson to Cosway, 24 Dec. 1786, 1 July 1787, 29 Apr. 1788, *Jefferson Papers*, 10:627, 11:520, 13:115; and Kaminski, *Jefferson in Love*, 75–76, 89, 105.

37. Maria Cosway to Jefferson, 30 Oct., 17 Nov. 1786, 15 Feb. 1787, *Jefferson Papers*, 10:494, 539, 11:148, 150; and Kaminski, *Jefferson in Love*, 65, 69, 83, 87.

38. Barnett, *Richard and Maria Cosway*, 102–8; and Lloyd, *Richard and Maria Cosway*, 50–51.

39. Jefferson to John Trumbull, 13 Nov. 1787, *Jefferson Papers*, 12:358.

40. *Memorandum Books*, 677–88, 680 n. 3, 684 n. 16, 691; Maria Cosway to Jefferson, "Saturday evening," 1 and 10 Dec. 1787, *Jefferson Papers*, 12:387, 403; and Kaminski, *Jefferson in Love*, 93, 95.

41. Maria Cosway to Jefferson, [7 Dec. 1787,] *Jefferson Papers*, 11:403; and Kaminski, *Jefferson in Love*, 94.

42. Maria Cosway to Jefferson, 10 and 25 Dec. 1787, *Jefferson Papers*, 11:403, 459; and Kaminski, *Jefferson in Love*, 95, 96.

43. Jefferson to Maria Cosway, 31 Jan. 1788, *Jefferson Papers*, 12:539–40; and Kaminski, *Jefferson in Love*, 98–99.

44. Jefferson to Maria Cosway, 24 Apr. 1788, *Jefferson Papers*, 13:104; and Kaminski, *Jefferson in Love*, 102–3.

45. Jefferson to Maria Cosway, 21 May 1789; Maria Cosway to Jefferson, 9 Oct. 1789, *Jefferson Papers*, 15:143, 513; and Kaminski, *Jefferson in Love*, 121, 129.

46. Lucy Ludwell Paradise to Jefferson, 2 Mar. 1790, *Jefferson Papers*, 16:198 (Jefferson received this letter on 27 Apr.).

47. Jefferson to Maria Cosway, 23 June 1790, *Jefferson Papers*, 15:550–51; and Kaminski, *Jefferson in Love*, 132–33.

48. Maria Cosway to Sir William Cosway, 24 May 1830, Barnett, *Richard and Maria Cosway*, 261; Maria Cosway to Jefferson, 17 Nov. 1786, *Jefferson Papers*, 10:539; and Kaminski, *Jefferson in Love*, 70. The daughter was named for her godmother, the countess of Albany, her godfather, General Paoli, and Maria Cosway's and Jefferson's mutual friend Angelica Schuyler Church (daughter of a New York manor lord and sister-in-law of Alexander Hamilton), who had married a wealthy Englishman.

49. Barnett, *Richard and Maria Cosway*, 118–24; Lloyd, *Richard and Maria Cosway*, 67–68; Horace Walpole to Mary Berry, 8 June 1791, *Horace Walpole's Correspondence with Mary and Agnes Berry and Barbara Cecilia Seton*, ed. W. S. Lewis and A. Dayle Wallace (New Haven, 1944), 1:285.

50. Cosway to Jefferson, 29 Apr. 1788, *Jefferson Papers*, 13:115; Kaminski, *Jefferson in Love*, 105; *Morning Post*, 2 July 1788, 20 and 26 Jan. 1789, quoted in Barnett, *Richard and Maria Cosway*, 111–12; and Williamson, *Richard Cosway*, 49.

51. Williamson, *Richard Cosway*, 50–51; and Barnett, *Richard and Maria Cosway*, 118–28. Williamson had access to the journal in the 1890s; a century later Gerald Barnett reported that its location was unknown. See *Richard and Maria Cosway*, 125.

52. Williamson, *Richard Cosway*, 53–64; Barnett, *Richard and Maria Cosway*, 172–93; Maria Cosway to Mrs. Chambers, 29 May 1816, Barnett, *Richard and Maria Cosway*, 182–84.

53. Barnett, *Richard and Maria Cosway*, 172–93; William Hazlitt, "Fonthill Abbey," in *Complete Works of William Hazlitt*, vol. 18, ed. P. P. Howe (London and Toronto, 1933), 179; and *Arnold's Library of Fine Arts*, 4:190, quoted in Barnett, *Richard and Maria Cosway*, 180.

54. Williamson, *Richard Cosway*, 63; Maria Cosway to Jefferson, 15 July 1821, Barnett, *Richard and Maria Cosway*, 194–95. I am grateful to Anna Berkes, research librarian at the Jefferson Library at Monticello, for locating the original at the Massachusetts Historical Society from which minor correc-

tions were made to Barnett's text. The auctions of her husband's art collections raised £12,000. See also Lloyd, *Richard and Maria Cosway*, 93.

55. Cosway to Chambers, 29 May 1816.

56. Jefferson to Angelica Schuyler Church, 27 Nov. 1793, TJP.

57. Barnett, *Richard and Maria Cosway*, 122–28.

58. Maria Cosway to Sir William Cosway, 24 May 1830.

59. By coincidence, Cosway died on the same afternoon in 1821 that his daughter's remains were being removed from his house for a conventional burial. See Williamson, *Richard Cosway*, 64.

60. Horace Walpole to Mary Berry, 16 Aug. 1796, Lewis and Wallace, *Walpole's Correspondence with Mary and Agnes Berry and Barbara Cecilia Seton*, 2:203.

61. Jefferson to Angelica Schuyler Church, 11 Jan. 1798, TJP. The informant was the Polish patriot and writer Julian Ursin Niemcewicz, one of Jefferson's guests at his "great dinner" on 2 Dec. 1787 and an immigrant to the United States.

62. Barnett, *Richard and Maria Cosway*, 156–63; Lloyd, *Richard and Maria Cosway*, 90–93; Christopher Hibbert, *Napoleon: His Wives and Women* (New York, 2002), 16, 332; and Williamson, *Richard Cosway*, 71–76.

63. Jefferson to Madame de Tessé, 20 Mar. 1787, *Jefferson Papers*, 11:226.

64. Gijsbert Karel van Hogendorp's profile of Jefferson, written in 1784, was published in *Brieven en Gedenkschriften van Gijsbert Karel van Hogendorp* (The Hague, 1866–1903), 1:343ff., and translated from Hogendorp's original manuscript in *Jefferson Papers*, 7:82–83n.

65. Jefferson to the marquis d'Chastellux, 26 Nov. 1782, *Jefferson Papers*, 6:203.

66. Malone, *Rights of Man*, 72.

67. Gary L. Cohen and Loren A. Rolak, "Thomas Jefferson's Headaches: Were They Migraines?" *Headache: The Journal of Head and Face Pain* 46 (2006): 494, revived Fawn M. Brodie's misguided effort to link "the old migraine" to his relationship with Maria Cosway in *Jefferson: An Intimate History*, 243. In the letter that Brodie cited as her source—written two full years after Mrs. Cosway had returned to London—Jefferson referred not to a headache (as he invariably did when he *was* suffering from one) but rather to "an illness which confined me to my chamber six days." See Jefferson to John Trumbull, 9 Sept. 1789, *Jefferson Papers*, 15:407.

68. John Walker's statement, 1805, app. A.

69. Jefferson to Page, 7 Oct. 1763, *Jefferson Papers*, 1:11–12.

70. Jefferson to Cosway, 12 Oct. 1786.

CHAPTER SIX: SALLY HEMINGS

1. *Richmond Recorder*, 1 Sept. 1802. The remainder of Callender's stories about Sally Hemings appeared in the *Recorder* on 22 and 29 Sept., 5 Nov., and 1 Dec. 1802.

2. The major texts in the recent debate over the evidence for a relationship between Jefferson and Sally Hemings include Annette Gordon-Reed, *Thomas Jefferson and Sally Hemings: An American Controversy* (Charlottesville, 1997); Thomas Jefferson Memorial Foundation, *Report of the Research Committee on Thomas Jefferson and Sally Hemings,* http://www.monticello.org/plantation/hemings_report.html; "*Forum:* Thomas Jefferson and Sally Hemings Redux," *WMQ,* 3d ser., 57 (Jan. 2000): 121–210; Helen F. M. Leary, "Sally Hemings's Children: A Genealogical Analysis of the Evidence," *National Genealogical Society Quarterly* 89 (2001): 165–207; Thomas W. Jones, "The 'Scholars Commission' Report on the Jefferson-Hemings Matter: An Evaluation by Genealogical Proof Standards," *WMQ,* 3d ser., 57 (Jan. 2000): 208–18; Joshua D. Rothman, "Can the 'Character Defense' Survive? Measuring Polar Positions in the Jefferson-Hemings Controversy by the Standards of History," *WMQ,* 3d ser., 57 (Jan. 2000): 219–33; and Jan Ellen Lewis and Peter S. Onuf, eds., *Sally Hemings and Thomas Jefferson: History, Memory, and Civic Culture* (Charlottesville, 1999). Cinder Stanton's and Josh Rothman's invaluable discoveries about the interracial world of Albemarle County and Andrew Burstein's insights about Jefferson's medical knowledge are cited later in this chapter.

The arguments of those who deny the relationship are presented in Eyler Robert Coates, Sr., ed., *The Jefferson-Hemings Myth: An American Travesty* (Charlottesville, 2001), and Cynthia H. Burton, *Jefferson Vindicated: Fallacies, Omissions, and Contradictions in the Hemings Genealogical Search* (Keswick, Va., 2005).

An imperfect but convenient summary of the earlier controversies over the Jefferson-Hemings relationship is Scot A. French and Edward L. Ayers, "The Strange Career of Thomas Jefferson: Race and Slavery in American Memory, 1943–1993," in *Jeffersonian Legacies,* ed. Peter S. Onuf (Charlottesville, 1993), 418–56. Like many other historians in the 1970s and 1980s, I regarded Douglass P. Adair's posthumously published study "The Jefferson Scandals," in *Fame and the Founding Fathers: Essays by Douglass Adair,* ed. Trevor Colbourn (New York, 1974), as more far reliable than Fawn M. Brodie, *Thomas Jefferson: An Intimate History* (New York, 1974). My skepticism about Brodie's misuse of evidence was expressed in an article written with the late Virginius Dabney, "The Monticello Scandals: History and Fiction," *Virginia Cavalcade* 29 (Autumn 1979): 52–61. In our conversations at the time, Dabney was more alarmed by the use he expected Gore Vidal to make of the matter in his historical novels than by Brodie's work or Barbara Chase-Riboud's *Sally Hemings: A Novel* (New York, 1979), which had prompted our article. Dabney routinely described the "alleged" relationship as "inconceivable," by which he literally meant that he could not imagine it to have happened. The grounds of my skepticism were different. In regard to the primary sources I then knew best, I was appalled by Brodie's sloppy handling of evidence for Jefferson's years in France. I had also accepted Adair's reading of the evidence (in ways that Annette Gordon-Reed perceptively critiqued in advance of the DNA tests).

When the managing editor of Dodd, Mead and Company approached Dabney and me about expanding our *Cavalcade* article into a book, however, I knew that we had already published everything upon which we agreed. I had reservations about the evidence; V. felt that the whole thing was inconceivable. Dabney's *The Jefferson Scandals: A Rebuttal* (New York, 1981) reflected the settled convictions of an elderly gentleman who had once stood bravely on the issue of race when that was not an easy thing to do, in Virginia or anywhere else in America. In the extensive and contentious literature about Thomas Jefferson and Sally Hemings, nearly every conclusion expressed in this chapter has probably been disputed by someone somewhere and especially by my late friend V. Dabney. So be it. I remain committed to learning what the primary-source evidence can reliably tell us.

Finally, lest anyone think these debates are about a dead past, see Sloan R. Williams, "Genetic Genealogy: The Woodson Family's Experience," *Culture, Medicine and Psychiatry* 29 (2005): 225–52; Byron W. Woodson, Sr., *A President in the Family: Thomas Jefferson, Sally Hemings, and Thomas Woodson* (Westport, Conn., 2001); and Shannon Lanier and Jane Feldman, *Jefferson's Children: The Story of One American Family* (New York, 2000).

3. *Memorandum Books*, 374; James Currie to Jefferson, 20 Nov. 1784, *Jefferson Papers*, 7:538–39; Elizabeth Wayles Eppes to Jefferson, 13 Oct. 1784, Francis Eppes to Jefferson, 14 Oct. 1784, *Jefferson Papers*, 7:441–42. Currie's letter reached Jefferson four months prior to the letters from Eppington, which arrived in May 1785.

4. Jefferson to Francis Eppes, 30 Aug. 1785, *Jefferson Papers*, 15:621–22.

5. Ibid.; Lucia Stanton, *Free Some Day: The African-American Families of Monticello* (Charlottesville, 2000), 58–60.

6. *Fredericktown* (Md.) *Herald*, reprinted in *Richmond Recorder*, 8 Dec. 1802.

7. Abigail Adams to Jefferson, 26 and 27 June 1787, *Jefferson Papers*, 11:501–3. Their correspondence about Polly Jefferson and Sally Hemings may also be found in Cappon, *Letters*, 178–86.

8. Scattered throughout the Virginia statute books are laws confirming private acts of manumission that suggest conjugal relationships, such as "an act to confirm to Anne and Margaret Rose their freedom and interest under the will of Walter Robertson, deceased." See William Waller Hening, ed., *Statutes at Large; Being a Collection of All the Laws of Virginia*, vol. 11 (Richmond, 1823): 362–63. See also n. 91 below.

9. Wilmer L. Hall, ed., *Executive Journals of the Council of Colonial Virginia, November 1, 1739–May 7, 1754* (Richmond, 1967), 141; and Philip D. Morgan, "Interracial Sex in the Chesapeake and the British Atlantic World, c. 1700–1820," in Lewis and Onuf, *Sally Hemings and Thomas Jefferson*, 532–36.

10. Memorandum of Dr. John Dove, 16 Sept. 1856, quoted in Morgan, "Interracial Sex," 57.

11. Diary of John Hartwell Cocke, 26 Jan.–15 Feb. 1853, 23 Apr. 1859, John Hartwell Cocke Papers, box 188, MSS 640, UVA; and Joshua D. Rothman, *Notorious in the Neighborhood: Sex and Families Across the Color Line in Virginia, 1787–1861* (Chapel Hill, 2003).

12. The comte de Volney quoted in Lucia Stanton, *Slavery at Monticello* (Charlottesville, 1996), 50 n., and in *Free Some Day*, 114.

13. Henry S. Randall to James Parton, 1 June 1868, in Gordon-Reed, *Thomas Jefferson and Sally Hemings*, 254. Randolph attributed the paternity of the children of Sally and Betsey Hemings, respectively, to Jefferson's nephews Peter and Samuel Carr, sons of his sister Martha—an attribution contradicted by DNA testing in the 1990s.

14. Charles Campbell, "Life of Isaac Jefferson of Petersburg, Virginia, Blacksmith," *WMQ*, 3d ser., 8 (1951): 567–68. Campbell's rendition of Isaac Jefferson's recollections was also published in Rayford W. Logan, ed., *Memoirs of a Monticello Slave, as Dictated to Charles Campbell in the 1840's by Isaac, One of Thomas Jefferson's Slaves* (Charlottesville, 1951), and reprinted in Bear, *Monticello*, 3–24.

15. Randall to Parton, 1 June 1868.

16. *Farm Book,* 9. In addition to sources cited below, biographical information is conveniently gathered in "Sally Hemings and Her Children: Information from Documentary Sources," app. H. of the Thomas Jefferson Memorial Foundation.

17. *Farm Book,* 9, 18; Lucia C. Stanton, "Sally Hemings," biographical sketch, Nov. 1989, rev. Oct. 1994, available on the Monticello website (www.monticello.org).

18. Edmund Bacon's recollections in Hamilton Wilcox Pearson, ed., *Jefferson at Monticello: The Private Life of Thomas Jefferson,* reprinted in Bear, *Monticello,* 100.

19. In her capacity as maid to Martha and Maria Jefferson, Sally Hemings was sufficiently acquainted with their friends to warrant two expressions of good wishes on her behalf in their letters: "Sally vous dit bien des choses" (Maria Jefferson to Angelica Schuyler Church, 7 May 1789, *Jefferson Papers,* 16:xxxi and facing p. 52) and "Dis bien des choses a Mlle. Sale" (Marie de Botidoux, a former classmate, to Martha Jefferson, Nov. 1789–Jan. 1790, UVA)—both quoted in Jefferson Foundation, "Sally Hemings and Her Children."

20. *Memorandum Books,* 685 and n.

21. Sally Hemings's responsibilities as "lady's maid to both sisters" were also affirmed by Jefferson's white descendants: Ellen Randolph Coolidge to Joseph Coolidge, 24 Oct. 1858, in Gordon-Reed, *Thomas Jefferson and Sally Hemings,* 259.

22. *Memorandum Books,* 690, 718, 721, 722, 725, 731; Memoirs of Madison Hem-

ings, *Pike County (Ohio) Republican*, 13 Mar. 1873, in Gordon-Reed, *Thomas Jefferson and Sally Hemings*, 246. Parisian maids were paid about $2.50 a month; Jefferson paid Sally's brother $4 a month; and his French servants earned between $8 and $12 a month. See Jefferson Foundation, "Sally Hemings and Her Children."

23. *Memorandum Books*, 729–34.
24. Jefferson to James Maurice, 16 Sept. 1789, *Jefferson Papers*, 15:433. I have replaced Jefferson's parentheses with commas.
25. "Maria's maid produced a daughter about a fortnight ago, and is doing well": Jefferson to John Wayles Eppes, 21 Dec. 1799, UVA, quoted in Stanton, *Free Some Day*, 113. "Despite her long association with Polly (after 1789 she became known as Maria) Jefferson," Stanton observed, "Sally Hemings was *not* one of the thirty slaves given by Jefferson to his daughter on her marriage" (emphasis added).
26. Memoirs of Madison Hemings, 248.
27. Edmund Bacon's recollections in Bear, *Monticello*, 100.
28. Jefferson to Thomas Mann Randolph, 19 May 1793, *Jefferson Papers*, 26:65.
29. Jefferson Foundation, "Sally Hemings and Her Children," describes the location as one of the " 'servants' rooms' in the South Dependencies, between the South Pavilion and the dairy." Jefferson's plan for the dependencies at Monticello shows two servants' rooms: one between the summer dairy and the kitchen at the corner of the south dependency and a second at the north end of the walkway beneath the main house between the saddle room and the stables under the North Terrace. See William Howard Adams, ed., *The Eye of Thomas Jefferson* (Washington, D.C., 1976), 275 (plates 471 and 472). As was customary on most plantations, some of the slaves assigned to the kitchen usually slept there. Archaeological evidence shows that Monticello slaves "lived in the smokehouse-dairy building, and in a building used to store nail rod." See Jack McLaughlin, *Jefferson and Monticello: The Biography of a Builder* (New York, 1988), 145.
30. Jefferson Foundation, "Sally Hemings and Her Children."
31. McLaughlin, *Jefferson and Monticello*, 256.
32. Randall to Parton, 1 June 1868; and Edmund Bacon's recollections in Bear, *Monticello*, 46.
33. McLaughlin, *Jefferson and Monticello*, 276.
34. Ibid., 444; McLaughlin, "The Blind Side of Jefferson," *Early American Life* 20, no. 2 (Apr. 1989): 30–33, 70.
35. McLaughlin, *Jefferson and Monticello*, 323.
36. Ibid., 326; McLaughlin, "Blind Side," 33; Leary, "Sally Hemings's Children," 204–6.
37. McLaughlin, *Jefferson and Monticello*, 444. Sally Hemings's children are listed in app. B.
38. *Richmond Recorder*, 1 Sept. 1802.

39. Memoirs of Madison Hemings, 246.

40. Freeing of James Hemings, 15 Sept. 1793, *Farm Book*, 15; and Stanton, *Free Some Day*, 126–29.

41. Jefferson to Paul Bentalou, 25 Aug. 1786, *Jefferson Papers*, 10:296.

42. Stanton, *Free Some Day*, 112. Julian Boyd cites no source for his statement in a terse footnote that "according to French law even TJ's status as a diplomat would not have permitted him to retain ownership of a slave on French soil if the issue had been raised." See *Jefferson Papers*, 10:296.

43. Annette Gordon-Reed ably summarized the debate over Thomas Woodson Hemings as it stood on the eve of the DNA testing in *Thomas Jefferson and Sally Hemings*, 67–77.

44. "Assessment of Thomas C. Woodson Connection to Sally Hemings," app. K of *Report of the Research Committee on Thomas Jefferson and Sally Hemings*; and Thomas Turner, "Letter, *Boston Repertory*, May 31, 1805," quoted in Gordon-Reed, *Thomas Jefferson and Sally Hemings*, 73. Writing prior to the DNA tests, Gordon-Reed observed that "Turner's omission of Tom Hemings is of great importance because [one of his informants] would have known if there was a Tom Hemings who had been sent away in the wake of the Callender scandal." See Gordon-Reed, *Thomas Jefferson and Sally Hemings*, 75. "The data do prove that Thomas Woodson was not the son of Thomas Jefferson or any close male-line relative of Jefferson. The Carr brothers are also excluded from being fathers of Eston [Hemings] or Thomas Woodson. Thus, as with modern day paternity testing, we can prove a man is/was not the father, but we cannot absolutely prove a man is/was the father." "Opinions of Scientists Consulted: Dr. Kenneth K. Kidd, Professor of Genetics, Yale University," app. B of *Report of the Research Committee on Thomas Jefferson and Sally Hemings*.

45. *Memorandum Books*, l–li, 878, 903.

46. Jefferson to James Madison, 9 June 1793, *Jefferson Papers*, 26:240; and Abigail Adams to Cotton Tufts, 8 Sept. 1784, *Adams Family Correspondence*, vol. 5, ed. Richard Alan Ryerson et al. (Cambridge, Mass., 1993), 458.

47. Jefferson to James Madison, 17 Apr. 1795, TJP.

48. Jefferson to Bowling Clarke, 21 Sept. 1792, *Farm Book*, 13; and "Recd. of Bowling Clark £55-5-6 = 184.26," *Memorandum Books*, 903.

49. Jefferson to Madison, 17 Apr. 1795.

50. Jefferson to the marquis d'Chastellux, 26 Nov. 1782, *Jefferson Papers*, 6:203.

51. Jefferson to Madison, 17 Apr. 1795.

52. Jefferson to James Madison, 9 June 1793, TJP.

53. Campbell, "Life of Isaac Jefferson," 567–68; Randall to Parton, 1 June 1868.

54. *Notes*, 162.

55. Samuel Auguste David Tissot, *Essay on Diseases Incident to Literary and Sedentary Persons* (1st English trans., Dublin, 1766), 61, 86. "The health of the learned is generally, though not always, as much hurt by bathing in warm water, as promoted by bathing in cold," Tissot wrote. "Riding is also useful,"

86–88. Andrew Burstein emphasized the significance of Tissot in *Jefferson's Secrets*, 34–37, 156–68, and passim.

56. Samuel Auguste David Tissot, *Onanism; or, A Treatise upon the Disorders Produced by Masturbation* (1st English trans., London, 1766), 52–53. For Tissot's reliance on Galen, see pp. 49–50. Countless editions of the popular manual *Aristotle's Master Piece* disseminated humoral theory throughout eighteenth-century America. See Otho T. Beall, Jr., "*Aristotle's Master Piece* in America: A Landmark in the Folklore of Medicine," *WMQ*, 3d ser., 20 (1963): 207–22.

57. Tissot, *Onanism*, 52. On the physiology of fluid balance, see also Thomas W. Laqueur, *Solitary Sex: A Cultural History of Masturbation* (New York, 2003), 190–99; Roy Porter, *Flesh in the Age of Reason: The Modern Foundations of Body and Soul* (New York, 2003); Roy Porter and Lesley Hall, *The Facts of Life: The Creation of Sexual Knowledge in Britain, 1650–1950* (New Haven, 1995), 106–21; Alex Comfort, *The Anxiety Makers: Some Curious Preoccupations of the Medical Profession* (London, 1967), 24–35; and Roy Porter, "Forbidden Pleasures: Enlightenment Literature of Sexual Advice," in *Solitary Pleasures: The Historical, Literary, and Artistic Discourses of Autoeroticism*, ed. Paula Bennett and Vernon A. Rosario II (New York, 1995), 75–98.

58. Dr. Nicholas Robinson, *A New Theory of Physick and Diseases, Founded on the Principles of Newtonian Philosophy* (London, 1725), 78–79; Voltaire quoted in Angus McLaren, "Some Secular Attitudes Toward Sexual Behavior in France, 1760–1860," *French Historical Studies* 8 (1974): 615. C. F. Volney, who had visited Monticello in the 1780s, wrote that "absolute continence is harmful to the health and causes grave illnesses," McLaren, "Secular Attitudes," 618. See also Burstein, *Jefferson's Secrets*, 34–37, 151–88.

59. Tissot, *Onanism*, 83–84; Burstein, *Jefferson's Secrets*, 157–58; Glen Baier, "A Proper Arbiter of Pleasure: Rousseau on the Control of Sexual Desire," *Philosophical Forum* 30 (1999): 249–68; Denis Diderot, "D'Alembert's Dream," in *Diderot's Selected Writings*, ed. Lester G. Crocker (New York, 1966), 216–19.

"Masturbation that is not habitual, not prompted by impulsive and passionate desires, and is, all things considered, *motivated only by need* is not in any way harmful and, therefore, in no way wrong." See *Encyclopédie ou Dictionnaire Raisonné des Sciences, des Arts et des Métiers*, 28 vols. (Paris, 1751–72), s.v. "Manstupration" (emphasis added). The translation is from Théodor Tarczylo, "Moral Values in 'La Suite de l'Entretien,'" trans. James Coke and Michael Murray, in *'Tis Nature's Fault: Unauthorized Sexuality During the Enlightenment*, ed. Robert Purks Maccubbin (Cambridge, 1987), 43–60. Conventional photocopies cannot safely be made from UVA's *Encyclopédie*, once owned by Catherine the Great. A more advanced machine at LVA enabled Tom Campden to make photocopies from its set of the *Encyclopédie* without damaging its bindings.

60. Campbell, "Life of Isaac Jefferson," 567–68. See also Burstein, *Jefferson's Secrets*, 145–49.
61. *Notes*, 138–39. A dozen years ago I noted that historians were often "squeamish about quoting and confronting texts that are filled with racial stereotypes" but that if Winthrop Jordan "was correct about the intensity of Jefferson's physical aversion to African Americans," his perspective needed to be taken "into account when they write about allegations of a liaison with Sally Hemings." See "The Irrelevance and Relevance of Saints George and Thomas," *VMHB* 102 (1994): 267 n. 20.
62. "Though for a century and a half we have had under our eyes the races of black and of red men, they have never yet been viewed by us as subjects of natural history," Jefferson wrote. "I advance it therefore as a suspicion only, that the blacks, whether originally a distinct race, or made distinct by time and circumstances, are inferior to the whites in the endowments both of body and mind." See *Notes*, 143, and Mia Bay, "In Search of Sally Hemings in the Post–DNA Era," *Reviews in American History* 34 (2006): 414.
63. Bertram Wyatt-Brown, *Southern Honor: Ethics and Behavior in the Old South* (New York, 1982), 307–8. "Eighteenth-century men who lost their composure in love were more likely to be held in contempt than celebrated," Wyatt-Brown observed. "Sexual intercourse was viewed as a natural biological function. For reasons of health, it was simply thought good policy for men to have a reasonably active sex life within marriage or, if necessary, outside it." See p. 309. See also Burstein, *Jefferson's Secrets*, 156–69.
64. *Farm Book*, 41, 49.
65. Trevor Burnard, *Mastery, Tyranny, and Desire: Thomas Thistlewood and His Slaves in the Anglo-Jamaican World* (Chapel Hill, 2004), 156. See also Burstein, *Jefferson's Secrets*, 183–84.
66. Biographical information about Sally Hemings's children is gleaned from Lucia Stanton and Dianne Swann-Wright, "Bonds of Memory: Identity and the Hemings Family," in Lewis and Onuf, *Sally Hemings and Thomas Jefferson*, 161–83; Stanton, *Free Some Day*, passim; Rothman, *Notorious*, 12–87; Gordon-Reed, *Thomas Jefferson and Sally Hemings*, 239–40; and Jefferson Foundation, "Sally Hemings and Her Children."
67. "Poor little Harriot . . . died a few days after you left us." See Martha Jefferson Randolph to Jefferson, 22 Jan. 1798, *Family Letters*, 153 (154 n. 1 transposed her birthday and her death date).
68. "I have not seen Jefferson," James Madison wrote James Monroe on 29 Sept. 1796, "and have thought it best to present him no opportunity of protesting to his friends against being embarked in the contest." See Malone, *Ordeal of Liberty*, 272–94 (quotation at 276).
69. Ellen Randolph Coolidge to Joseph Coolidge, 24 Oct. 1848, in Dumas Malone, "Mr. Jefferson's Private Life," *Proceedings of the American Antiquarian Society* 84 (1975): 69; and Memoirs of Madison Hemings, 246. Critics of

Gordon-Reed's book have identified three errors in the published text of Ellen Coolidge's letter: "indignant belief" should read "indignant disbelief" (258); "to be in public gaze" should read "to be there and none could have entered without being exposed to the public gaze" (259); and "such things, after" should read "such things, after all" (259). The other variants involve so-called accidentals, on which Malone and Gordon-Reed sometimes agree. I am grateful to Richard E. Dixon for a copy of his typescript and collation notes.

70. Edmund Bacon's recollections in Bear, *Monticello*, 102. See also *Memoirs of Madison Hemings*, 246.

71. By Virginia statute as codified in 1792: "Every person other than a negro . . . who shall have one fourth part or more of negro blood, shall . . . be deemed a mulatto." Samuel Shepherd, ed., *Statutes at Large of Virginia*, vol. 1 (Richmond, 1835), 123.

72. Jefferson to Francis Calley Gray, 4 Mar. 1815, TJP; also printed in Albert Ellery Bergh, ed., *The Writings of Thomas Jefferson*, 20 vols. (Washington, D.C., 1907), 14:270. See also Burstein, *Jefferson's Secrets*, 147–49.

73. Jefferson to Gray, 4 Mar. 1815; Rothman, *Notorious*, 53–56; and Stanton, *Free Some Day*, 107.

74. Jefferson to Gray, 4 Mar. 1815.

75. F.-A.-F. La Rochefoucauld-Liancourt, *Voyage dan les États-Unis d'Amérique* (Paris, 1798–99), trans. and quoted in Stanton, *Slavery at Monticello*, 20, and in *Free Some Day*, 114.

76. E.g., 1 Kings 11:3, 2 Chr. 11:21; Laura Betzig, "Politics as Sex: The Old Testament Case," *Evolutionary Psychology* 3 (2005): 326–46; Beryl Rawson, "Roman Concubinage and Other De Facto Marriages," *Transactions of the American Philological Association* 104 (1974): 279–305; and Thomas A. M. McGinn, "Concubinage and the Lex Iulia on Adultery," *Transactions of the American Philological Association* 121 (1991): 335–75. See also Judith Kelleher Schafer, " 'Open and Notorious Concubinage': The Emancipation of Slave Mistresses by Will and the Supreme Court in Antebellum Louisiana," *Louisiana History* 28 (1987): 165–82; Burstein, *Jefferson's Secrets*, 5, 162–64, 185; and John Boswell, *Same-Sex Unions in Premodern Europe* (New York, 1994), 28–52.

77. C. Vann Woodward, ed., *Mary Chesnut's Civil War* (New York, 1981), 29–30; C. Vann Woodward and Elizabeth Muhlenfeld, eds., *The Private Mary Chesnut: The Unpublished Civil War Diaries* (New York, 1984), 42.

78. Woodward, *Mary Chesnut's Civil War*, 169; Burstein, *Jefferson's Secrets*, 145–49.

79. George Green Shackelford, "Maria Jefferson and John Wayles Eppes," in *Collected Papers to Commemorate Fifty Years of the Monticello Association of the Descendants of Thomas Jefferson* (Princeton, 1965), 154–66.

80. Thomas Jefferson's Will and Codicil, 16 and 17 Mar. 1826, acc. no. 5145, UVA, printed in Ford, *Writings*, 12:478–83, and in Bear, *Monticello*, 118–22.

81. Ibid.
82. Ibid. See Philip J. Schwarz, *Slave Laws in Virginia* (Athens, Ga., 1996), 54–62.
83. Jefferson's will complied with the spirit and letter of the 1782 Virginia statute governing the manumission of slaves, which required that slaves "not being . . . of sound mind and body, or being above the age of forty-five years, or being males under the age of twenty-one, or females under the age of eighteen years, shall respectively be supported and maintained by the person so liberating them, or by his or her estate." See Hening, *Statutes,* 11:39.
84. Jefferson's Will and Codicil.
85. Ibid. (emphasis added).
86. Hening, *Statutes,* 11:39.
87. Jefferson's Will and Codicil.
88. Ibid.
89. Memoirs of Madison Hemings, 248; Ervin Jordan, Jr., " 'A Just and True Account': Two 1833 Parish Censuses of Albemarle County Free Blacks," *Magazine of Albemarle County History* 53 (1995): 137.
90. Based on his conversations with Martha Randolph's children, biographer Henry Stevens Randall wrote that the manumission of Wormley Hemings Hughes, "should he desire it, was orally recommended to Mrs. Randolph." See Stanton, *Free Some Day,* 143.
91. Martha Randolph's Will, 18 Apr. 1834, ibid., 143. After Sally Hemings died in 1835, Martha Randolph removed her name from the final version of her will, which was proved after her death in 1836. See Lucia C. Stanton, "Monticello to Main Street: The Hemings Family and Charlottesville," *Magazine of Albemarle County History* 55 (1997): 107–8.

  The practice of granting "time" in lieu of formal manumission is illuminated by the provisions of a will proved in 1818 in Chesterfield County, immediately south of Richmond. Louis Ducos Lahaille directed his executor to "purchase a little boy by the name of William who is about the age of two years, and the son of Nancy, which little boy and his mother belong to Gervase Storrs esquire of Henrico county, and which boy I consider and believe to be my child." Lahaille directed his executor to "keep the said little boy William with him untill he shall attain the age of twenty one years and bring him up to gardening as a trade and profession." When William reached age twenty-one, Lahaille specifed that he was "to have and enjoy the full and absolute benefit of his time and labour . . . in the same manner as free men are entitled to the same, but if the said William shall think proper to leave the Commonwealth of Virginia, or if at his age of twenty one the laws of Virginia shall permit the emancipation of slaves, then and in either event, it is my will and desire that the said William shall be absolutely and forever free." See Chesterfield County Will Book 8, 1813–1818 (LVA microfilm reel 29), 510–11. I am indebted to Michael L. Nicholls for this reference.

92. Recollections of Thomas Jefferson Randolph, UVA, in Stanton, *Free Some Day*, 142.

CHAPTER SEVEN: AMAZONS AND ANGELS

1. Abigail Adams to Elizabeth Shaw Peabody, 10 June 1808, quoted in Lynne Withey, *Dearest Friend: A Life of Abigail Adams* (New York, 1981), 4.

2. Abigail Adams to Francis van der Kemp, 3 Feb. 1814, quoted in Judith Pulley, "The Bittersweet Friendship of Thomas Jefferson and Abigail Adams," *Essex Institute Historical Collections* 108 (1972): 220.

3. John Adams to Abigail Adams, 27 May 1776, *Adams Family Correspondence*, ed. Lyman H. Butterfield et al. (Cambridge, Mass., 1963), 1:420; Betsy Erkkila, "Revolutionary Women," *Tulsa Studies in Women's Literature* 6 (1987): 198; and Withey, *Dearest Friend*, 73–74. For the evolution of Abigail Adams's views in the context of America's post-1776 retreat from the feminist implications of revolutionary rhetoric, see Pauline Schloesser, *The Fair Sex: White Women and Racial Patriarchy in the Early American Republic* (New York, 2002), 114–53.

4. Abigail Adams to Mary Smith Cranch, 8 May 1785, *Adams Family Correspondence*, vol. 5, ed. Richard Alan Ryerson et al. (Cambridge, Mass., 1993), 119.

5. Ibid. Jefferson and the Adamses were frequently together. "On Thursday I dine with him at his house," Abigail told her sister one week, "on Sunday he is to dine here, on Monday, we all dine with the Marquis, and on Thursday we dine with the Swedish Ambassador."

6. Abigail Adams to Jefferson, 6 June 1785, Cappon, *Letters*, 28.

7. Jefferson to Abigail Adams, 25 Sept. 1785; Abigail Adams to Jefferson, 23 July 1786, Cappon, *Letters*, 71, 145.

8. Jefferson to Abigail Adams, 21 June 1785, Cappon, *Letters*, 34. My thanks to Holly Brewer for making sure that I did not overlook this important passage.

9. For their agreement about women's education, see Abigail Adams to John Adams, 14 Aug., and his reply on 25 Aug. 1776, Butterfield et al., *Adams Family Correspondence*, 2:94, 109–10.

10. Abigail Adams to John Adams, 31 Mar. 1776, ibid., 1:370.

11. Ibid.; Abigail Adams to Mercy Otis Warren, 27 Apr. 1776, ibid., 1:370, 397.

12. John Adams to Abigail Adams, 14 Apr. 1776, ibid., 382; John Adams to James Sullivan, 26 May 1776, *Papers of John Adams*, ed. Robert R. Taylor et al. (Cambridge, Mass., 1979), 4:208–13.

13. Abigail Adams to Warren, 27 Apr. 1776.

14. Cappon, *Letters*, 28–338, 268–82; Kaminski, *Jefferson in Love*, 11–136. The 2:1 ratio holds for all 58 letters in the correspondence between Cosway and Jefferson from 1786 to 1824. When Abigail Adams initiated a brief correspondence with Jefferson in 1804, she wrote 4 letters to his 3 replies.

15. Maria Cosway was utterly perplexed by Jefferson's references to Sterne; Abigail Adams alluded to him in her letters. See Jefferson to Cosway, 24 Apr., and Cosway to Jefferson, 29 Apr. 1788, Kaminski, *Jefferson in Love*, 102, 104; and Abigail Adams to Jefferson, 11 Feb. 1786, Cappon, *Letters*, 119.

16. Jefferson to Abigail Adams, 25 Sept. 1785, and Abigail Adams to Jefferson, 7 Oct. 1785, Cappon, *Letters*, 69–71, 80.

17. Abigail Adams to Jefferson, 20 May 1804, ibid., 168–69.

18. Ibid., 169. For clarity, a few commas are omitted and a comma substituted for Adams's colon after *Being*.

19. Jefferson to Abigail Adams, 13 June 1804, ibid., 270–71.

20. Abigail Adams to Jefferson, 1 July 1804, ibid., 271–74.

21. Ibid.

22. Jefferson to Abigail Adams, 22 July 1804, ibid., 274–76.

23. Abigail Adams to Jefferson, 18 Aug. 1804, ibid., 276–78.

24. Jefferson to Abigail Adams, 11 Sept. 1804, ibid., 279.

25. Abigail Adams to Jefferson, 25 Oct. 1804, ibid., 281–82.

26. Jefferson to Benjamin Rush, 16 Jan. 1811, quoted ibid., 268. A final chance for reconciliation between Jefferson and Abigail Adams was derailed in 1813 by Jefferson's pained silence after the death of the Adamses' daughter. See Pulley, "Bittersweet Friendship," 214–16.

27. Jefferson to Abigail Adams, 21 June 1785, Cappon, *Letters*, 34.

28. Abigail Adams to Lucy Cranch, 5 Sept. 1784, Butterfield et al., *Adams Family Correspondence*, 5:436; and Susan Stabile, "Salons and Power in the Era of Revolution: From Literary Coteries to Epistolary Enlightenment," in *Benjamin Franklin and Women*, ed. Larry E. Tise (University Park, Penn., 2000), 129–48.

29. Abigail Adams to Lucy Cranch, 5 Sept. 1784; to Mercy Otis Warren, 10 May 1785; to Mary Smith Cranch, 9 Dec. 1784, Butterfield et al., *Adams Family Correspondence*, 5:436, 6:14–16, 139. Abigail read French with "much more facility" than she spoke it, for, as her daughter wrote, "there is nothing easier than to learn to *read* French . . . by translating a Page every day from French to English with . . . the dictionary, and in three months any Person may insure to themselvs knowledge enough to *read* the Language." Adams to Mary Cranch, 9 Dec. 1784, Abigail Adams 2d to Lucy Cranch, 6 May 1785, Butterfield et al., *Adams Family Correspondence*, 6:15, 128 (emphasis added). Jefferson, Franklin, and John Adams spoke French *passablement*. See Paul M. Spurlin, "The Founding Fathers and the French Language," *Modern Language Journal* 60 (1976): 85–96.

30. J.-P. Brissot de Warville, *New Travels in the United States of America, 1788*, ed. Durand Echeverria (Cambridge, Mass., 1964), 85–86.

31. Jefferson to John Banister, Jr., 15 Oct. 1785, *Jefferson Papers*, 8:636; and Martha Jefferson to her father, 9 Apr. 1787, *Jefferson Papers*, 11:282. See also Elizabeth Wirth Marvick, "Thomas Jefferson and the Ladies of Paris," *Pro-*

ceedings of the Annual Meeting of the Western Society for French History 21 (1994): 81–94.

32. Abigail Adams to Mary Smith Cranch, 4 Sept. 1784; and to Mercy Otis Warren, 10 May 1785, Butterfield et al., *Adams Family Correspondence*, 5:439, 6:139.

33. Benedetta Craveri, *The Age of Conversation*, trans. Teresa Waugh (New York, 2005), 296; Alan Charles Kors, "The Myth of the Coterie Holbachique," *French Historical Studies* 9 (1976): 587; and Joan B. Landes, *Women and the Public Sphere in the Age of the French Revolution* (Ithaca, 1988), 23.

34. Jefferson to Adams, 21 June 1785; George Green Shackelford, *Thomas Jefferson's Travels in Europe, 1784–1789* (Baltimore, 1995), 37–42; and Malone, *Rights of Man*, 14–20.

35. Robert Darnton, "The High Enlightenment and the Low-Life of Literature in Pre-Revolutionary France," *Past and Present* 51 (May 1971): 92–93. See also Dena Goodman, "Filial Rebellion in the Salon: Madame Geoffrin and Her Daughter," *French Historical Studies* 16 (1989): 28–47; and Steven D. Kale, "Women, Salons, and the State in the Aftermath of the French Revolution," *Journal of Women's History* 13 (2002): 54–80.

36. *Memorandum Books*, 598.

37. Jefferson to Madame de Tessé, 20 Mar. 1787, *Jefferson Papers*, 11:226; Marvick, "Jefferson and the Ladies of Paris," 88–89. Crèvecoeur published *Letters from an American Farmer* under the pseudonym J. Hector St. John.

38. Madelyn Gutwirth, *The Twilight of the Goddesses: Women and Representation in the French Revolutionary Era* (New Brunswick, N.J., 1992), 51, 77–132.

39. Jefferson to Anne Willing Bingham, 11 May 1788, *Jefferson Papers*, 13:151–52.

40. Ibid.

41. Jefferson to David Humphreys, 18 Mar. 1789, ibid., 14:676.

42. Jefferson to George Washington, 4 Dec. 1788, ibid., 14:330. "Possessing the confidence and intimacy of the leading [French] patriots," Jefferson wrote in his autobiography, "I learnt with correctness the views and proceedings of that party; while my intercourse with the diplomatic missionaries of Europe at Paris, all of them with the court, and eager in prying into it's councils and proceedings, gave me a knolege of these also." Peterson, *Writings*, 97.

43. The recipient's copy of Jefferson's letter is in the George Washington Papers at the Library of Congress and may be consulted online through the American Memory website.

44. Jefferson to Washington, 4 Dec. 1788.

45. Jefferson to Maria Cosway, 24 Apr. 1788 and 21 May 1789, *Jefferson Papers*, 13:104, 15:143, 513; and Kaminski, *Jefferson in Love*, 102–3, 121, 129.

46. Jefferson blamed Queen Marie Antoinette for *all* the horrors of the French Revolution because she led "the king on with her, and plunged the world into crimes and calamities." Had Jefferson been in a position to do so, he reflected in his autobiography, "I should have shut up the Queen in a Con-

vent, putting harm out of her power, and placed the king in his station, investing him with limited powers, which I verily believe he would have honestly exercised, according to the measure of his understanding. In this way no void would have been created . . . nor occasion given for those enormities which demoralized the nations of the world, and destroyed, and is yet to destroy millions and millions of its inhabitants." Peterson, *Writings,* 92–93.

47. Ibid.

48. Jefferson to Anne Willing Bingham, 7 Feb. 1787, *Jefferson Papers,* 11:122–24.

49. Jefferson to James Madison, 30 Jan. 1787, ibid., 95.

50. Anne Willing Bingham to Jefferson, 7 Feb. 1787, ibid., 392–94; and Robert C. Alberts, *The Golden Voyage: The Life and Times of William Bingham, 1752–1804* (Boston, 1969), 464–66.

51. Jefferson to Bingham, 11 May 1788.

52. Alberts, *Golden Voyage,* 157–69; Susan Branson, *These Fiery Frenchified Dames: Women and Political Culture in Early Philadelphia* (Philadelphia, 2001), 6, 135–40.

53. Catherine Allgor, *Parlor Politics: In Which the Ladies of Washington Help Build a City and a Government* (Charlottesville, 2000), 18–20; Harold Donaldson Eberlein, "190, High Street (Market Street Below Sixth): The Home of Washington and Adams, 1790–1800," *Transactions of the American Philosophical Society,* n.s., 43 (1953): 168–71; and Patricia Brady, *Martha Washington: An American Life* (New York, 2005), 161–69.

54. *Philadelphia Aurora and General Advertiser,* 22 Aug. 1795; (New London, Conn.) *Bee,* n.d., quoted in (*New York*) *Time Piece,* 29 Nov. 1797; (Boston) *Independent Chronicle and Universal Advertiser,* 14 Dec. 1797; and (Brattleboro, Vt.) *Federal Galaxy,* 16 Jan. 1798. Also George L. Montagno, "Congressional Cakewalk," *WMQ,* 3d ser., 17 (1960): 349.

55. Allgor, *Parlor Politics,* 21; Jefferson to Washington, 4 Dec. 1788; and Thomas Jefferson, "Etiquette of the Court of the U.S.," reprinted in Malone, *First Term,* 499–500.

56. "Jefferson to William Short on Mr. and Mrs. Merry, [23 Jan.] 1804," *American Historical Review* 33 (1928): 832–35.

57. Malcolm Lester, *Anthony Merry Redivivus: A Reappraisal of the British Minister to the United States, 1803–6* (Charlottesville, 1978), 30–31, and Joel Larus, "Growing Pains of the New Republic: III, Pell-Mell Along the Potomac," *WMQ,* 3d ser., 17 (1960): 349–57.

58. Malone, *First Term,* 378; and Allgor, *Parlor Politics,* 36.

59. Lester, *Merry Redivivus,* 32–33. Jefferson's conduct remained vivid in Merry's memory when he recounted these details to a diplomatic colleague in Denmark in 1807.

60. Ibid., 34, 36–40.

61. Ibid., 34; Allen Culling Clark, *Life and Letters of Dolly Madison* (Washington, D.C., 1914), 61–62; and Allgor, *Parlor Politics,* 36–40.

62. Catherine Allgor, *A Perfect Union: Dolley Madison and the Creation of the American Nation* (New York, 2006), 84–100.

63. Jefferson to Washington, 4 Dec. 1788.

64. Margaret Bayard Smith, *Forty Years of Washington Society*, ed. Gaillard Hunt (London, 1906), 46.

65. Ibid.; Jefferson to James Monroe, 8 Jan. 1804, Ford, *Writings*, 8:290.

66. Jefferson to Monroe, 8 Jan. 1804 (emphasis added).

CHAPTER EIGHT: ALL MEN ARE CREATED EQUAL

1. Abigail Adams to John Adams, 31 Mar. 1776, *Adams Family Correspondence*, ed. Lyman H. Butterfield et al. (Cambridge, Mass., 1963), 1:370; and Pauline Maier, *American Scripture: Making the Declaration of Independence* (New York, 1997), 97–153.

2. *Virginia Gazette* (Rind), 15 Sept. 1774, quoted in Cynthia A. Kierner, *Beyond the Household: Women's Place in the Early South, 1700–1835* (Ithaca, 1998), 79 (emphasis added); and Sandra Gioia Treadway, "Anna Maria Lane: An Uncommon Common Soldier of the American Revolution," *Virginia Cavalcade* 37 (1988): 134–43.

3. Andromache in the *South Carolina Gazette and Country Journal*, 16 Aug. 1774, quoted in Kierner, *Beyond the Household*, 81.

4. *Virginia Gazette* (Dixon and Hunter), 21 Sept. 1776; and Cynthia A. Kierner, "Governor Henry's Dependents: Women and Families in Revolutionary Virginia," Fifth Annual Governor Henry Lecture, 17–18 Apr. 2005, *Newsletter of the Patrick Henry Memorial Foundation*, Spring 2005.

5. *Virginia Gazette* (Dixon and Hunter), 21 Sept. 1776. "Terrel's revolutionary consciousness outlived the excitement of 1776. In 1781, she named her eighth child George Washington Terrel, to honor the leading hero of the American Revolution." See Kierner, "Governor Henry's Dependents."

6. Louise Belote Dawe and Sandra Gioia Treadway, "Hannah Lee Corbin: The Forgotten Lee," *Virginia Cavalcade* 26 (1988): 70–77; Richard Henry Lee to Hannah Lee Corbin, 17 Mar. 1778, *Letters of Richard Henry Lee*, ed. James Curtis Ballagh (New York, 1911–14), 1:392–93; Kierner, "Hannah Lee Corbin," *DVB*.

7. Mary Willing Byrd to Jefferson, 23 Feb. 1781, *Jefferson Papers*, 4:691; Sara B. Bearss, "Mary Willing Byrd," *DVB*; and Julian P. Boyd et al., app. I: "The Affair of Westover," *Jefferson Papers*, 5:671–705.

8. Byrd to Jefferson, 23 Feb. 1781; and Byrd to [Thomas Nelson?], 10 Aug. 1781, *Jefferson Papers*, 4:691, 5:704.

9. John G. Kolp and Terri L. Snyder, "Women and the Political Culture of Eighteenth-Century Virginia: Gender, Property Law, and Voting Rights," in *The Many Legalities of Early America*, ed. Christopher Tomlins and Bruce H. Mann (Chapel Hill, 2001), 272.

10. Maier, *American Scripture*, 126–27, 166, 189–99.

11. *Oxford English Dictionary,* s.v. "man." The *OED*'s inclusive examples date from the tenth century.

12. Maier, *American Scripture,* 197.

13. Jefferson to John Hampden Pleasants, 19 Apr. 1824, Ford, *Writings,* 10:303. "Yet among the men who either pay or fight for their country," Jefferson continued, "no line [restricting suffrage] of right can be drawn."

14. "Bills Reported by the Committee of Revisors," *Jefferson Papers,* 2:329–665 (quotation at 394). "With independence, one might expect to find a bit of legal innovation in married women's property rights. No such luck: the new state of Virginia confirmed most of the colonial restrictions on married women's property, even restricting the dower rights of widows to slaves." See Linda L. Sturtz, *Within Her Power: Propertied Women in Colonial America* (New York and London, 2002), 181.

15. Jefferson to Nathaniel Burwell, 14 Mar. 1818, *The Works of Thomas Jefferson,* ed. Paul Leicester Ford, 12 vols. (New York, 1905), 10:104. See also Catherine Kerrison, "Jefferson's Daughters and the American Republic of Letters," unpublished paper, SHEAR conference, Providence, 22–25 July 2004; and Gene Crotty, *Jefferson's Legacy: His Own University* (Charlottesville, 1996).

16. Marie Jean Antoine Nicolas Condorcet, *On the Admission of Women to the Rights of Citizenship* (Paris, 1790), reprinted in John Avery, *Progress, Poverty and Population: Re-reading Condorcet, Godwin and Malthus* (London and Portland, Ore., 1997), 121–27.

17. Immanuel Kant, "An Answer to the Question: What Is Enlightenment?" (1784), in *Basic Writings of Kant,* ed. Allen W. Wood (New York, 2001), 135–41, quoted at p. 135 (emphasis added). Of course, Kant also retained gender distinctions in his *Observations on the Feeling of the Beautiful and Sublime* (1764), *Anthropology* (1798), and other works. In a British and American context, the concept of "the fair sex" tended to exclude poor and nonwhite women; Pauline Schloesser, *The Fair Sex: White Women and Racial Patriarchy in the Early American Republic* (New York, 2002), 12–81.

18. Theodor Gottlieb von Hippel, *On Improving the Status of Women,* ed. and trans. Timothy F. Sellner (Detroit, 1979), 62; Mary Wollstonecraft, *A Vindication of the Rights of Woman; with Strictures on Political and Moral Subjects* (London, Dublin, and Boston, 1792); and Eleanor Flexner, *Mary Wollstonecraft* (New York, 1972), 147–66.

19. Jefferson to Albert Gallatin, 13 Jan. 1807, TJP. The only things in Jefferson's papers from this period that had anything to do with women were a letter and printed prospectus from the Philadelphia educator Maria Rivardi, dated a week earlier, seeking the president's endorsement of her seminary for young ladies.

20. Maria Rivardi to Jefferson, 6 Jan. 1807, TJP. William Staughton, *An Address, Delivered October, 1807, at Mrs. Rivardi's Seminary on the Occasion of the Examination of the First and Middle Classes* (Philadelphia, 1807); Mary John-

son, "Madame Rivardi's Seminary in the Gothic Mansion," *Pennsylvania Magazine of History and Biography* 104 (1980): 3–38.

21. Jefferson to John Hampden Pleasants, 19 Apr. 1824; to Edward Coles, 25 Aug. 1814; and to Samuel Kercheval, 12 July 1816, Peterson, *Writings,* 1345, 1402. In 1803 Jefferson wrote that the inhabitants of Louisiana also were "as incapable of self-government as children." See Jefferson to De Witt Clinton, 2 Dec. 1803, Ford, *Works,* 10:55; and Jon Kukla, *A Wilderness So Immense: The Louisiana Purchase and the Destiny of America* (New York, 2003), 310–11, 336, 411 n. 4.

22. Jefferson to Gallatin, 13 Jan. 1807 (emphasis added).

23. Conference Report, 1777, *Jefferson Papers,* 2:46; Jefferson to John Dickinson, 6 Mar. 1801, Peterson, *Writings,* 1085; Bergh, *Writings,* 3:379; and Jefferson to Kercheval, 12 July 1816.

24. Carole Pateman: *The Disorder of Women: Democracy, Feminism, and Political Theory* (Stanford, 1989), 33–89; " 'God Hath Ordained to Man a Helper': Hobbes, Patriarchy and Conjugal Right," *British Journal of Political Science* 19 (1989): 445–63; " 'The Disorder of Women': Women, Love, and the Sense of Justice," *Ethics* 91 (1980): 20–34; "Women and Consent," *Political Theory* 8 (1980): 149–68; and "Democracy and Democratization," Presidential Address: XVIth World Congress, IPSA, *International Political Science Review* 17 (1996): 5–12. Susan Moller Okin: "Reason and Feeling in Thinking About Justice," *Ethics* 99 (1989): 229–49; "Political Liberalism, Justice, and Gender," *Ethics* 105 (1994): 23–43; "Patriarchy and Married Women's Property in England: Questions on Some Current Views," *Eighteenth-Century Studies* 17 (1983–84): 121–38; "Rousseau's Natural Woman," *Journal of Politics* 41 (1979): 393–416; "Philosopher Queens and Private Wives: Plato on Women and the Family," *Philosophy and Public Affairs* 6 (1977): 345–69; "Women and the Making of the Sentimental Family," *Philosophy and Public Affairs* 11 (1982): 65–88; "Justice and Gender," *Philosophy and Public Affairs* 16 (Winter 1987): 42–72; " 'The Soveraign and His Counsellours': Hobbes's Reevaluation of Parliament," *Political Theory* 10 (1982): 49–75; and "Gender Inequality and Cultural Differences," *Political Theory* 22 (1994): 5–24. Sherry B. Ortner: "Is Female to Male as Nature Is to Culture?" *Feminist Studies* 1, no. 2 (Autumn 1972): 5–31, and "The Virgin and the State," *Feminist Studies* 4, no. 3 (Oct. 1978): 19–35.

25. Pateman, "Justifying Political Obligation," in *Disorder of Women,* 60; Mary Beth Norton, *Founding Mothers and Fathers: Gendered Power and the Forming of American Society* (New York, 1996), 9–13, 60–62, 296–98; Holly Brewer, *By Birth or Consent: Children, Law, and the Anglo-American Revolution in Authority* (Chapel Hill, 2005).

26. John Locke, *Two Treatises of Government,* rev. ed., ed. Peter Laslett (Cambridge, 1963), Second Treatise, §4, p. 309; and Thomas Hobbes, *Leviathan,* ed. C. B. Macpherson (Harmondsworth and Baltimore, 1968), chap. 13, p. 185.

27. Locke, *Two Treatises*, Second Treatise, §116, p. 390.

28. William Blackstone, *Commentaries on the Law of England*, quoted in Pateman, "Women and Consent," 155.

29. Rousseau, *Discourse on the Origins of Inequality* (1755), quoted in Okin, "Rousseau's Natural Woman," 399, and Susan Moller Okin, *Women in Western Political Thought* (Princeton, 1979), 144.

30. Carol Berkin, *Revolutionary Mothers: Women in the Struggle for America's Independence* (New York, 2005), 155; Linda K. Kerber, "Daughters of Columbia: Educating Women for the Republic, 1787–1805" and "The Republican Mother: Women and the Enlightenment—an American Perspective," in *Toward an Intellectual History of Women* (Chapel Hill, 1997), 23–62; Susan Branson, *These Fiery Frenchified Dames: Women and Political Culture in Early Philadelphia* (Philadelphia, 2001); Jan Lewis, "The Republican Wife: Virtue and Seduction in the Early Republic," *WMQ*, 3d ser., 44 (1987): 689–721; and Ruth H. Bloch, "American Feminine Ideals in Transition: The Rise of the Moral Mother, 1785–1815," in *Gender and Morality in Anglo-American Culture, 1650–1800* (Berkeley, 2003), 57–77. I am grateful to Megan Schockley, of Clemson University, for her observation (after hearing a preliminary version of this chapter at the 2006 conference of the Southern Association of Women Historians in Baltimore) to the effect that Jefferson's attitude seems to have skipped Republican Motherhood and leapt to the antebellum Cult of Domesticity. For southern women, the "image of politicized domesticity, now known as republican womanhood," competed with the "rival feminine ideals" of the "genteel lady" and the "virtuous helpmeet." See Kierner, *Beyond the Household*, 109.

31. Quoted in Mary Beth Norton, *Liberty's Daughters: The Revolutionary Experience of American Women* (Boston, 1980), 247. Sheila L. Skemp, *Judith Sargent Murray: A Brief Biography with Documents* (Boston, 1998); and Jeanne Boydston, "Making Gender in the Early Republic: Judith Sargent Murray and the Revolution of 1800," in *The Revolution of 1800: Democracy, Race, and the New Republic*, ed. James Horn, Jan Ellen Lewis, and Peter S. Onuf (Charlottesville, 2002).

32. Judith Apter Klinghoffer and Lois Elkis, " 'Petticoat Electors': Women's Suffrage in New Jersey, 1776–1807," *Journal of the Early Republic* 12 (1992): 159–93.

33. Darlene Gay Levy, Harriet Branson Applewhite, and Mary Durham Johnson, eds., *Women in Revolutionary Paris, 1789–1795: Selected Documents Translated with Notes and Commentary* (Chicago, 1980), 75–77. See also Dominique Godineau, *The Women of Paris and Their French Revolution* (Berkeley, 1998); Joan B. Landes, *Women and the Public Sphere in the Age of the French Revolution* (Ithaca, 1988); Shirley Elson Roessler, *Out of the Shadows: Women and Politics in the French Revolution, 1789–95* (New York, 1996); Olwen H. Hufton, *Women and the Limits of Citizenship in the French Revolution*

(Toronto, 1992); Harriet B. Applewhite and Darline G. Levy, eds., *Women and Politics in the Age of the Democratic Revolution* (Ann Arbor, 1990).

34. Levy, Applewhite, and Johnson, *Women in Revolutionary Paris*, 87–96.

35. Ibid., 213–17.

36. Ibid., 220, 271. The orator Etta Palm d'Aelders fled to Holland but was imprisoned from 1795 to 1798.

37. Rousseau, *Origins of Inequality*, quoted in Okin, "Rousseau's Natural Woman," 399.

38. Catherine Allgor, *Parlor Politics: In Which the Ladies of Washington Help Build a City and a Government* (Charlottesville, 2000), 21–22, Thomas Jefferson, "Etiquette of the Court of the U.S.," reprinted in Malone, *First Term*, 499–500; Jan Lewis, "Politics and the Ambivalence of the Private Sphere: Women in Early Washington, D.C.," in *A Republic for the Ages: The United States Capitol and the Political Culture of the Early Republic*, ed. Donald R. Kennon (Charlottesville, 1999), 122–51; Merry Ellen Scofield, "The Fatigues of His Table: The Politics of Presidential Dining During the Jefferson Administration," *Journal of the Early Republic* 26 (2006): 449–69. Charles Cullen is preparing a documentary edition of Jefferson's dinner records from the manuscripts at the Massachusetts Historical Society, Boston.

39. Margaret Bayard Smith, *Forty Years of Washington Society*, ed. Gaillard Hunt (London, 1906), 388–89; James Sterling Young, *The Washington Community, 1800–1828* (New York, 1966), 167–70 (emphasis added); Branson, *These Fiery Frenchified Dames*, 124–42; Fredrika J. Teute, "Roman Matron on the Banks of Tiber Creek: Margaret Bayard Smith and the Politicization of Spheres in the Nation's Capital," in *A Republic for the Ages*, 89–121.

40. Smith, *Forty Years*, 387–91.

41. Everett Somerville Brown, ed., *William Plumer's Memorandum of Proceedings in the United States Senate, 1803–1807* (New York, 1923), 123; Lynn W. Turner, *William Plumer of New Hampshire, 1759–1850* (Chapel Hill, 1962), 456.

42. Manasseh Cutler to Dr. Joseph Torrey, 4 Jan. 1802, in Scofield, "Fatigues of His Table," 465.

43. Jefferson to Thomas Jefferson Randolph, 24 Nov. 1808, *Family Letters*, 364; Jefferson to David R. Williams, 31 Jan. 1806, TJP.

44. Jefferson to James Monroe, 8 Jan. 1804, in Scofield, "Fatigues of His Table," 465 (emphasis added). David B. Mattern and Holly C. Shulman write that Dolley Madison "would often serve as Thomas Jefferson's hostess on the relatively few occasions when he found it necessary to include women at his dinner table," and her most recent biographer notes that "Dolley served as the president's occasional hostess." See Mattern and Shulman, *Selected Letters of Dolley Payne Madison* (Charlottesville, 2003), 39; and Catherine Allgor, *A Perfect Union: Dolley Madison and the Creation of the American Nation* (New York, 2006), 43.

45. Alexander Hamilton to Edward Carrington, 26 May 1792, *Papers of Alexan-

der Hamilton, ed. Harold Syrett et al. (New York, 1961–73), 11:439; Smith, *Forty Years,* 5–6; Henry Adams, *History of the United States of America During the Administrations of Thomas Jefferson* (1889; New York, 1986), 100; Joseph J. Ellis, *American Sphinx: The Character of Thomas Jefferson* (New York, 1996), 305–6; Joyce Appleby, "Thomas Jefferson and the Psychology of Democracy," in Horn, Lewis, and Onuf, *Revolution of 1800,* 168; and Andrew Burstein, *Jefferson's Secrets: Death and Desire at Monticello* (New York, 2005), 87–92.

APPENDIX A

1. Henry Lee's 18 Sept. 1806 letter stated that John Walker wanted from Jefferson "a written paper"—its authenticity attested by the signatures of two witnesses—"going only to his, & his Ladys entire exculpation," so that he could, if necessary, defend himself and his wife from insult prior to Jefferson's "retirement from public life." It seems likely (in accord with his implicit assurances in the two "conditions" mentioned in Lee's letter) that Walker destroyed the more detailed documentation after Jefferson's retirement from the presidency in Mar. 1809, after Elizabeth Walker's death on 10 Sept. 1809, or shortly before his own death on 2 Dec. 1809.
2. Joanne B. Freeman notes that "contemporaries considered it an affair of honor" and that "some charged that Walker even sent Jefferson a challenge." See *Affairs of Honor: National Politics in the New Republic* (New Haven, 2001), 115, 269–70, and quoted at 317 n. 19.
3. (Hudson, N.Y.) *Balance and Columbian Repository,* 26 Feb. 1805, printed Hulbert's speech "as reported by the Boston Centinel."
4. The contemporary docketing reads: "(Copy) Thomas Jefferson to John Walker, April 13, 1803."
5. Not known to be extant.
6. Jefferson returned from France in 1789.
7. The editors mentioned are Elias Boudinot Caldwell, James Thomson Callender, William Coleman, Samuel Relf, Benjamin Russell, and Caleb Parry Wayne.
8. The newspapers mentioned are the (New York) *American Citizen* (Philadelphia) *Aurora,* and (Hudson, N.Y.) *Bee.*
9. Not known to be extant.
10. The contemporary docketing reads: "A letter from Col. Walker to Genl. Lee giving an acct. of Mr. Jefferson's attempts upon Mrs. Walker's virtue."
11. Interlined: "[illegible] part of any cancelled all." Dumas Malone omitted the remainder of this sentence and the interlineation from the transcription he published in *Jefferson the Virginian,* 449; he marked the omission with ellipsis points.
12. Jefferson's wedding was on 1 Jan. 1772.
13. Interlined: "October."

14. The first house the Walkers built at Belvoir, in 1764, was moved first to Milton and then to "the Creek." The Walkers built a larger house at Belvoir about 1790 that was destroyed by fire in 1836. See Nancy S. Pate, "Belvoir," Works Progress Administration of Virginia Historical Inventory, 6 Sept. 1937, LVA.

15. Martha Wayles Jefferson died on 6 Sept. 1782. Jefferson departed Monticello on 16 Oct. 1783, spent several months in Congress at Philadelphia and Annapolis, and sailed for France from Boston on 5 July 1784.

16. Transcribed from the original and printed by permission of the Henry E. Huntington Library and Art Gallery.

17. Lee devoted most of this letter to an unrelated dispute over a land transaction; the relevant text resumes at the middle of the final page.

18. Replying to Lee's letter of 24 Feb., Jefferson devoted most of his letter to the land transaction involving Lee, Strode, and Washington.

19. Possibly the fragment written upside down on the final page of this letter was intended to be inserted here.

20. Gerard W. Gawalt, ed., " 'Strict Truth': The Narrative of William Armistead Burwell," *VMHB* 101 (1993): 118–20, is based on the original manuscript at the Library of Congress.

21. The *New-England Palladium* of Boston published on 18 Jan. 1805 "a broad attack on Jefferson's personal morality, including the Walker affair, Jefferson's behavior during the British invasion of Virginia, and his alleged irreligion." See Gawalt, "Strict Truth," 120n.

APPENDIX C

1. Jon Kukla, "Flirtation and *Feux d'Artifices:* Mr. Jefferson, Mrs. Cosway, and Fireworks," *Virginia Cavalcade* 26 (Autumn 1976): 52–63.

2. Kaminski, *Jefferson in Love,* 38–39.

3. Ibid.

4. Kaminski's wrote that Maria Cosway "loved Paris, and, in the handsome, intelligent, and charming American diplomat, she found the perfect man to paint her into her exquisite new world. For *six weeks* she was happy" (ibid., xii–xiii, 12; emphasis added). Dumas Malone accepted mid-August from Bullock as the date for Jefferson's encounter with the Cosways at the Halle au Blé and wrote that "in the month that followed he saw or heard some thing beautiful with her nearly every day" (Malone, *Rights of Man,* 70–71). Fawn M. Brodie relied on Boyd's early-August date for the first meeting; she also drew inferences about Jefferson's feelings from texts written weeks before they actually met. See *Thomas Jefferson: An Intimate History* (New York, 1974), 204–7, especially quotations at nn. 22–34. Gerald Barnett, *Richard and Maria Cosway: A Biography* (Cambridge, 1995), used Bullock's dates both for their first meeting and for Jefferson's injury (92).

5. *Jefferson Papers,* 10:454n.

6. Helen Duprey Bullock, *My Head and My Heart: A Little History of Thomas Jefferson and Maria Cosway* (New York, 1945), 11, 24; and Marie Kimball, *Jefferson: The Scene of Europe, 1784 to 1789* (New York, 1950), 161, 168.

7. *Jefferson Papers,* 10:454n; Jefferson to Maria Cosway, 12 Oct. 1786, *Jefferson Papers,* 10:445. With no supporting evidence whatsoever, Fawn M. Brodie contended that their intimate meetings continued for two weeks after Jefferson's injury because "the absence of letters is evidence not of their failure to see each other but the contrary." See *Intimate History,* 208. Although a close reading of the other letters contradicts Brodie's contention, it remains true that proximity can affect the nature of surviving written evidence, as it did for some of Jefferson's contemporaries in Congress in 1785–86. See Jon Kukla, *A Wilderness So Immense: The Louisiana Purchase and the Destiny of America* (New York, 2003), 64.

8. *Memorandum Books,* 637.

9. Jefferson to Maria Cosway, 24 Apr. 1788, *Jefferson Papers,* 13:104; and Kaminski, *Jefferson in Love,* 103. Pierre-François Hugues d'Hancarville had secured an audience for Richard and Maria Cosway with Louis XVI. When the Cosways left Paris on 6 Oct., it was d'Hancarville who accompanied them and Jefferson in the carriage to Saint-Denis.

10. Lucy Ludwell Paradise to Jefferson, 5 May 1789, *Jefferson Papers,* 15:95.

11. Jefferson left a long space in lieu of a new paragraph.

12. The word *domes* was written over *vaults; Jefferson Papers,* editor's note.

13. The word *comedienne* was partially struck through and *forter* inserted above the line.

14. The words *a little* were inserted above the line.

15. Again, Jefferson left a space in lieu of a new paragraph.

16. Translation: "Without wit, without sentiment / without beauty or youth / in France one may have the greatest lover: / For this Pompadour is proof." Bullock, *My Head and My Heart,* 42n.

ACKNOWLEDGMENTS

Many fine people inhabit Clio's mansion. *Mr. Jefferson's Women* benefited from historians who commented on preliminary versions of the text on four occasions: Christine Heyrman and Janet Moore Lindman at the 2005 meeting of the Society for Historians of the Early American Republic; Martha J. King, Cynthia A. Kierner, Teresa Murphy, and Megan Shockley at the 2006 meeting of the Southern Association of Women Historians; Peter S. Onuf, Andrew Jackson O'Shaughnessy, Richard B. Bernstein, Annette Gordon-Reed, Andrew Burstein, and others at Gene A. Smith's "Thomas Jefferson for Today" conference at Texas Christian University in April 2006; and Peter V. Bergstrom, Holly Brewer, Robert M. Calhoun, Victor Carnes, Don Higginbotham, Jeff Lucas, John Nelson, John Wood Sweet, and Peter H. Wood at the Research Triangle Early American History Colloquium in October 2006.

For research assistance I am deeply indebted to Anna Berkes, Dori Williams, and Jack Robertson at the Jefferson Library of the Thomas Jefferson Memorial Foundation; James Horn, Gail Greve, and George Yetter at the John D. Rockefeller Jr. Library of the Colonial Williamsburg Foundation; Patricia A. Howe at Longwood University; Dennis Northcott at the Missouri Historical Society; John Rhodehamel, Olga Tsapina, and Bert Rinderle at the Henry E. Huntington Library and Art Gallery; Tom Camden and Sara Bearss at the Library of Virginia; Robert Johnson at the Tompkins-McCaw Library of Virginia Commonwealth University; and Iris Trivilino of the *Cleveland Clinic Journal of Medicine*. I am grateful to John H. Peterman for permission to quote from *The Peterman Owner's Manual*.

Lorri Glover offered guidance on marriages involving siblings of a deceased spouse, Barbara Oberg on Jefferson's 1807 note to Gallatin, Joseph O'Connor on Greek passages in Jefferson's early letters, Fraser D. Neiman on conception dates, Eve S. Gregory and Joyce Browning on Tidewater families, Michael L. Nichols on manumissions, and Richard E. Dixon on Ellen Randloph Coolidge's

1858 letter to her husband. My notes testify to the invaluable scholarship of Andrew Burstein, Lucinda C. Stanton, and Joshua D. Rothman. Jennifer Anne Kukla was my translator and indefatigable guide during our exploration of Jefferson's Paris, assisted by Alice Jouve. Long drives between Richmond and Red Hill gave me the benefit of in-depth conversations with Cynthia A. Kierner and Carol Berkin during their visits as Governor Henry Lecturers in 2005 and 2006. And, after struggling to make sense of primary sources about male honor, misogyny, or race, there were moments when I discovered that some hard-earned conclusions had been anticipated long ago by Bertram Wyatt-Brown and the late Winthrop D. Jordan.

Andrew Burstein, John P. Kaminski, and Lucia C. Stanton generously read and commented upon chapters that engage their own incisive scholarship. The final text is clearer and stronger because W. W. Abbot, Connie Kukla, Suzanne Lebsock, Aixa Martinez, Mimi Melcher, James F. Sefcik, and Sandra Gioia Treadway read the entire manuscript—and Virginia J. Laas, Amy Kukla Chelgreen, Elizabeth Ross Kukla, and Jennifer Anne Kukla various chapters.

Sandra Gioia Treadway shared her research about Hannah Lee Corbin, Anna Maria Lane, Elizabeth Moore Walker, Martha Jefferson's fund-raising, and so much more. My editor Jane D. Garrett and agent Rafe Sagalyn supported the project from the outset. Leslie Levine, Ellen Feldman, Margaret Wimberger, and Jane's design and production team at Alfred A. Knopf are a writer's dream.

When I told Susan Larson that I was thinking about writing this book, she grinned and warned that I was going to learn a lot about myself. History should always offer that benefit to its writers and readers. My dedication reflects my appreciation for five generations of women who have enriched my life—and demonstrated by their examples that Jefferson's underestimation of women's talents and destiny was profoundly misguided.

INDEX

A NOTE ABOUT THE AUTHOR

A native of small towns in Wisconsin, Jon Kukla accepted his B.A. from Carthage College (1970) and his M.A. (1971) and Ph.D. (1980) from the University of Toronto. In Richmond, Virginia, from 1973 through 1990, he directed historical research and publishing at the Library of Virginia and dabbled in documentary editing, historic preservation, archaeology, and public history. He spent the next decade in the French Quarter, as director of the Historic New Orleans Collection from 1992 to 1998, adding museum exhibits, television, and historic building renovation to his bag of tricks. He returned to the Old Dominion in 2000 as director of the Patrick Henry Memorial Foundation in Charlotte County, a position he held until 2007. Mr. Kukla currently resides in Richmond, Virginia.

A NOTE ON THE TYPE

This book was set in a modern adaptation of a type designed by the first William Caslon (1692–1766). The Caslon face, an artistic, easily read type, has enjoyed over two centuries of popularity in our own country. It is of interest to note that the first copies of the Declaration of Independence and the first paper currency distributed to the citizens of the new-born nation were printed in this typeface.

Composed by North Market Street Graphics, Lancaster, Pennsylvania

Printed and bound by Berryville Graphics, Berryville, Virginia

Map by David Lindroth Inc.

Book design by Robert C. Olsson